Using
Your Mac

Todd Stauffer

que

Using Your Macintosh

Library of Congress Catalog No.: 95-67126

ISBN: 0-7897-0094-8

98 97 96 95   6 5 4 3 2 1

Interpretation of the printing code: the rightmost double-digit number is the year of the book's printing; the rightmost single-digit number, the number of the book's printing. For example, a printing code of 95-1 shows that the first printing of the book occurred in 1995.

Publisher: David P. Ewing

Associate Publisher: Stacy Hiquet

Associate Publisher—Operations: Corinne Walls

Director of Product Series: Charles O. Stewart III

Publishing Director: Brad R. Koch

Managing Editor: Sandra Doell

Credits

Publishing Manager
Thomas H. Bennett

Acquisitions Editor
Cheryl D. Willoughby

Product Director
Stephanie Gould

Production Editor
Heather Kaufman

Technical Editor
Todd Knowlton

Figure Specialist
Cari Skaggs

Book Designer
Amy Peppler-Adams
Sandra Stevenson

Cover Designer
Jay Corpus

Acquisitions Assistant
Ruth Slates

Operations Coordinator
Patty Brooks

Editorial Assistant
Andrea Duvall

Graphic Image Specialists
Becky Behler
Steve Carlin
Brad Dixon
Jason Hand
Denny Hager
Clint Lahnen
Cheri Laughner
Michael Reynolds
Laura Robbins
Dennis Sheehan
Craig Small
Jeff Yesh

Production Team
Claudia Bell
Karen Gregor
Daryl Kessler
Beth Lewis
Steph Mineart
G. Alan Palmore
Kris Simmons
Scott Tullis
Mary Beth Wakefield

Indexer
Rebecca Mayfield

Composed in *ITC Century*, *ITC Highlander*, and *MCPdigital* by Que Corporation.

Dedication

About the Author

Todd Stauffer has been writing non-stop about computers since he graduated from Texas A&M University, where he studied a bizarre combination of English literature, Management Information Systems, and quite a bit of golf. Since that time he has worked as a technical writer, advertising copywriter, and freelance writer—all in the personal computer industry.

Todd's work appears frequently in *Texas Computing* magazine, industry catalogs, radio advertisements, training publications, and national magazines. Todd himself often appears in local Dallas coffee shops trying to convince his friends to buy Macintosh computers, quit their jobs, and run away to Colorado. He can reached at TStauffer@aol.com (where he actually reads his mail) or stauffer@connect.net (where he does not actually read his mail).

Trademarks

Acknowledgments

This book took countless people to work, rework, and finally get it relatively right—to say that I had much of a hand in its production is really an overstatement at best. Thanks to everyone at Que for helping me push through a difficult schedule and sitting back patiently while I consistently blundered along.

Specifically I'd like to thank Cheryl Willoughby, Tom Bennett, and Stephanie Gould for walking me through the process and helping me get all the materials I needed for this project. A couple of your phone calls and e-mail messages kept me from making days worth of mistakes!

Thanks also to Lary Anderson and Larry Groebe for help and understanding back at the old "day job." If it hadn't been for some well-placed vacation time and a few "personal" days, I might still be writing this book!

A big nod again to Larry Groebe and David Filbey, fellow Mac-lovers and a couple of guys who know a whole lot more about this stuff than I do. Thank you for your insights into and explanations of all those deep, dark Mac secrets. Also, thank you both for *not* explaining System 6 fonts to me. I don't think I would have ever left my home again.

Thanks to Katie Mitchell, Ray Rose, Liz Stauffer (Mom), and Chris Stauffer (Dad), for each of you, in your own ways, letting me vent frustrations and helping me to stay sane during this ordeal. I only wish I'd called some of you collect.

Finally, amazingly special thanks to Amy Dennis for reading absolutely every single word of this book, making sure what I submitted was at least twice as good as what I'd actually written, and saying everything was great when it was clearly nothing more than very, very good (wink). Your hard work, your special eye for *repetitious redundancies*, and your unfailing belief in me was the biggest part of what made this whole thing possible.

We'd like to hear from you!

As part of our continuing effort to produce books of the highest possible quality, Que would like to hear your comments. To stay competitive, we *really* want you, as a computer book reader and user, to let us know what you like or dislike most about this book or other Que products.

You can mail comments, ideas, or suggestions for improving future editions to the address below, or send us a fax at (317) 581-4663. For the online inclined, Macmillan Computer Publishing has a forum on CompuServe (type **GO QUEBOOKS** at any prompt) through which our staff and authors are available for questions and comments. The address of our Internet site is **http://www.mcp.com** (World Wide Web).

In addition to exploring our forum, please feel free to contact me personally to discuss your opinions of this book: on CompuServe, I'm at 73602,2661, and on the Internet, I'm **sgould@que.mcp.com**.

Thanks in advance—your comments will help us to continue publishing the best books available on computer topics in today's market.

Stephanie Gould
Product Development Specialist
Que Corporation
201 W. 103rd Street
Indianapolis, Indiana 46290
USA

Contents at a Glance

{Table of Contents}

Introduction

Welcome to Using Your Macintosh!

Why should I use this book?

How to use this book

Part I: Welcome to Macintosh

Chapter 1: Welcome to the Macintosh

Chapter 2: Some Assembly Required

How to set up your Mac

see page 20

Chapter 3: Meet the Mac

*What's the
Machintosh
hard drive?*

see page 29

Chapter 4: To Key or to Click?

Part II: Taking Your Mac for a Test Drive

Chapter 5: Touring the Desktop and Using Menus

Chapter 6: Folders, Windows, and the Finder

How can I get organized?

see page 70

Chapter 7: Finding a Place for Your Stuff: Floppy Disks and Hard Drives

Tips for managing your disks

see page 89

Chapter 8: Getting Help When You Need It

Part III: This Mac Is Mine!

Chapter 9: Getting Organized with the Apple Menu and Aliases

Chapter 10: Banish the Bland Mac!

Chapter 11: The Macintosh Memory Tune Up

*What if I
don't have
enough
memory?*

see page 143

Chapter 12: Cool Customizing Software

Chapter 15: The Printed Page and Applications that Create Them

*Why is
word
processing
so great?*

see page 189

*The
Macintosh
as a
printing
press*

see page 203

Chapter 16: Number Crunching and Managing Lists

Chapter 17: Getting It All with Works Applications

*What's
the best
financial
software?*

see page 218

Part V: Getting Your Stuff in Print

Chapter 18: Setting Up and Using Your Printer

How do I print a document?

see page 245

Chapter 19: What You Need to Know About Fonts

Part VI: My Mac Can Do That?

The best games and edutainment CDs for Mac

see page 277

Making music with your Macintosh

see page 285

Chapter 24: Presenting Information on the Mac

Part VII: Getting on the Information Superhighway

Chapter 25: The Online Essentials

Create a family album with music, sound, and video

see page 312

Chapter 26: Finding Your Superhighway Ramp

*How do
I connect
to the
Internet?*

see page 345

Chapter 27: In the Fast Lane—Using the Internet

Part VIII: Keep Your Mac Smiling

Chapter 28: Inside the System Folder

Chapter 29: Keeping Your Mac Happy

Part IX: Indexes

Introduction

Welcome to *Using Your Mac*!

The first time I used a computer, it was a little green screen with a keyboard, connected who-knows-how, to some room-sized monolith with flashing lights and buzzers and people running around it like lion trainers. I sat down at it, typed some cryptic commands, hit some buttons, and walked down the hall to get my printout. Of course, everything I'd done was wrong.

One day, quite a few years later, I was introduced to the Macintosh. I'd been using little green screens and keyboards for quite some time—and I'd gotten used to them. When I saw the little Mac (Macs were all "little" back then) with its mouse sitting beside it and pictures on the screen, I thought it was kind of silly. It didn't look like a computer.

But, oh, is it a computer! Any Macintosh is a powerful machine, useful for literally thousands of different tasks. And the incredible thing is—it really is easy to use! Once you get a feel for the little pictures on your screen and how to move them around with your mouse, you'll be on your way to getting any Mac task done.

My goal with *Using Your Macintosh* is to explain to you some of the theories behind why the Macintosh works the way it does. If I can help you get familiar with your Mac, let you in on some of ways you can use it, and let you know some of the pitfalls to avoid, I'll count this book a success.

The Macintosh is already a highly-intuitive and very friendly computer. Once you understand a little about how the Mac works, you'll find that it's a pleasure to work with, a great tool for exploring new ideas, and it might just make life a little easier.

Why should I use this book?

This book has one simple mission. Get you using a Macintosh computer as quickly as possible—ready to perform basic tasks and capable of learning more complex ones. It's that easy.

I've tried to keep a nice-sized city block between us and techno-babble. Most of the words in this book will have appeared in an English dictionary 20 years ago. The ones that haven't (or, words like network that have been confounded by the Computer Age) will be called out, pointed at, defined, and then utterly humiliated (if we have time). After all, it's not us that's the problem. It's clearly the word's fault.

How to use this book

This book has been arranged to begin with very basic concepts and work up to more complex ideas. If you'd like, feel free to read straight through this book. I've tried to have a little fun in the text, so hopefully it won't be a completely dull read. Plus, chances are that even if you do know a lot about the Macintosh, you'll pick up some good tips or learn something that you didn't know before.

Granted, some parts of this book are more exciting than others. If you're already familiar with a concept—or if you just need to find a quick solution to a problem you're having—just jump straight to that chapter. Each chapter has a roadmap at the beginning to let you know what's covered, and callouts throughout the text to point you to what you need to know.

The chapters follow a logical order: They start out discussing the Macintosh in general, move on to elements of the Macintosh interface, and end with different things you can accomplish with your Mac. There is also an index at the back of this book that will lead you directly to the troubleshooting (Q&A) tips scattered throughout these pages.

Part I: Welcome to Macintosh

In the first part of the book we'll hit most of the basics. We put the computer together, turn it on and off, get used to the mouse and keyboard, and figure out what everything on the screen does. If you've never used a Mac or if you just bought one, you may want to start here.

Part II: Taking Your Mac for a Test Drive

Here's where we'll actually start *doing things* with the Mac. We talk about how to create and find your files, how to print, how to store your work for safekeeping, and how to get your Mac to help you when you run into trouble or just need some advice.

Part III: This Mac Is Mine!

In this section we'll talk about the different ways to customize your Mac, from jazzing up your color scheme to organizing your Macintosh for speed and ease. We also talk a little about "tuning up" your Macintosh to make it run efficiently. We'll even talk about some cool stuff you can buy to help you make your Mac more personal, more efficient, and more fun.

Part IV: Getting a Little Work Done

Lights, bells, pictures, whistles. How do you get something done?! With your Mac, you can create printed pages and art, crunch numbers, store information, and communicate with the world. Crammed into these chapters are some of the basics you need to deal with all those software programs that make your Mac go.

Part V: Getting Your Stuff in Print

Chances are this is one of the major reasons you're using a computer at all—to create printed documents. To do that, you've got to get all the right cables hooked up and then convince your Mac and your printer to talk. If you need help, head to this section.

Part VI: My Mac Can Do That?

Ready to be amazed at what a Macintosh can do? We'll talk about working with other computers (like DOS and Windows computers) and using multimedia. Heard that word before? The Mac's a master at using things like photos, video, sounds, electronic music, and graphics to create business presentations, professional-looking home videos, or the world's most high-tech family photo album. Get ready to say "cool."

Part VII: Getting on the Information Superhighway

These chapters might just be everything you need to know about getting online. It's the latest computer craze for a good reason—it's useful, educational, *and* entertaining. You really can hook your Mac up to your phone line and dial out to the world. Exchange electronic mail messages, get the news headlines, ski reports, buy jewelry, and chat with folks just like you. I'll even show you how to send me an electronic message—just in case you need extra help!

Part VIII: Keep Your Mac Smiling

Our last section talks about the insides of your Mac and how to keep things running smoothly. If you're having a little trouble with your Mac, or if you just want to know more about its inner-workings, here are the chapters for that.

See you down the Information Superhighway

If you've just bought a new Macintosh or decided to learn to use the Macintosh at school or in the office, congratulations! You've made the right choice. The Macintosh is an "insanely great" tool that will give you years of productivity, education, and entertainment.

Plus, if you get to know the basics of the Macintosh, you're a long way down the road to understanding computing in general. I hope that the time you spend in front of your Macintosh will be time you consider well spent as you look past the images on your screen and into an incredible new world of information. Good luck...and don't forget to have fun!

Special elements

Each chapter has special sections to help you move more quickly to the information you need. These elements let you decide how much or how little you want to know about a given subject. Here's a quick breakdown:

(Tip)

Tips are where you'll get shortcuts, often overlooked ideas, or just a quick way to remember something. Hopefully you'll find that these tips improve the way you work with the Macintosh and make your sessions run more smoothly. If you already basically understand what's covered in a chapter, you may still want to scan these tips quickly to pick up something that will make life easier.

{Note}

I've also sprinkled some little notes around these pages, just to call out items that might be of special interest or reminders of what is important in the surrounding text.

<Caution>

Just about anyone and everyone should read these. Cautions let you know when you could potentially do something to harm yourself, harm your computer equipment, affect your Macintosh's low-level system files, or lose valuable data. Hopefully, reading these callouts will make you feel more at home with your Mac. Also, the cautions may help you avoid some costly mistakes.

Q&A

What's a Q&A?

These questions and answers are problems and concerns I hear all the time from new Mac users. Most of the time these questions relate to troubleshooting your Macintosh and figuring your way out of jams. Sometimes they'll just be hints or advice that point you in the right direction—but their ultimate goal is to solve any problems you may have.

 Plain English, please!

These notes define **computer-nerd lingo** when I'm forced to use it. If you already know a word, skip the definition and keep reading.

I've also used some typographical clues to let you know what is going on. Words in **boldface** are either an important new term or something that you should type exactly as it is written. Things in the `special typeface` are what appear on your computer screen.

If you see the names of two keyboard keys separated by a plus sign, like Option+A, that just means you should press and hold the first key, press the second key, and then release both keys.

Sidebars are things you don't need to know!

Every once in a while I'll go shooting off on a tangent. The Macintosh Universe is so full of interesting things and ideas that sometimes I just get excited and start typing away. I don't want to waste all that precious time with my Macintosh, so I've put those excursions into little sidebar sections. Read the ones that interest you and completely ignore the ones that don't. Generally speaking, if you miss a sidebar, it shouldn't adversely affect your ability to use the Mac. But reading these sidebars may just enhance your appreciation for the Mac!

Part I

Welcome to Macintosh

Welcome to the Macintosh

In this chapter:

- What makes the Mac friendly and easy to use?

- Why is there more than one Mac?

- How do I know which Mac is right for me?

- Are there Macs designed for people who travel?

The Macintosh is powerful and easy to work with because, most of the time, it simply makes sense.

A computer should work the way we do. That's what Apple Computer, Inc. thought when it set out to build a totally new computer in the early 1980s. They thought a computer should look like the everyday tools that people use at their desks—like desktops, pens, paper, and file folders. And because all these things have to be presented on a TV-like screen, the computer should use pictures to represent those tools. You'd save your electronic documents using pictures that looked like file folders and delete them using a picture that looked like a trash can.

The result of this idea was a computer called **Macintosh**. During the last decade, the Mac has been improved and redesigned, but Apple's original vision has not changed. Even though the Macintosh has become more powerful, it's easy to work with because, most of the time, it simply makes sense. And talk about friendly...it even smiles at you when you turn it on!

Which Macintosh do I need?

Apple Computer currently offers four different "models" of Macintosh in retail stores, each geared to a different type of user. These are the model names and their target customers:

- **Performa**—Home and home/office users

- **Quadra**—Business users

- **Power Macintosh**—Business users, professionals, and "power" users

- **PowerBook**—Portable computer users

Many of these models overlap in ability and design—for instance, there are Performa computers that are as powerful as Power Macintosh computers, and Quadra models that are less powerful than some PowerBooks. The name of the computer doesn't necessarily mean it's more or less powerful than another model. Essentially, these model names suggest two things: how these computers are sold and what's included with them.

At home with the Performa

The **Performa** line of computers is most often found in home electronics stores, department stores, and warehouse-style discount stores. If you buy a Macintosh at Sears, Best Buy, or WalMart, chances are it's a Performa. And here's why: In most cases, the Performa comes with everything you need to get started (see fig. 1.1). You get the computer itself, a keyboard, a video monitor, and software programs like word processors, checkbook managers, and games. Almost all the latest Performas also include extra features like a CD-ROM drive and modem, plus the software you need to use them.

 Plain English, please!

You need a modem in your computer if you want to exchange programs, messages, or other information with other computer users over a phone line. So, for example, you'll need a modem if you want to join one of the online services like America Online or CompuServe.

Fig. 1.1
Most Performas come with everything you need to get started. Some even include extras like a modem or CD–ROM drive. (Pictured: the Performa 630CD)

In general, a Performa can be a very good purchase, especially for first-time buyers and home computer buyers. Most Performas are flexible enough for a family environment—good for games and education for the kids—but still powerful enough to run business applications and home finance software. Plus, Performas come prepackaged to take a lot of the guesswork out of computer buying.

◑ (Tip)

Apple offers different combinations of programs (often called software bundles) for retail stores to sell with the Performa based on what the store believes its customers want. If you think the software included at one store isn't right for you, call around to other stores that offer Performas. Chances are you can find a Performa with software that more closely fits your needs.

The Quadra in the office

The **Quadra** shown in figure 1.2 is a good choice for business users and experienced users who want more options than the Performa offers. But, Apple may soon stop introducing Quadra models as more and more people buy Power Macintosh computers.

Fig. 1.2
The current Quadra models are designed for users interested in a more customized computer system. Monitor, keyboard, and software are all choices the individual buyer has to make.

The reason the Quadra is still attractive to business customers is Apple's "bare-bones" marketing approach for selling Quadras. New Quadras are offered with very few extras at a very low price. All you get is the computer, a mouse, and the System software. You buy everything else yourself. This gives you the flexibility to add non-Apple products (perhaps a special keyboard), products the rest of your company uses (like special monitor or networking add-ons), or extras that don't come with the Performa. It also helps you avoid paying for options you may not need, like a CD-ROM drive.

⊛ {Note}

When Quadra and Performa models have similar names, chances are their "brains" are similar, too. For instance, the only major difference between the Quadra 630 and Performa 630 (aside from the extras included) is the Quadra's floating point unit, which enables it to process decimal-point math (often used in finance and graphics-oriented programs) more quickly.

Power Macs for power users?

In the last few years, Apple has begun to offer Macintoshes that use a new processor. By designing their computers around the new PowerPC processor, Apple was able to take a leading role in the entire personal computer industry. The transition has gone well, and a **Power Macintosh** is a truly wonderful choice for a new computer buyer (see fig. 1.3).

Plain English, please!

The "brain" of any personal computer is called the microprocessor, or processor for short, because it's the computer chip that "processes" the information that you and your programs give it.

Fig. 1.3

The latest and greatest Macintosh computers are called Power Macintosh because they are based on the new PowerPC processor developed jointly by Apple, IBM, and Motorola.

So why is the Power Macintosh such a great computer? Reason one: It's faster! The new processor gives a Power Mac fantastic new speed and power—especially for users interested in the graphic arts and new technologies like digital video and music. The Power Macintosh is quickly becoming very popular with folks who create TV and movie animation, music videos, and multimedia presentations (stuff like mall kiosks, touch-screen information booths, and interactive movies).

Reason two: It's the Mac's future. For the average user, the Power Macintosh offers the capability to complete any standard computing task like word processing or number crunching—plus, the promise of growth in the future. It's the standard that Apple will eventually incorporate into every Mac it makes. Buying a Power Macintosh now means you get the most advanced Macintosh available—and, you'll be ready for future innovations.

 *{Note}*___ In fact, many programs available today for the Macintosh come in two versions (sometimes in the same box). One version is for regular Macs like the Quadra and most Performas. The other version is Power Mac accelerated—designed to take advantage of the Power Mac's extra speed.

On the road with PowerBook

Here's the other factor you should consider in choosing your Macintosh: Ever think you might want to take it with you? That's what the PowerBook is designed for (see fig. 1.4). These little machines pack the same power as most other Macintosh computers, but they fold up and fit in your briefcase. It's something that's definitely worth thinking about.

Fig. 1.4
Top: The full-sized PowerBook has most of the features of a desktop Mac. Bottom: The tiny PowerBook Duo turns into a desktop computer when used with a Duo Dock.

PowerBooks are targeted toward many different users, from low-power machines directed at college students to high-end presentation computers directed at traveling professionals. You can get stereo sound, color screens, and processors that make them as fast as the newest Quadra and Performa models. PowerBooks run the same programs as desktop Macintosh computers, but they allow you the flexibility of taking your computer with you. Apple has also announced plans for upgrading some PowerBooks to PowerPC technology. This means that, after buying a special add-on product, PowerBook owners will be able to use the same programs that Power Macintosh computers use—faster programs with more features and new capabilities: like TV-quality video and speech recognition.

The PowerBook Duos

You might also want to take note of some special PowerBooks called **PowerBook Duos**. These notebooks are designed to give you the best of both worlds—a "sub-notebook" or "superportable" and a desktop computer. The notebook sacrifices a few luxuries (like a built-in floppy drive for your disks) to slim it down to around 4 lbs or less when you travel. But when you get home, you simply slide your PowerBook Duo into the Duo Dock and you have a desktop computer with a floppy drive and a full size monitor.

Did I buy the right Mac?

Deciding what computer fits your style can be a difficult process. It's comforting to remember that Apple and other companies have a multitude of ways for you to upgrade your computer to faster technology if you start to outgrow it. And making sure you exploit the full potential of your Mac is what this book's all about!

2

Some Assembly Required

In this chapter:

- Where should I put my new Mac?

- What do I do with all these cables?

- How do I turn it on?

- What happens now?

Fortunately, putting your Macintosh together is much easier than learning to program a VCR!

How many times have we heard the joke about people not being able to program their VCRs? It seems to be one of those jokes of the decade, right up there with "I've fallen and I can't get up."

Fortunately, putting your Macintosh computer together is much easier than learning to program a VCR. Getting your Mac up and running may require a quick study of the symbols Apple uses to represent various ideas, but, with just a few moments of study, you'll be able to connect and troubleshoot your Mac's connections with ease.

Does it matter where I put my Mac?

Of course, if you're using a Macintosh portable computer, a PowerBook, or PowerBook Duo, you can use it almost anywhere. However, you don't want to move a full-size computer too often, so give some thought to where you will be most comfortable. Also, you should consider safety issues such as keeping the electrical cords out of the way and reducing glare.

> Computers and monitors get warm while they're on so it's a good idea to allow a few inches on all sides for air to circulate.

Keep those cords out of the way

Most people back their computer tables up against the wall, and with good reason—the cords and cables behind a computer can be pretty unsightly, and it's important to keep cords out of high-traffic areas.

> It's a good idea to use a **surge protector** to plug your computer components in to. And, buy a surge protector whose manufacturer offers insurance. Power surges due to lightning strikes and other variables can ruin your thousands of dollars worth of computer equipment—which the manufacturer's insurance would cover.

Put yourself in a good position

Many studies have been done on how your sitting position and hand positions affect you when you use a computer. The best advice I can give you is to use a little common sense, and, if you start to feel strain, change your setup.

> Your monitor should be at a comfortable viewing angle, preferably at eye level. You may prefer to look slightly down on your monitor to avoid direct glare and reflections in the glass. And remember to look away from your monitor occasionally so that your eyes can relax.

The desk or table you choose for your keyboard and mouse should allow you to sit comfortably with your elbows bent at about a 90° angle. Just for convenience sake, you should try to position your mouse close to your keyboard and on the same level. You may also want to invest in an ergonomic keyboard if you do a good deal of typing, as newer keyboards are designed to allow your hands to fall in a more natural position.

Look out for glare

One of the most annoying problems you can have with a computer is monitor glare. Apple monitors, as well as many made by other manufacturers, often provide a glare-reducing coating on the screen that should help a little. But the best thing you can do to avoid glare is consider your lighting. You never want harsh lighting directly behind your monitor (so that you look into it) or directly in front of your monitor (behind your back).

It's best to have overhead lighting that is concentrated on your workspace in general. If you have a window that gets a fair amount of sunlight, it's a good idea to choose a spot that will put that window on your left or right, as opposed to behind or in front of you. That way you won't be directly affected by the sunlight—and that window will give you a good excuse to turn away from your monitor every so often.

*(Tip)*

Available from various manufacturers are "glare guards" that fit over your monitor to help reduce glare from light sources. These vary widely in effectiveness, so it would be to your advantage to test several before buying one.

From the box to the desk

Depending on which Macintosh model you have, you'll need to connect a certain number of its components when you first set up the computer. The Macintosh makes this relatively easy to do—most Apple products use a universal picture scheme that's a lot like those international street signs you find in Europe (see the graphics page "How to set up your Mac"). These pictures tell you which port, or input/output connection, you're dealing with and what goes there. To help you identify these symbols, an illustration is included in the margin next to the text where the connection is explained.

How to set up your Mac

The placement of the ports on the back of Macs varies, but you'll have at least some—if not all—of these ports on the back panel of your Mac.

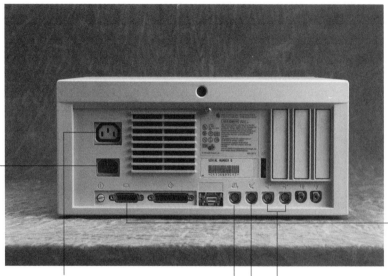

On most Macintosh computers, the monitor cable plugs directly into the monitor and into the **monitor port**.

Plug the power cable for your Mac in the **AC power connector** and into a surge protector.

Plug your monitor's power cable into the **monitor AC connector** if your Mac has one and it will automatically get power when your computer is turned on and automatically turn off when you shut down your Mac. If you don't have a monitor AC port, you should plug your monitor into a surge protector.

Connect your keyboard to one of the two **ADB ports** on the back of the computer. It doesn't really matter which one you use. The mouse can either connect to the other port or you may be able to connect it to the same type of port on your keyboard if it has one.

Connect the modem cable to the modem and to the **modem port**. This one is easy to recognize because the symbol looks like the handset from a phone. Then you'll need to connect the modem to the phone line.

If you have a standard Apple printer, simply connect your printer cable to the **printer port** on the back of your printer, and then plug the other end into this printer port. Plug the power cable from the printer either into the wall or your surge protector.

Connecting the keyboard and the mouse

 Next you'll want to hook up your keyboard. The keyboard connects to what Apple calls the ADB port. Some Macs have more than one ADB port, but it doesn't really matter which one you use.

The mouse can either connect to the other ADB port on the back of the computer or it can connect to a similar port on your keyboard. Some Macintosh keyboards offer two mouse ports, depending on whether you want the mouse on the left or the right. There's no rule here—either side works the exact same as the other.

 Plain English, please!

What's a **port**? Well, aside from a place to pull your ship into for the night, a port is just a connector on the back of your computer for plugging in other things. In fact, it's a little like a ship's port—you're transferring data from your computer to a printer, monitor, or other device just like you transport goods from a dock onto a ship.

Connecting the monitor

 On most Macintosh computers, the monitor cable plugs directly into the monitor and into a port on the computer's back panel.

⊗<Caution> Always make sure your Macintosh is turned off before you connect or disconnect cables. Also, never force a cable or plug into a port on the back of your Macintosh. For the most part, connectors should fit together easily. If things don't seem right, step back and look at what you're doing. You may be trying to plug in a connector upside down, sideways, or into the wrong port!

You also need a power cord to plug the monitor into a power outlet. Some monitors have to be connected to a grounded power outlet, not to the computer, so you should check the information that came with your monitor. Other monitors, however, can be plugged in to the back of your Macintosh.

Your computer may have what looks like two power connections in the back. One has "male" pins that stick out like the end of a power cord—this connection is for your Macintosh's power cord. If there is a second power connection, it should look like a wall socket with slots instead of prongs. This port can take your monitor's power cord, if the cord is correctly designed. Plug your monitor into this port, and it will automatically come on when your computer is turned on and automatically turn off when you shut down your Mac.

 Power Macintosh computers work a little differently. All Power Macs have a monitor connection designed specifically to work with the Apple AudioVision (or AV) monitor, which has built-in speakers and a microphone. Because all these features must connect through the monitor port, it uses a special connection. If you're using this special monitor, simply plug it in to that port. If youre using a different monitor, you'll have to plug your monitors connector into the *other* monitor port on the back of your machine (or use the Video Adapter that comes with your Power Mac 6100).

Connecting the keyboard and mouse

 Next, you'll want to hook up your keyboard to a port on the back of the computer. Some Macs have more than one port labeled with this symbol, but it doesn't really matter which one you use.

The mouse can either connect to the same type of port on the back of the computer or it can connect to a similar port on your keyboard. Some Macintosh keyboards offer two mouse ports, depending on whether you want the mouse on the left or right. There's no rule here—either side works exactly the same as the other.

Connecting a modem

 If your Macintosh came with a modem, or if you bought one to add on, you'll start by connecting the modem cable to the modem and to the modem port on the back of your Mac. This one is easy to recognize, the symbol looks like the handset from a phone.

Then you'll need to connect the modem to the phone line. The modem uses standard telephone cable with modular plugs (RJ-11 plugs). On the modem, look for a connection that either shows a picture of a modular plug or is labeled "data" or "line." Plug your phone cable in to this port, and then plug the other end of the phone cable into a wall-mounted phone jack, just like a telephone.

If you want to use your phone on the same extension, then connect the phones cable to the port on the modem that's labeled with a picture of a phone or "phone." Now you can pick up your phone to test it. If you hear a dial tone, even with the computer off, you're in business.

You may not need a modem to connect!

If you own a Power Macintosh or Macintosh AV computer, all you need is a GeoPort Adapter designed for your computer. Both Power Mac and Mac AV computers have the built-in ability to dial-up online services and send or receive faxes without a modem. And, unlike most standard modems, these computers can act as a phone answering machine and speaker-phone, too.

Why are these Macs unique? They have the ability to run software programs that act like a modem, instead of requiring an additional device. The GeoPort Adapter connects the computer directly to the phone lines, just as you would a telephone, fax machine, or answering machine.

The advantage is, all you need is new software to add a new feature like voice mail, teleconferencing, or other emerging technologies. Plus, when a faster modem or fax standard is established in the industry, you just load a new software program. No need to buy a whole new modem!

Connecting a printer

 There are a number of different ways to connect your printer to your Macintosh, and these are covered in more depth in chapter 18, "Setting Up and Using Your Printer." If you have a standard Apple printer, you'll most likely want to hook it up using the printer port. Simply connect your printer cable to the printer port on the back of your printer, and then plug the other end into the printer port on the back of your Mac. Plug the power cable from the printer either into the wall or your surge protector and you're ready to go!

How do I turn it on?

In most cases, you use the power key on your keyboard to start your Mac. The keyboard power key is either located at the very top right corner, or across the very top of your keyboard in the middle. Either way, you simply press the key to start your computer.

❶(Tip)

> Apple has a habit of changing the way you turn on different Macintosh models. The easiest way to know exactly how to turn yours on is to consult the manual that came with your Mac. Consulting the manual is a good way to get troubleshooting tips if you can't seem to get your Mac to start.

❓Q&A

What if my keyboard power key doesn't work?

Apple uses the same keyboard with different Mac models. So, just because you have a keyboard power key doesn't mean that's how you turn your Mac on. Try it, and if it works, great! If not, you'll need to look for another power switch. On some models, the power switch is a rocker switch (like a wall switch for lights) and on others its a round button found under the floppy drive opening. If you throw the switch and your Mac *still* doesn't power up, try hitting the keyboard power again (especially on all-in-one Performa models).

Wow, it works!

If your Macintosh powers up correctly, you should hear the famous "Macintosh Chord," and your monitor should come alive. After a few moments, your monitor screen will turn gray, and if everything goes well, you'll see the "Happy Mac." Then, you'll hear your hard drive clicking while little pictures show up on the bottom of your screen. These are **extensions**, or little programs that add additional features to your Mac like screen savers. (We discuss extensions in more depth in chapter 28, "Inside the System Folder.")

⊗**<Caution>** Do not turn off your computer with the power switch. The Mac is designed to be turned off using a special Shutdown command, so that it can complete some necessary chores before the power disappears. See the section "How do I turn this thing off" in chapter 5 for more information.

If everything's successful up to this point, you should end up with a screen that looks something like figure 2.1. Did it work? Congratulations! Welcome to Macintosh.

Fig. 2.1
We've arrived! I like to call this screen the "Bland Mac." It's the default arrangement of everything we'll be working with for the next few chapters.

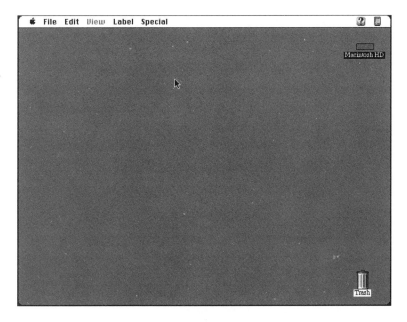

Q&A

> **I turned it on, but nothing happened. What do I do now?**
>
> If there's no response from the computer when you turn it on, check that all the cables are pushed firmly into the ports and electrical outlets, and try again.

3 Meet the Mac

*Think of the Mac's screen
as a desktop—you can
write, read, draw,
set up a filing system
with folders, and use the
calculator.*

In this chapter:

- I've seen the Happy Mac. Now what am I looking at?

- What do these pictures mean?

- Why does my Mac need memory?

- Where do I store stuff I want to keep?

When you finally set up your Macintosh, get all the cables connected, and turn it on, what you're met with looks almost exactly like your desktop on the first day at a new job. No pictures, no baseball pennants—and no work-in-progress or phone messages. Just bare desktop space, a rudimentary filing system, and the Trash. Of course, in the office, you'd probably put the trash under your desktop—but we'll let that slide (it's your first day).

It's what I call the "Bland Mac." Everything is exactly to factory specs, with nothing customized and nothing changed. So have a seat at your new desktop and let's explore!

What is the Desktop?

At its most basic, the **Desktop** is the solid color or pattern that's behind everything else on your Macintosh's display. That's why it's called the Desktop—it's what you put all your stuff on. Everything else (like folders, the menu bar, and the Trash) is on top of the Desktop.

If you think of the Desktop just as you would a standard desk at the office, you can start to see the parallels (see fig. 3.1). Icons represent storage spaces, in-boxes, and tools like a calculator or address book. Menus are where you choose what type of pen to use or what color of paper you want. And windows are pieces of paper—for writing, reading reports, or drawing. Windows can be stacked one on top of the other, so, for instance, you can address an envelope with the letter beneath it.

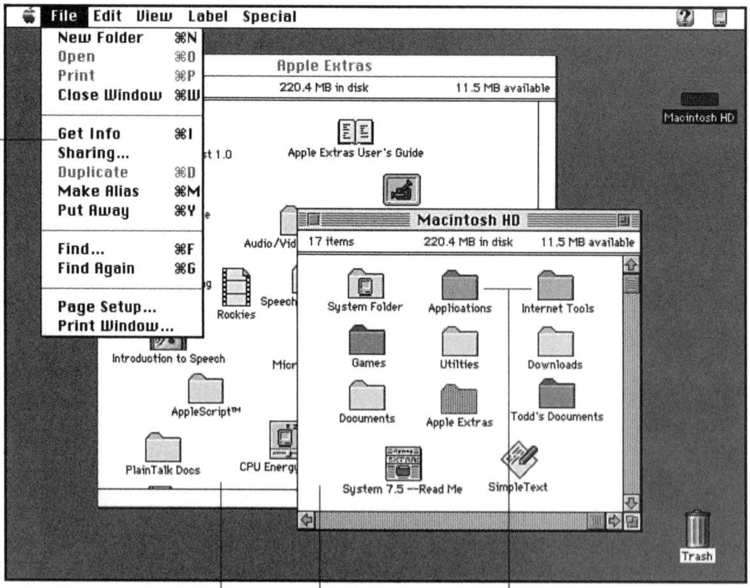

Fig. 3.1

A real-world desktop is represented by pictures on the Mac's screen.

Menus are drawers full of choices

Windows are stackable sheets of paper

Icons represent storage and tools

In the real world, all these pens, pieces of paper, and in-boxes are kept on your desk. On the Mac, all your icons, menus, and windows are kept on the Desktop, too.

Plain English, please!

Icons, basically, are little pictures or symbols on your computer screen that represent things. The Trash, for instance, is an icon. So is the little picture with the words "Macintosh HD." And, icons have only one real purpose. They let you see and manipulate things on-screen with a mouse.

What's the Macintosh hard drive?

The **Macintosh HD icon** represents the internal hard disk. Try thinking of this as a filing cabinet, as it's where you'll keep stuff, including folders.

What are the words at the top of the screen?

If the Macintosh HD icon is really my main filing cabinet, then what are those words at the top of my screen? They're the drawers in your desk. It's called the **menu bar,** and it's where you tell the Mac what you want to do and what tools you want to use. To open a desk drawer, move the pointer to the word in the menu bar by moving the mouse on the mouse pad, and then click and hold the mouse button. Chapter 4, "To Key or to Click?" covers in-depth how to work with the mouse. For now, notice in figure 3.2 how nearly all the words in a menu are "action" words. When I open the File "drawer" I get selections like **Open, Close,** and **Quit.** It's the same in the other drawers, too.

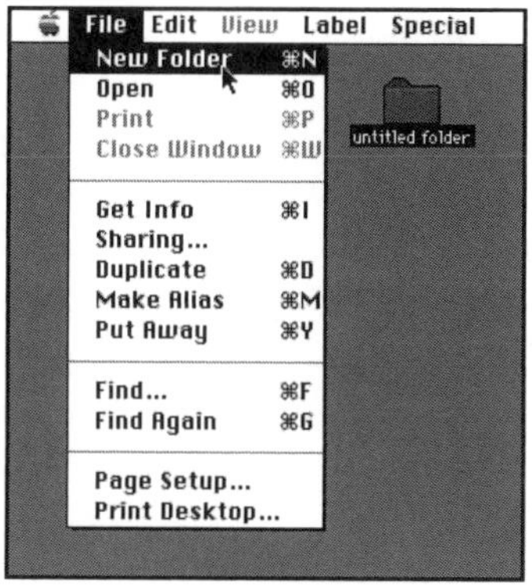

Fig. 3.2
Here I've opened the File "drawer" to look at its contents. If I choose New Folder, that's what Mac will give me.

File	Edit	View	Label	Special

New Folder	⌘N
Open	⌘O
Print	⌘P
Close Window	⌘W
Get Info	⌘I
Sharing...	
Duplicate	⌘D
Make Alias	⌘M
Put Away	⌘Y
Find...	⌘F
Find Again	⌘G
Page Setup...	
Print Desktop...	

untitled folder

What you're choosing on the menu bar are **commands**, or instructions for the Mac. If you select New Folder, for instance, Mac will create a new folder (untitled folder) and drop it on the Desktop. If you tell the Macintosh to open that folder, that's what will happen. Then you can see and manipulate the contents of that folder.

Yes, the Trash is for throwing stuff away

 The easiest thing to recognize on the Desktop is the **Trash**. The Trash is significant because it's the only way you can throw things away on a Mac. Why is that? Because if you have to do it deliberately, consciously, and the same way every time, you are not likely to throw something away by accident.

The Macintosh Trash works very much like any real trash. Throw something away, and, if you absolutely have to, you can dig it back out. Empty the Trash, however, and it's gone for good. (There's no "dumpster" on the Mac!) The Trash also has a cute way of telling you it's got something in it—its sides bulge out to indicate that it's waiting to be emptied (see fig. 3.3).

Fig. 3.3
No question about it, there's something in the Trash.

What are icons for?

We already know that icons are just pictures that represent things on the Desktop. What things? Well, there are four basic elements that can be represented by icons. These are (in no particular order) **disks**, **folders**, **programs**, and **documents**. Once you understand these four elements, it won't feel like your first day in the office anymore. You'll be ready for a promotion!

⊛ {Note}___

Just so that you Mac-maniacs don't send me hate mail, I'll point out that icons can represent other things, too. For instance, in applications (like Microsoft Word), icons can represent toolbar commands that let you open files and change font styles. For now, however, we're discussing *Desktop icons.*

Remember the Macintosh HD icon? It's the perfect example of a disk icon where you store files, documents, applications, and all that other stuff. There are different types of disks including hard disks, floppy disks, and CD-ROMs. Whenever the Mac recognizes a new disk (like when you put a floppy disk in the floppy drive), a new icon will show up on the Desktop automatically.

❝❝ *Plain English, please!*

A **CD-ROM** (Compact Disc-Read Only Memory) is a compact disc from which your Macintosh can read data. Just like an audio CD stores digital music, a CD-ROM stores digital information, like text, pictures, and digital movies. With a special CD-ROM drive, you can use these CD-ROM discs with your Mac. **❞❞**

The Desktop uses folder icons to organize other icons, just like you use folders in a filing cabinet. When you open a folder icon, you can view what's in that folder. And it's usually more folders, documents, or program icons.

⊗<Caution>___

You may notice that one folder stands out from all the others. It's the System folder, which is a special folder the System software uses to store programs that control the Macintosh. It's definitely not a good idea to poke around in the System folder until you're very comfortable with your Macintosh. For an in-depth look at the System folder, see chapter 28, "Inside the System Folder."

What do all these little pictures do?

Disk icons represent the disks that are available on your computer for you to store folders, documents, programs, and all that other stuff.

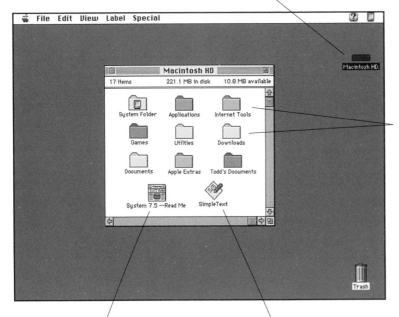

The Desktop uses folders to organize other icons. When you open a folder icon, you can view what's in that folder. And it's usually more folders, document icons, and program icons.

The System 7.5 "Read Me" icon represents a document. In this case, it's a note I can read in SimpleText.

Application icons are usually pretty easy to pick out, because they almost always have a meaningful picture and name.

The third way that the Mac uses icons is to represent programs. There are two kinds of programs on the Mac: System programs, which make the computer work, and application programs that you use to do stuff like writing letters or calculating budgets. Program icons are usually pretty easy to pick out, because generally they have a meaningful picture.

Another element that an icon can represent is a document. In Mac lingo, a document is anything that you work on in an application program. So, a note written in SimpleText can be a document, as can a picture file that I create in ClarisWorks. When I'm done creating a document in one of these programs, I'll tell it to save the document. It will then create a document icon and put it in the folder that I specify.

 Plain English, please!

When you're working in a program, it's always a good idea to tell that program to **save** your work to a disk. Saving writes the information on the disk so that you can read it again later. The Save command is found under **File** on the menu bar.

What's memory and what good is it?

If I meet you tomorrow in the computer bookstore, and you tell me your name, I'll probably remember it the entire time we're talking. I'll say, "Oh, Bob, you're right," and "Hey, Bob, it was nice chatting with you." Then, the second I get back in my car, I'll probably completely forget your name. It's nothing personal, Bob. It's just that, if I don't write something down, after a while I'm going to forget it.

Well, your Macintosh is the exact same way. The second you turn it off, it'll forget everything it knows. Unless, of course, you tell it to write something down. It's the difference between leaving something in the Mac's memory and storing it on a disk.

Where is the memory?

Memory or **Random Access Memory** (**RAM**) is the "active" storage area in your Macintosh for programs and documents. It's where the Mac puts the application you're using and information about the work you're doing at the particular moment that you're doing the work. But memory is volatile. Things can only stay in memory as long as your computer is on.

 Remember, you can't see memory, but everything that you do see on the screen is using RAM. If it's "in memory," that means it is currently being used or shown on the screen by your Mac.

That's why you have disks. If you need to keep something for more than a few minutes, it needs to be "written down" to a disk, usually your hard disk. That saves it permanently so that you can use it again later. And, it's important to save things regularly. If you turn off your Mac or a power surge or blackout affects power to your Mac, anything that is in memory at the time will be lost. And, if it wasn't already saved to disk, it will be lost for good.

How much memory do I have on my computer?

These days, memory is measured in **megabytes** (**MB**), which means (very approximately) millions of characters. Sounds like a lot, right? Well, the most recent version of the Macintosh System software, System 7.5, takes up between 2 and 5 megabytes of memory just to keep your computer running! That's before you begin working with programs and documents. If you'd like to see how much memory your Mac has and how much is being used, here's how.

With the mouse, move the pointer (on-screen) up to the "Apple" in the upper-left corner (see fig. 3.4). Click and hold the mouse button over the Apple. A menu appears. Keep holding down the mouse button and move the pointer down slightly. When the words **About This Macintosh** reverse color, let go of the mouse button. Now you should see a box that tells you how much memory is installed and how much memory the System software is using. If using the mouse isn't something you're familiar with, check out chapter 4, "To Key or to Click?"

Fig. 3.4
The About This
Macintosh box is an
easy way to see how
your memory is being
used.

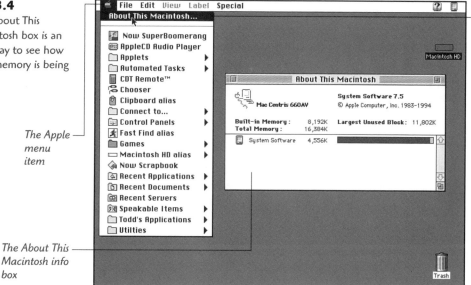

Selecting
About This
Macintosh...

The Apple
menu
item

The About This
Macintosh info
box

The "About This Macintosh" box is also useful for determining how much
memory is being used by your programs. Any time you select this box, it shows
you both memory in use by the System software and memory being used by any
open programs.

When is enough memory really enough?

The memory requirement in Macintoshes just
keeps going up. System 7.5, Apple's most recent
version of the Macintosh system software, has
raised the bar even higher by requiring 3 megabytes or more.

Macintoshes have another feature that can
affect how much memory you need. It's called
multitasking, and it means having more than one
program going at one time. The idea is, you can
have a word processing program open while you

work on a report. Then, you can open a spreadsheet to check on the latest sales figures. To have
both of these programs open at the same time,
however, uses more memory.

Currently, the standard for decent performance is
8 megabytes. But your mileage may vary. If you
often find that your Mac tells you that it can't
open a program because you've run out of
memory, it may be time to buy more.

How much memory do I need?

The requirements for memory continue to increase as computers become more powerful. These days, most Macintosh models ship with 8 megabytes of memory standard. For many beginners, this is enough. Once you get more heavily into working with your Mac, however, you may find you need more. See the sidebar for more on memory and your Mac.

4

To Key or to Click?

The mouse is like a remote control for your hand. It lets you pick up and move icons, shuffle documents, and toss things in the Trash.

Normally, you use your hands to pick things up and move them around. On the Mac's screen, you don't have that luxury. The **mouse** is the next best thing, providing a remote control for your hand on the Mac Desktop. It lets you pick up and move icons, shuffle documents, and toss things in the Trash.

Should I use the mouse or the keyboard?

The mouse and keyboard are specifically designed for different tasks on the Macintosh Desktop. The mouse is your "virtual hand" on the Desktop. It is designed to move stuff around in the Mac environment, like picking things up and putting them down again. The mouse is also good for choosing items on the menu bar, throwing things in the Trash, and generally putting your mouse pointer where you want to work (see fig. 4.1).

It's through the keyboard that most things are "accomplished" on your Mac. If you want to write a letter, calculate a mortgage, or create a database, most of the words, numbers, and data will be entered using the keyboard. Until speech recognition (see sidebar) or some other technology makes using a computer more "natural," the keyboard will be the best way to get ideas into your Mac. We'll talk more about the keyboard later.

Should you name your Mac "Hal"?

The HAL9000 in the movie *2001: A Space Odyssey* didn't require a keyboard or mouse for interaction. It spoke and recognized the voices of the crew members of the *Discovery*. So why name your Macintosh "Hal"? Because, if it's an AV Macintosh or Power Macintosh, it can recognize and carry out speech commands, too.

When equipped with a microphone, these Macintosh models can listen in and execute commands based on what you say. For instance, with Speech Recognition turned on, you can say "Macintosh, open SimpleText" and it will happen automatically. You can also write simple programs of your own. On my Mac, when I say "Macintosh, who is Todd?" he responds, "Todd is my master and comrade." Makes me feel kinda special.

One of the many faces of Macintosh, awaiting my command. Notice the words in italics—those are voice commands that my computer recognized and executed.

Icons, the menu bar, and windows
are best left to the mouse

Fig. 4.1
Here are a few
examples of when
to use what.

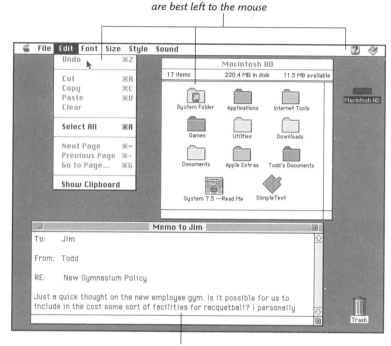

Save the keyboard for serious thought!

How do I work with a mouse?

If you're sitting near your Macintosh, take a moment and look at the mouse. Touch it. Feel it. Wrap your hand around it and hold it tight. (I promise I'm going somewhere with this.) Does it feel like an extension of your hand? It should, at least to a certain degree. Moving the mouse pointer around on the screen should feel just about as natural as pointing at things with your index finger on the screen. If it doesn't, don't worry. It soon will.

 <Caution> Relax that wrist to avoid painful mousing injuries! If your hands are relatively average-sized, your fingertips should rest comfortably toward the very front of the mouse button. The mouse should fit into the palm of your hand, with your wrist resting just behind the mouse on your desktop (or mousepad). This does two things: it keeps your wrist relaxed and gives you a better "feel" for pointing with the mouse.

Rolling it around the Desktop

Why do you roll the mouse around? To get the mouse pointer where you want it to go. If you use a mousepad with your mouse, you may notice that your mousepad somewhat resembles the shape of your screen. Try rolling your mouse from one corner of your mousepad to the other and back again. See how the pointer scoots across the screen?

 Q&A

> ### What if I reach the edge of the mouse pad but the pointer hasn't reached the target?
>
> Don't worry. Just lift the mouse, place it back in the center of the mouse pad, and try again.

One click or two?

If you *could* use your hand to move stuff around on the Desktop, there are a few basic movements you would probably make. You would point at items to tell Mac that you want to work with them. You would pick things up and move them around on the screen. And you'd "open" things. You'd open disks, you'd open folders, and you'd open applications.

You can do all these things using the mouse and the mouse button. Since Mac's mouse only has one button, though, we'll have to remember a few rules for different manipulations. They're pretty simple though. And the best part is, they work every time!

Click once to select something

Selecting is how you tell Mac that you'd like to focus more closely on something. If, for instance, I drag my mouse pointer up to Macintosh HD and click once, that tells Mac that I'm focusing on that particular icon. If I then choose a command from the File menu, Mac knows that I want that command to affect the Macintosh HD item (see fig. 4.2).

Clicking is pressing the mouse button while the pointer is on an icon.

(Tip)

Want to select more than one icon at a time? Hold down the Shift key as you click to select. Now, whatever you do to one of these icons is done to the rest of them. To de-select them all, click the window's background or click on the Desktop.

Fig. 4.2
By clicking once on an icon I give it focus. Now it's clear to Mac which object I want to work with.

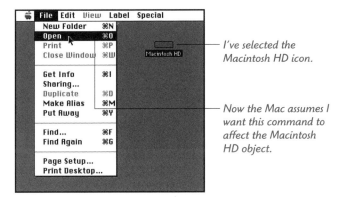

— *I've selected the Macintosh HD icon.*

— *Now the Mac assumes I want this command to affect the Macintosh HD object.*

*{Note}*

Notice that when you give something "focus," the Macintosh acknowledges this by changing the color of the object you've selected. In the case of Macintosh HD, Mac turned the icon from white to gray (see fig. 4.3).

Click once and drag to move an icon

To "pick up" an icon and move it around, position the mouse pointer over the icon, press and hold the mouse button, and move the mouse. This is called **dragging**. The Mac lets you know when you're dragging by showing you an outline under the mouse pointer of the object being dragged. When you're done moving, release the button and the item "drops" back to the Desktop.

Plain English, please!

What does **drag-and-drop** mean? Well, we just saw dragging, which is simply moving an icon. And dropping is releasing the mouse button to put the icon in a new place. Drag-and-drop, then, is using these two concepts to accomplish something more than just moving. For instance, throwing something in the Trash is a drag-and-drop action. If you *drag* an icon to the Trash and *drop* it by releasing the mouse button, it's "trashed"(the icon disappears inside the Trash and the Trash bulges).

Click once to open a menu

Click once on any of the words in the menu bar at the top of the screen and hold down the mouse button to view the menu options. Keeping the mouse button down, you can drag the pointer to other words in the menu bar and those menus will open. To select an option from the menu, drag until the item is highlighted and release the mouse button.

Click twice to find out what's inside folders and disks

The third thing we do with items on the Desktop is open them. The easiest way to do that is by double-clicking the mouse button. **Double-clicking** means clicking the mouse button twice in rapid succession. This may take a little practice, but, again, it works any time. If you want to open a disk, a folder, or even the Trash (to drag stuff out), you do it by double-clicking (see fig. 4.3).

Click twice to start a program

You also double-click to start a program. If I double-click on the SimpleText icon, it will start the application SimpleText, which is a text file editor (or, a very simple word processing program). Then, I can type away.

Fig. 4.3

I've double-clicked on both the Macintosh HD and the Trash. Now I can see what I've kept and what I've thrown away!

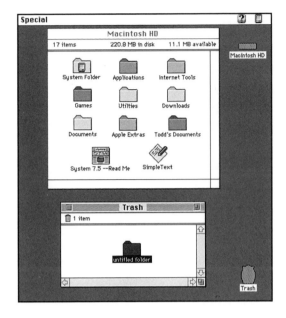

Practicing with the Puzzle

Okay, now we're ready to put some of this mousing to practice. We'll use the Puzzle to get in a little wrist action.

Let's start by opening the Apple menu.

1 Move the mouse pointer over the Apple icon in the top left corner of the screen.

2 Press and hold the mouse button to open the menu and drag until Puzzle is highlighted.

3 Release the mouse button. Up pops the Puzzle (see fig. 4.4).

Fig. 4.4

With the Puzzle, you select each piece you want to move by clicking once. Plus, you can also get in some great dragging practice.

Close box

So, how do you play with the Puzzle? It's one of those little slider puzzles where you have one slot open, and you try to move all the pieces around to make a picture. (In this case, it's the Apple Computer logo.) Just select a piece (single-click on it) to move it. If it's next to the open slot, it should slide right over. This is also a good time to practice some dragging. If you'd like to move the Puzzle around the screen, press and hold the mouse button on the word "Puzzle" at the top of the Puzzle's window. Now, keep holding the button and move the mouse around. See the outline? When you're ready to drop the Puzzle, just release the button and the Puzzle shows up in its new position.

Done with the Puzzle? Almost every application written for the Macintosh can be closed with the Quit command, including the Puzzle. How? First, click once on the Puzzle to make sure it has focus. Then, press and hold down the mouse button on the File menu bar item. Keep holding and drag the pointer down to Quit. Release the mouse button and the Quit command executes.

Special keys on the Apple keyboard

Computer keyboards are all pretty much the same, with an alpha-numeric keypad, arrow keys, and sometimes a separate number pad (the bit that looks like a calculator). Often there are keys labeled F, called **function keys**, that programs use to carry out particular procedures. As a general rule, the Mac doesn't make much use of the function keys. However, there are a few special keys on the Mac that you will want to use.

{Note}

Your Mac will have one of two keyboards, the standard or the extended. The extended keyboard has some additional features: height adjustment, function keys, a separate section for the arrow keys, a numeric keypad, and additional keys including Help, Home, End, Page Up or Page Down, and Forward Delete.

These special keys are Command or ⌘ (sometimes called the Apple key), Option, and Control (see fig. 4.5). In the same way you press the Shift key and a letter to get uppercase letters, you use Command, Option, and Control with letters to accomplish almost everything you can do with the Mac and its programs.

Fig. 4.5

Special keys on an Apple extended keyboard.

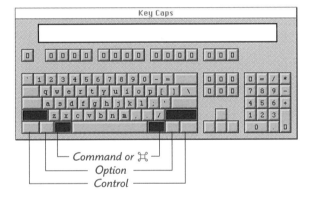

Used in combinations, these keys provide you with **keyboard shortcuts** to common commands. They allow you to make selections and perform commands without using the menus or the mouse. For instance, ⌘+O is the keyboard command for **Open**, which does the same exact thing as double-clicking with the mouse. We'll talk more about command keys in chapter 5, "Touring the Desktop and Using Menus."

Part II

Taking Your Mac for a Test Drive

5

Touring the Desktop and Using Menus

In this chapter:

- What's on the menu?

- Where do I put stuff I want to keep?

- How do I get rid of stuff I don't want?

- How do I empty the Trash?

- How do I turn my Mac off without losing anything?

Using menus and other things on the Desktop is how you get stuff done! How the Desktop looks, though, is up to you.

E verybody's desk is a little different. Some people like to keep their's neat, with boxes, folders, and little file-o-things to keep everything in their rigidly structured, orderly systems. Other people wouldn't think twice about taking a Ginsu knife and chopping away at sushi on their desktop. The different ways that people work are what make their Macintoshes different, too (see fig. 5.1). But, then again, the Mac was designed to be different.

Fig. 5.1

Top: Here's how System 7.5 sets up your Desktop. It's bland Mac!

Bottom: By the time you've gotten used to your new Desktop, you'll have it customized for convenience and productivity.

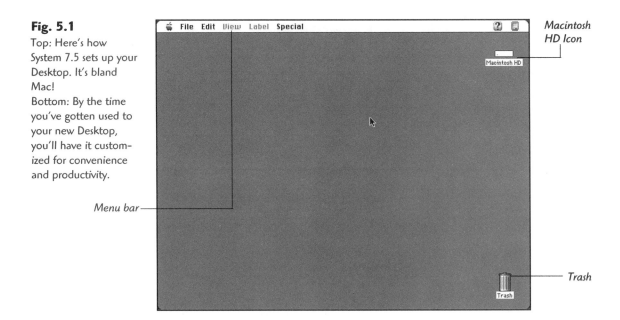

Macintosh HD Icon

Menu bar

Trash

Customized Drive icon: Make it meaningful.

Folder icons: Take advantage of drag-and-drop

Desktop Icons: Put things where you can see them.

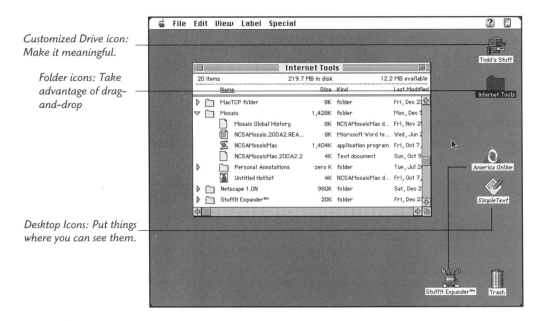

Just sitting there and staring at the Bland Mac can be a little intimidating. There doesn't seem to be much to do. All you have is a little hard drive icon, the Trash, and the menu bar.

So how do you get anything done? Well, that drive icon, Trash, and menu bar actually make up one of the most powerful filing systems ever created—the Macintosh **Finder**. The Finder helps you find things you've stored on your computer by showing you icons, allowing you to create new folders, and giving you a way to delete things. You can start programs, move documents, and organize folders from the Finder. In short, anything you do with your Mac starts with the Finder. (We'll discuss the Finder in more depth later in chapter 6, "Folders, Windows, and the Finder.")

What's on the menu?

At the heart of the Finder, as well as all other Macintosh programs, is the **menu bar**. The menu bar is where you decide what to do and how you want to do it. In the case of the Finder, it's how you manage your files and applications. In other applications, it might be where you decide what font to use, when to print, or what formula to use in a spreadsheet (see fig. 5.2).

Fig. 5.2

In any application, the menu bar is where all the action is. Just press, hold, drag, and release.

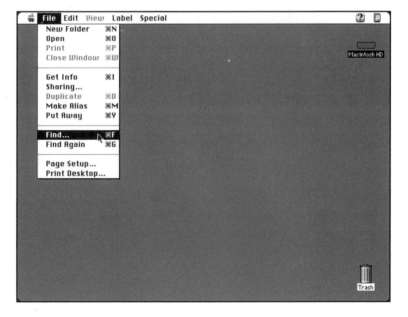

Because the Macintosh is designed so that programs look and work alike, the menu bar generally acts the same in every application. You'll notice that when you switch from one application to another, the menu bar switches with you. And whether it's the Finder or Microsoft Word, you choose menu items the same way.

How do I select from a menu?

Press, hold, drag, and release.

The menu bar uses a system of **pull-down menus** (sometimes called drop-down menus) that's a lot like opening a drawer in your desk. The menu item (or drawer) labeled File, for instance, pulls down a menu of commands (stuff in that drawer) that enable you to create new documents, save them, and print them. And opening that drawer is easy.

Let's try it with File in the Finder.

1 **Press** and hold the mouse button with the mouse pointer on the word File. Its pull-down menu appears.

2 **Hold** down the mouse button and drag the pointer down the menu. This reveals the **highlight bar**, which shows what's selected.

3 **Drag** the highlight bar until you get to what you want to do, like Find.

4 **Release** the button. The highlight bar blinks a few times to let you know it's executing that command.

Why are some options black and others gray?

All commands are not equal. In the Finder and many applications, you will sometimes find that a command is **grayed**, or appears lighter than the other commands. This is the Macintosh way of telling you that there's no reason to select this command now. A good example of this is trying to choose Print before you've opened a document in your word processor. The Print command will be gray until you open up a document or start a new one. If you don't have a document open, you can't print, so you can't choose the command.

What does the ... mean?

You'll notice in many pull-down menus that the options are followed by an **ellipsis** (...), like Find... back in figure 5.2. The ellipsis means what it usually means in English grammar—essentially, "more to come." It's the Mac's way of telling you that if you select this command, a **dialog box** will appear asking you for more information (see fig. 5.3). If you select the Find... command, for example, a dialog box appears asking you to type in the name of the file you want to find.

Fig. 5.3

The Find dialog box appears after you select the Find... command in the Finder's File menu.

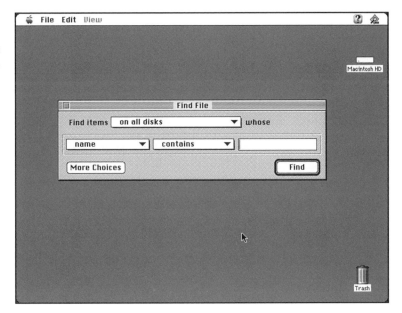

> **Plain English, please!**
>
> A program uses a **dialog box** to ask you a specific question or get more detailed information from you. It's information that the program needs before it can continue, so a dialog box doesn't work the same way as a window. Sometimes you can move dialog boxes around on the screen, but you usually can't work with anything else until you tell it what it wants to know. Often a dialog box requires a yes or no answer, usually giving you options like **OK** or **Cancel** (see fig. 5.4).

Fig. 5.4
Here's a typical dia-
log box asking you
whether it's okay to
continue or whether
you would like to
change your mind
and Cancel.

The Trash contains 10 items, which use 1.9
MB of disk space. Are you sure you want
to permanently remove these items?

[Cancel]   [OK]

See the exclamation mark in figure 5.4? That means this dialog box is actually
an **alert**, letting you know that you are about to do something you should
think twice about. It's just Mac's way of making sure you know what you're
doing.

What are the symbols on the right of the menu?

Another thing you might have noticed in the typical pull-down menu is that
many commands have symbols and letters next to them. For instance, in
figure 5.2, the Finder's File pull-down menu has New Folder ⌘N as one of its
commands. The ⌘N means that pressing these keys simultaneously on your
keyboard while working in the Finder allows you to create a new folder
without touching the mouse. See the sidebar "Save time and wrists!" for
more info on keyboard shortcuts.

Here's how it works

Every time I write a letter, I go through a certain number of steps. I sit down
at my desk. I open a drawer. I get a piece of paper. I get a pen. I write the
letter. I get an envelope...and so on. I go through a similar process to write
a grocery list, write a memo to my boss, or balance my checkbook.

There are minor differences, of course, but many parts of the process are the
same. That's something the designers of the Macintosh noticed about how
people work, and it's why nearly every Macintosh program has a core set of
menu items that are the same from one program to another (see fig. 5.5). Use
one program and you're on your way to understanding how nearly every Mac
program works!

Fig. 5.5

Notice how the menu bar changes for each application. Yet, some of the menu items are the same. Learn one Macintosh application, and you've learned some of every Macintosh application!

The Finder's menu bar

Microsoft Word's menu bar

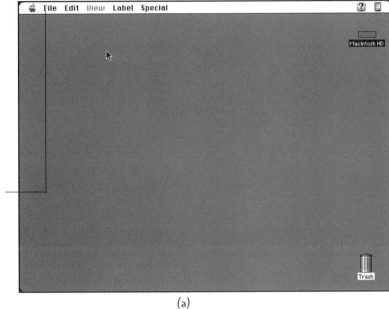

(a)

(b)

*Lotus 1-2-3's
menu bar*

☀ File Edit Worksheet Range Graph Data Style Tools Window	② 🅿🅱

Untitled

	A	B	C	D	E	F	G	H	
1									
2									
3									
4									
5									
6									
7									
8									
9									
10									
11									
12									
13									
14									
15									
16									
17									
18									
19									
20									

Ready   7:12:50 PM

(c)

Save time and wrists!

Going to the mouse every time you want to get something done is a little like getting up and walking across the room every time you want to change the channel on your TV. The Macintosh provides you with a few "remote control" buttons that allow you to keep working with your hands on the keyboard. Get to know a few of the more important keyboard shortcuts, and you'll have much more productive sessions at the Macintosh. The cool thing is that these shortcuts work in nearly every Macintosh program! What are the top five most useful? Depends on how you use your Mac...but try these for starters:

⌘Q	Quit a program
⌘S	Save a document
⌘C	Copy to clipboard
⌘V	Paste into document
⌘P	Print

Here are a few of the common menu items that appear in nearly every Macintosh application.

Start and end with the File menu

Every standard Macintosh program has a **File menu** (refer to fig. 5.5). It's usually where you start and end every session with a program. With your word processor, for instance, you'd likely find options like **New**, **Open**, **Save**, and **Print**. And, the File menu is where you'll always find the **Quit** option. Sometimes it's convenient to think of the File menu as the menu that contains most of the "computer-oriented" decisions. Taking care of files, printing them, moving them around—that's the File menu.

Change your mind in the Edit menu

The **Edit menu** is another standard to which most Mac applications adhere (refer to fig. 5.5). The Edit menu is where you find the **Undo** command (if your application has one). Depending on the program, selecting this command will undo the last change you made to a document, or the last few changes. If you ever make a huge mistake (like deleting a paragraph or page) go straight to the Edit menu and look for an Undo command.

In general, the Edit menu is also where you'll find the **Cut**, **Copy**, and **Paste** commands. These are for moving text, numbers, and other objects around in your documents. It's also one way to share information between programs. For instance, if you have figures in a spreadsheet that you'd like to put in a memo (written using your word processor) you'd use these functions to copy the text from the spreadsheet and paste it into the word processor.

Take another look in the View menu

The third standard menu bar item is the **View menu** (refer to fig. 5.5). The View menu is where you go when you don't like the look of things. In the Finder, for instance, you can choose how you'll look at the contents of a folder, with options like **By Small Icon**, **By Icon**, or **By Name**. In your word processor, you might get options like **Outline**, **Page Layout**, and **Zoom**. As a general rule, if you want to look at something in your program a little differently, head to the View menu.

Options that are always available

We've already discussed how one of the unique things about the Macintosh is that the menu bar changes when we switch applications. Some options stay the same, some change. The Finder, for instance, has certain options that are not available in Microsoft Word or Lotus 1-2-3, even though all three menus have some selections that are the same. There are, however, a few items on the menu bar that never change. These menu items are always on the menu bar, no matter what the application is.

The Apple menu

Do you have a "utility" drawer at home? You know the kind—it's the drawer you always go to when you can't find something. It's got flashlights, birthday candles, fingernail clippers, stenopads, and lots of duct tape. If you don't find it there, it can't be found and it's not worth using. Right?

The Macintosh equivalent is the **Apple menu**. Here's where you'll find all the utility items and most of the tidbits. Press and hold the mouse button on the Apple menu icon and you'll see what I mean (see fig. 5.6). Its got little applications ("applets") for doing things like adding a clock to your desktop. It also gives you access to the **Control Panels**, where you change settings and customize your Macintosh. (See chapters 9-11 for Control Panel details.) In System 7.5 and above, you may also notice that the Apple menu works a little differently than other menus. Instead of symbols and letters next to menu items, some of them show a black arrow. These are called **cascading menus**—a relatively new feature that lets you do some interesting things with the Apple menu (see fig. 5.6). See the sidebar "Sliding down cascading menus" for details.

For now, get used to thinking of the Apple menu as a good place to go when you need a tidbit or a utility. Soon, it'll be the best place to go for nearly everything! We'll discuss customizing the Apple menu and how to take complete advantage of cascading menus in chapter 9, "Getting Organized with the Apple Menu and Aliases."

Fig. 5.6

If the menu item
has a little arrow,
then it will
"cascade" out

The Apple Menu icon

The Main menu

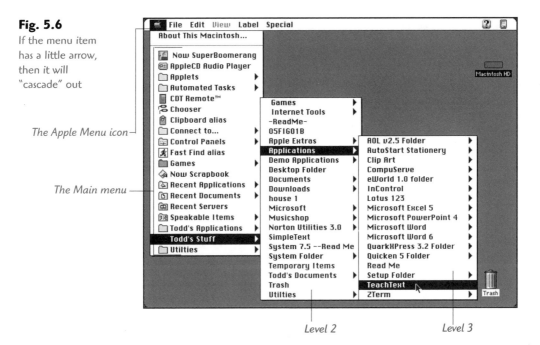

Level 2   *Level 3*

The Application menu

You may already know that your Macintosh System Software has the ability
to run more than one program at a time (it's called multitasking). You
manage these open programs through Mac's **Application menu** (see fig. 5.7).
Every time you start a new application, it gets added to the Application
menu. By clicking and holding on the Application menu icon, you can see
every application that is currently running. Dragging your highlight bar down
the menu and releasing on an application name takes you to that application
window.

 Plain English, please!

> **Multitasking** is your Mac's ability to run more than one program at one time.
> For instance, you can have both Microsoft Word and Lotus 1-2-3 open at the
> same time, and you can switch between the two. The Macintosh uses a system
> called cooperative multitasking, where applications have to "agree" to
> multitask, depending on how much of the computer's power each application
> decides it wants to use.

Fig. 5.7
Working away in
Microsoft Word,
I decide I'd like
to switch to Lotus
1-2-3 to check some
numbers. I do that with
the Application menu!

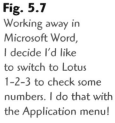

Microsoft Word,
currently in use.

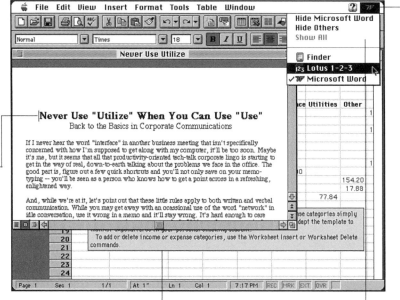

Lotus 1-2-3, in the background.   The Application menu in action.

The icon of the currently selected program appears here.

Sliding down cascading menus

Cascading menus are also often called hierarchical menus, because, just like in a paper-based filing system, they allow you to have more than one level of organization. For instance, in a paper-based filing cabinet, you may have a file drawer labeled "Contacts."

Within that drawer, however, you wouldn't necessarily find just a bunch of file folders with people's names on them. You might find folders grouped by location, by company, or by how long it's been since you called them. It's the same with the Apple menu. Menus within the Apple menu cascade out to the side to give you more levels of organization—making it easier to find things.

Switching applications

Let's say you were working on a memo in Microsoft Word, and you wanted to consult sales figures in Microsoft Excel. Click on the Application menu, pull your highlight bar down to **Microsoft Excel**, and release. The Macintosh brings Excel to the front, giving it the selected application. It's just like laying your sales report on top of your handwritten memo so that you can study it more closely.

Don't get lost while multitasking applications! Your Macintosh has a great way of keeping you focused on your work. The Application menu displays the icon for the application that is currently selected. If you're using Microsoft Word, you'll see the Microsoft Word icon (as shown in fig. 5.7). Switch to Finder, and the Application menu changes to a Finder icon. Talk about helpful!

Hiding and showing applications

Here's another similarity to your real desk—your Macintosh Desktop can get pretty cluttered. Open enough documents and applications and you could have a real mess on your hands. That's why the Application menu includes the **Hide** command. This command is for hiding applications that you don't need to use at that moment, but would like to keep open. It eliminates clutter.

Let's say you're working on your memo in Microsoft Word, and you have Microsoft Excel open behind it. You could go to the Application menu and choose **Hide Others**. This will hide all open windows that weren't created by Microsoft Word. Now there's a nice, clean screen, with just the Microsoft Word window and your Desktop icons. And nothing's lost! Go back to the Application menu and select **Microsoft Excel**, and you'll see that all of Excel's windows are still available. Or, to get everything back, choose **Show All**. Then, your clutter reappears and you can see everything.

The Hide command works just as well for hiding applications you just want off your screen. Whether it's Poker Solitaire or a confidential report, just choose Hide from the Application menu and it's gone.

The ? (Help) menu

The last of our universal menu bar items is the **? menu**, the first place to go when you need a little help (see fig. 5.8). Generally speaking, help under the ? menu is specific to the application with "focus." If the Finder currently has focus, the ? menu will offer you help specific to the Finder's menus and abilities (stuff like icons and folders). If you're working in Microsoft Word, you'll get Word-type help (stuff like fonts and spacing). See detailed coverage on Balloon Help and Apple Guide in chapter 9.

{Note} In System 7.5, the ? menu has been renamed the Apple Guide menu. It's still the menu you use for all different kinds of help.

Fig. 5.8
All the help you'll ever need. Here's where you get Apple Guide and Balloon help, along with any help files supplied by your application.

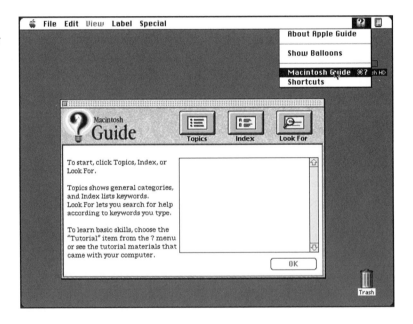

{Note} You can also hit the Help key (on an extended keyboard, it's right next to the Home key) to get help in many applications. Generally, the Help key will give you whatever type of help is most applicable in your situation.

How do I clean up and throw stuff away?

If you're in your office and you have a memo you'd like to get rid of, you probably do what most of us do. Throw it in the trash. You really can't get rid of stuff any other way. And, there's an advantage to throwing something in your trash. Sick as it may seem, if you need to, you can dig that memo out again. At least, you can that same day. In my office, the janitorial staff comes back and empties my trash every evening. The next morning, that memo's gone.

For the most part, that's exactly how the Finder's **Trash** works. You don't delete files using the menu, the Delete key, or anything else. You delete things by pointing to their icon, pressing and holding down the mouse button, dragging the file to the Trash, and releasing the mouse button (see fig. 5.9). It's done this way to avoid confusion. Because there's no other way to delete things, you have to make this very deliberate movement to throw things away. That way, at least on a Macintosh, files and documents can't "just disappear!"

Fig. 5.9

To throw things away I just drag them to the Trash (see it bulging?). I can recover them by double-clicking on the icon and dragging them out of the Trash window, unless I've already emptied it!

The Trash window: Drag it back out to use again.

The Special menu: Empty the trash and you can't get it back.

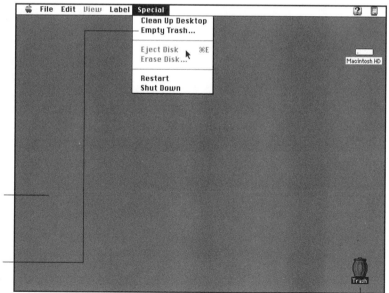

The Trash: Just drag it here and it's trash!

What if I make a mistake?

And, if you must, you can dig through the Trash. Notice that after you've dragged something to the Trash, its icon bulges a little to suggest it's full. If you want to see what's in there, just double-click on the bulging icon. A window pops up and shows you what's there, as shown in figure 5.9. Want to recover something you dropped in by mistake? Drag it to the Desktop, a folder, or your hard drive icon. It jumps right out of the Trash, squeaky clean and ready to use.

How do I empty the Trash?

With the Finder, it's your responsibility to throw out the Trash. You do this by pulling down the Special menu on the Finder's menu bar and choosing **Empty Trash...** (see fig. 5.10). This will bring up a dialog box that tells you how many items are in the Trash, how much disk space they take up, and asking if you're sure you want to delete those files. If you're sure, click on **OK**. If you'd like to think about it some more, click on **Cancel**.

Fig. 5.10

The Special menu is where you find the commands to Empty the Trash, Shut Down, and Restart.

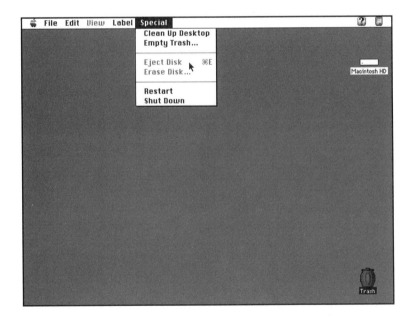

 **<Caution>** Once you've emptied the Trash, it is gone and unrecoverable without using a special utility program. Some programs (like Central Point's TrashBack) may be able to help, but empty the Trash at your own risk!

How do I turn off my Mac?

There are two important commands in the Special menu you should get to know the first time you use your computer. Those are the **Shut Down** and **Restart** commands (refer to fig. 5.10). The Shut Down command is the "safe" way to turn most Macs off—when you get ready to leave the office for the day, for instance. The Restart command is there to let you safely "reload" the System software without shutting down and powering back up. This is especially useful after you add new System software features (see chapter 28) or after you install new applications or utility programs on your Mac. Either way, it's very important to use these commands instead of just throwing your Mac's power switch or shutting off power to your Mac.

②Q&A

I got a meassage stating that my computer may not have shut down correctly. What happened?

It's important to remember to always use the Shut Down commands in the Finder's Special menu to turn off your Mac. The Shut Down command lets your Mac know that you're ready to end your session and allows the Mac to do vital housecleaning before being powered down. Since the Mac often keeps important system files in RAM while you're working, shutting the power off without warning can damage those files, resulting in the loss of data and an unhappy Mac.

The Shut Down and Restart commands also check to make sure that you have saved any work in progress that you leave in open applications. To use these commands, just move your mouse pointer up to the Special menu item and press and hold the mouse button. Now drag your mouse down to either Restart or Shut Down and release the mouse button.

Shut Down properly and you'll be much less likely to lose your work or mess up your Mac's System software. Isn't that reason enough? If you're really looking for destruction and heartache, I'd suggest unplugging your telephone answering machine in the middle of a recording. Now, plug it back in and try to figure out how to get the time/date voice stamp to work properly.

Folders, Windows, and the Finder

In this chapter:

- What is the Finder and why should I care?

- How can I see what's on my disks?

- If I want to use a program, what do I do?

- How can I organize my stuff?

Almost everyone hates filing, but the Mac makes it quick and easy. You can even color-code your folders!

No matter if you're a glutton for efficiency or a normal human being who hates filing (like me), you'll have to do some filing on your Mac. That's what the **Finder** is for. The Finder is Mac's filing system, and it's actually pretty powerful.

What is the Finder?

Simply put, the **Finder** is the application or program that starts and displays the Desktop every time you turn on your Mac (see fig. 6.1). The Finder lets you see and organize the icons that represent your folders, documents, and programs. The Finder also provides you with the basic tools for organizing your Mac's icons. Although the organization is up to you, there are some basics we discuss later in this chapter.

Fig. 6.1
See? The Finder really is an application, just like SimpleText or Microsoft Word.

 {Note}

Although the Finder may seem like it's part of the Desktop, it's actually an application, like Microsoft Word or Lotus 1-2-3. In fact, if you'd like proof, check the Application menu (refer to fig. 6.1). You'll see the Finder sitting right there.

 (Tip)

Although you can use the Application menu to change from another application to the Finder, you don't have to. One quick way is just to move the mouse pointer over an exposed part of the Desktop and click.

How can I find out what's on my disks?

You've got to open your filing cabinet to get at your folders, and in the Finder, you have to do the same thing with your disks. Let's start with your hard drive icon. My hard drive icon, Macintosh HD, is floating there at the top right corner of figure 6.2. When I double-click on it, a window pops up that allows me to see all my "first-level" folders that I use for organizing applications and documents. To look inside another folder, say Applications, all I do is double-click again. Suddenly, there are folders and icons for all the applications I use on a regular basis.

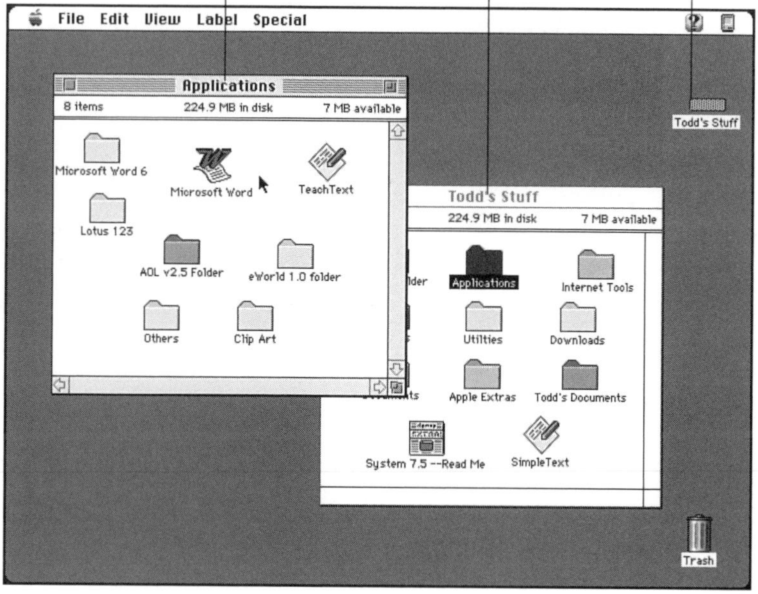

Folder window—getting warmer!

Hard Drive window—first level of organization

The Hard Drive icon— where it all begins

Fig. 6.2
Looking into drives and folders is as easy as a double-click. But make sure your folders are well organized, or you may have to dig deep to find what you want.

How do I start a program?

Let's say I want to create a listing of all the paperback books I own. Since I haven't worked on this document before, I'll just double-click on the Microsoft Word icon (refer to fig. 6.2). This starts the Microsoft Word application, complete with a new document called "Untitled." In general, any application can be started in this fashion. Just find the program icon and double-click.

 **{Note}**

Although I'm using Microsoft Word for my list, there are much more powerful programs for list management. We'll discuss database programs and list management software in chapter 16, "Number Crunching and Managing Lists."

The truth is, however, I have already started a listing of all the books I own. From my hard drive window, I double-click on the folder called Todd's Documents (see fig. 6.3). In the Todd's Documents folder is another folder called Lists. Double-click on that, and, what-do-ya-know, there's an icon named List of My Books.

Fig. 6.3
List of My Books looks just like a Microsoft Word icon! That means double-clicking on that document will start Microsoft Word, and then it'll load my List.

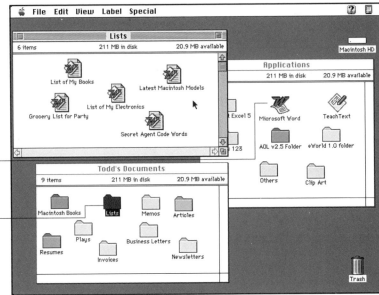

Microsoft Word Program icon

Document created in Microsoft Word

⊛ *{Note}* _____ | Notice that my list's icon looks a lot like the Microsoft Word application icon. That's because the Finder remembers what application you created a document in. So, if I double-click on List of My Books, the Finder starts Microsoft Word, and then tells Word that I want to work on List of My Books. Word, in turn, brings up that document.

How can I get organized?

The Finder is your application for organizing stuff on your Mac, so we might as well start with some of the filing tools provided. One of the Finder's main tasks is the creation of **folders**. Just like standard filing folders in a cabinet, you'll need to pull out a fresh one every once in a while and stick a label on it.

Creating folders

If you want a new folder, all you have to do is drag your mouse pointer up to the Finder's menu bar, pull down the File menu, and select **New Folder**. Do that, and up pops a new folder labeled "Untitled Folder." Be aware, though, that any time you create a folder, it will pop up in the window that is currently selected (where you clicked before selecting from the menu).

? Q&A *I created a folder, but now I can't find it?*

Untitled folders appear in the window that's currently selected. If you have a window open on your Desktop, it's probably in there. If not, it may have appeared on the Desktop. If that's the case, you can simply drag it wherever you need it.

Giving your folders names

The next step in creating your Mac filing system is giving your folders a more meaningful label. You have up to 31 characters to work with, and you can use any character except a colon (:), so use numbers and letters freely. There's no stick-em here, just a little electronic wizardry.

First, make sure the Finder is "active" using the Application menu or by clicking on the Desktop. Then, click once on the name of the folder (see fig. 6.4). After a short pause, the current name will be highlighted and change color. Once it's highlighted, you can just start typing your new name, or you can click inside the name and use the arrow or Delete keys to edit the current name.

 **{Note}** Actually, this is the procedure you follow for renaming *any* icon. You can rename your disks, documents, or even your programs the exact same way.

Fig. 6.4
Rename folders for a
more effective filing
system.

⊗<Caution>__ Avoid beginning the names of folders or icons with a period (.). A period can occasionally confuse the Macintosh into believing your file is an important system file and it will try to use it, potentially destroying data on your hard drive.

Color-coding your folders

The Label menu on the Finder's menu bar allows you to organize your folders by color (see fig. 6.5). If your Macintosh is a busy workplace, it helps to get to know these colors. Select a folder by clicking once on its icon. Then, pull down the **Label menu** and choose a color (red for "hot," blue for "personal," etc.) and you'll know instantly the importance of a folder in the grand scheme of things. (See chapter 13, "Develop Your Personal Filing System," for more on using labels to organize your Desktop.)

Fig. 6.5
Use these labels, or
make your own, to
help organize folders
and files with the
Finder.

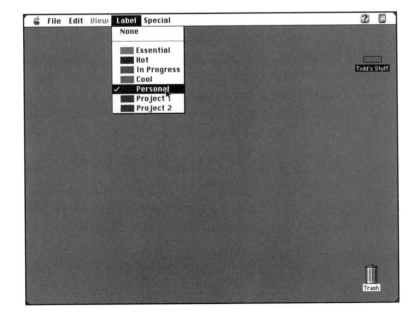

Getting rid of folders

There's one way to delete things on the Mac, and it works the same with folders as with any icon. From the Finder, place your mouse pointer over the folder you want to delete, and then click and hold down the mouse button. Drag that folder over the Trash and let go of the mouse button when the Trash changes colors. It's in the Trash, now, waiting to be emptied.

 **<Caution>** When you Trash a folder, anything in that folder is Trashed, too. Just like in the real world, all the documents or applications you stored in that folder will disappear when you empty the Trash. So, make sure nothing important is hiding in a folder you plan to toss out.

What are windows

Windows are like pieces of paper on your Desktop that you can stack on top of one another, move around, and hide. They allow you to view information from different folders, different documents, or even different applications at the same time.

A window is generally created by an application or the Finder when you "open" something. Open the Macintosh HD container icon (by double-clicking on it) and the Finder will generate a window to show you what folders and applications that disk holds. If you double-click on a Microsoft Word document, the Finder will start Word and Word will create a window to hold that document.

How do I move a window?

To move a window, press and hold down the mouse button on the window's **title bar** (see the graphics page "The elements of Mac's standard window"). Now you've got a faint, dotted outline of your window. Move the mouse pointer around the screen, and the outline will follow along with it. When you have the outline where you want it, release the mouse button. The outline disappears and the window takes its place.

Microsoft Windows and the Mac

You've probably heard a lot about Microsoft Windows, and perhaps you've wondered exactly what it is, and what it has to do with the Macintosh.

Microsoft Windows is an operating environment for IBM-compatible computers that works in conjunction with the MS-DOS operating system. Microsoft Windows gives these computers a slightly more Macintosh look and feel, complete with menu bars and movable windows.

Programs have to be written specifically to work with Microsoft Windows, although it allows (non-graphical) DOS-based programs to run in their own windows on the Microsoft Windows desktop. Newer versions of Microsoft Windows are promised in 1995 that are expected to more effectively rival the Macintosh Finder in ease-of-use and friendliness.

The Microsoft Windows environment, the IBM-compatible computer's answer to the Macintosh.

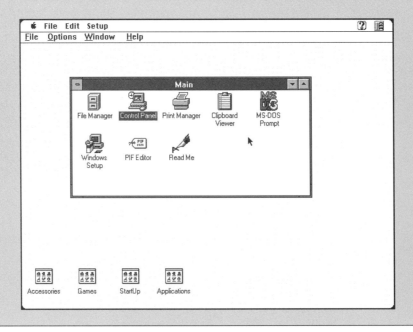

The elements of Mac's standard window

Close box: *When you've seen everything you want to see, click once here and the window's gone!*

Title bar: *Press and hold down the mouse button here. Move the mouse pointer around the screen and an outline of the window will follow it. When you have the outline where you want it, release the mouse button.*

Zoom box: *Click once and the window resizes to show you all available information, while taking up the least amount of screen space. Click again and your window will return to the size it was before the first click.*

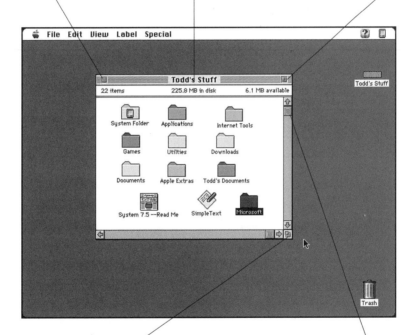

Size box: *Press and hold down the mouse button on the size box. Again you'll get an outline. Drag the mouse pointer around the screen until the outline's size looks about right and release.*

Scroll bars: *If you need to see something that's not currently in the window, put your mouse pointer over the scroll box and press the mouse button. You can then either drag the mouse down to move the contents of the window up, or up to move the contents of the window down. The horizontal scroll bar works the same way, but moves things from left to right.*

Can I change the window's size?

There are two ways to resize a window. Press and hold the mouse button on the **size box** (refer to "The elements of Mac's standard window"). Again you'll get an outline. Drag the mouse pointer around the screen until the outline's size looks about right. Release the button, and there's your new window size.

Another way to resize a window is by clicking on the Zoom box. The **Zoom box** is basically a switch—it resizes your window two ways. The first time you click on it, it returns the window to its default state. The default is defined by each individual application to show you all available information, while taking up the least amount of screen space. If you're not happy with the way things look, click on the Zoom box again. It will return your window to the size it was before your first click. Call it the pre-default state.

> The Zoom box on a folder's window will attempt to show you everything in that folder in the least amount of space. If you've got icons that have scrolled off your folder window, try clicking the Zoom box first.

What if there's stuff there I can't see?

The scroll bars on your standard window work a lot like the paper feeder on a typewriter. Sometimes there's too much information to show in a window, and you'll need to move "the page" up or down. If you need to see something that's not currently in the window, put your mouse pointer over the **Scroll box** (refer to "The elements of Mac's standard window") and press and hold the mouse button. Now, you can move the Scroll box up and down the scroll bar to see up and down in the window. Release the mouse button when you see what you are looking for.

?Q&A

I can't see my window anymore. How do I get it back?

Depends on how you lost it. If you see the title bar but no window, you may have accidentally activated Windowshade. Try double-clicking the title bar. (Chapter 10, "Banish the Bland Mac!" has more on Windowshade.)

If you clicked the close box, you'll have to use your program's Open command to reopen the document (or, you may need to restart your program by double-clicking its icon). Finally, you may have switched applications and hidden the window. See chapter 5 for more info on switching and hiding applications.

Is this the only view through the window?

The Finder allows you to look at folder windows in many different ways, depending on which organization makes you the most comfortable. The default view for most Finder windows is "By Icon," which gives you standard-sized icons in a window. Others may prove more or less useful, depending on your taste and needs. Just experiment with what works best for you. See chapter 13, "Develop Your Personal Filing System," for information on taking advantage of Finder views.

How do I close the window?

When you've seen everything you want to see, you're ready to get rid of a window. Just click the mouse button once with your mouse pointer on the **Close box** (refer to "The elements of Mac's standard window").

That's all there is to paper shuffling on your Mac. It's just like in your office—once you've got your file folders labeled, your filing cabinet organized, and plenty of blank paper handy, you're ready to get some work done!

Finding a Place for Your Stuff: Floppy Disks and Hard Drives

In this chapter:

- What happens to a file when I save it?

- Why do I need a hard drive?

- When should I use a floppy disk?

- How do I copy and move stuff between disks?

- How do I know if I'm running out of storage space?

Storing stuff is easy when you've got plenty of space. But disks are like closets; they fill up fast!

O n your Macintosh, just as in apartment living, storage is a premium. You generally start out small—just like you do with your first apartment. But you keep collecting stuff. Documents, applications, games, and utility programs all have to be stored somewhere. That's why your Macintosh has a hard drive and a floppy disk drive. You use these for storage.

What is a hard drive?

If you took your Macintosh's case apart and looked inside, you'd see the **hard disk drive** (or just *hard drive* for short). It's a metal case connected to a bunch of wires. Inside the metal case are a number of metal platters coated in magnetic material. But who cares about that, right?

What the hard drive *does* is provide a holding area or container where a large number of documents and applications can be safely stored for a long period of time. On the Desktop, your hard drive is represented by an icon, like the Macintosh HD icon shown in figure 7.1.

Fig. 7.1

The Macintosh HD disk icon represents the internal hard drive of my Macintosh. The open window is a graphical representation of the stuff on that hard drive.

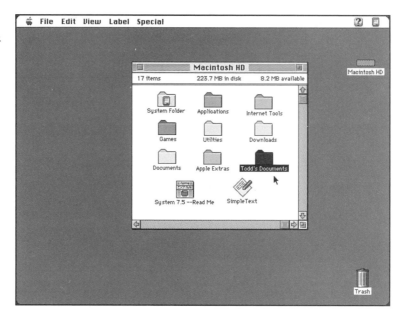

How much space is enough?

Hard drives range in the amount of data they can hold. The smallest hold about 20 MB of data, the largest (for a Macintosh) can hold thousands of megabytes. What's a **megabyte** (**MB**)? It's around 1 million bytes, or characters, of data. That's roughly equivalent to around 400 pages of text. New Macintosh systems generally ship with between 160 and 1,000 MB of hard drive space.

Is that a lot? Well, that's a little tough to figure. Big-name productivity applications like word processing and spreadsheet programs can take between 5 MB and 15 MB each on your hard drive. Some of the latest movie-style games and educational programs can take up as much or more than that. Even a single graphics file (like a digital picture) can take up 1 MB or more.

So, how much space you need depends on what you have to store. Storage requirements will continue to grow over the next few years as the requirements for new technologies take hold. Someday, even gigabytes (thousands of megabytes) of storage will seem small!

What's so hard about it?

It's called the *hard disk* drive because the **platters**, or disks, inside the drive case are made of a rigid aluminum. The mechanism inside a hard drive is kind of like a phonograph record, with a **head** that, like a stylus, reads information from the platter. The heads on a hard drive read the information magnetically instead of physically, as does a phonograph's stylus.

How do I use it?

Any time you save a document or put a new folder in the Macintosh HD window, you are using the hard drive. For the most part, items on the Desktop are stored on your hard drive, even if you access them outside of your Macintosh HD window.

Saving in applications

One way you get data onto your hard drive is by **saving** it in an active application. So where is the data until you save it? While you're working on a document, it's stored in memory (or RAM), your Mac's temporary storage. When you save, the Mac writes that data from memory to the hard drive so that it can be used again later (see fig. 7.2).

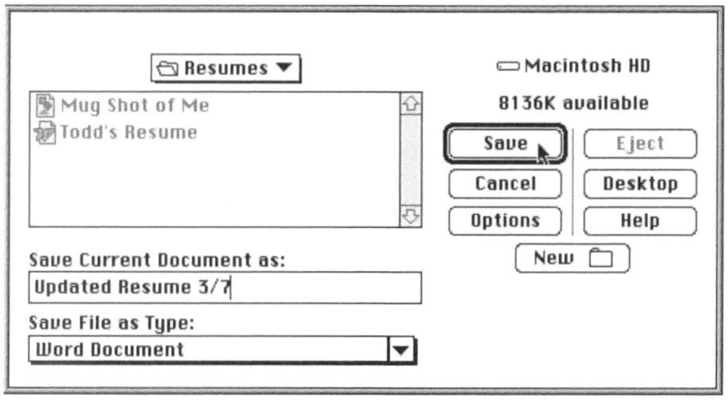

Fig. 7.2
Microsoft Word's Save dialog box. When you save, you're storing the data that's in RAM on your hard drive.

Saving work to your hard drive is a little like using a microcassette recorder for dictation. While you're thinking about something, it's foremost in your mind and you can concentrate all your attention on it. Take a quick nap, though, and you may lose those thoughts. So, you record the thoughts for use later.

Same with your hard drive. While you work on a document on the screen, it's all there (in Mac's memory) for rearranging and formatting. Turn your Mac off, though, and it's gone. To use it later, you need to save it to the hard drive.

{Note}

Most Macintosh programs are designed to remind you to save your work, especially before you close the document or shut down. But it's still a good idea to save periodically—just to make sure your work is safe if someone trips over Mac's power cord!

Copying from the floppy drive

The other way you get files on your hard drive is by copying files from some other kind of disk or storage device, usually the floppy disk drive. A little later in this chapter, we'll talk about how to copy files from floppy disks to your hard drive and back again.

What is a floppy disk drive?

Basically, the **floppy disk drive** is the slot on the front of your computer that takes floppy disks. The floppy disk drive is an internal mechanism that accepts floppy disks and allows your Mac to read them in a way that is somewhat similar to the hard drive. Floppy disks for the Macintosh are thin, square cartridges that are about 3.5" square (see fig. 7.3). They store considerably less data than your hard drive, but they have the added advantage of being portable.

Fig. 7.3
A standard floppy disk. What's so floppy about it? The disk inside the hard plastic case.

Files for my Mac

 **{Note}** Most Macintosh floppy disk drives accept high-density floppy disks that can hold about 1.4 MB of data. When you consider how much space some applications require (see sidebar "How much space is enough" earlier in this chapter), it's easy to see why many applications come on multiple floppy disks or even high-capacity CDs.

What's a floppy disk?

Although a **floppy disk** has a rigid plastic shell, inside there is a small, circular disk that really is floppy. It's similar to the platter in a hard drive in that it stores data magnetically, but it's physically more flexible, and it stores considerably less data.

Inserting a floppy disk

Remember one quick rule: *Label up and out.* That's the rule for inserting a floppy disk (see fig. 7.4). You want the floppy disk's label to be facing up and closest to you, so that the first part of the disk that enters the drive is the metal slider.

What type of disks does a Mac use?

 The first Macs used single-sided disks that could hold about 400,000 bytes of data. Later, floppy disk drives that could use double-sided disks and hold 800,000 bytes were added to systems. The current Apple SuperDrives can read and write to single-sided, double-sided, and high-density disks. High-density disks (the kind you should probably get) can hold about 1.4 MB of data. Apple SuperDrives can also read high-density disks formatted for IBM-compatibles.

Fig. 7.4
Be careful that you put
the disk in correctly.
And don't force it.

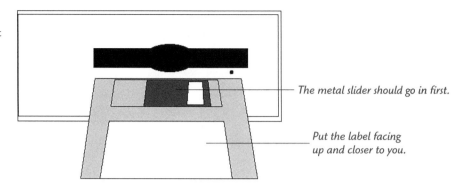

The metal slider should go in first.

Put the label facing
up and closer to you.

There are two types of floppy disk drives found in Macs. Each type works a
little differently. If your Macintosh is new, you probably have a manual-inject
drive. You should be able to just push the disk in slowly until it "clicks" into
place. If your Mac is a few years old or an older model, it may have an auto-
inject drive. This type of floppy disk drive grabs the disk and pulls it into the
drive. Your car's cassette deck may work in a similar way, by "grabbing" the
cassette and pulling it in.

<Caution> Don't force the disk into the drive until you're sure which type you have. Insert
the floppy disk slowly until it either stops with a click or gets pulled in.

Preparing a new disk

When you insert a new disk in the floppy drive, the Macintosh will do one of
two things. It will either place a new icon on the Desktop that looks just like
a floppy disk, or it will ask you if you want to initialize the disk (see fig. 7.5).

66 *Plain English, please!*

Initializing (sometimes called formatting) puts a basic filing system on the disk
that the Macintosh can use to manage the files that you want to store. Since
the same 3.5" disks can be used with a number of different computers, they
must be specifically initialized to work with the Mac. 99

Fig. 7.5

Give the Mac a disk it doesn't recognize and you'll have to answer a dialog box like this one.

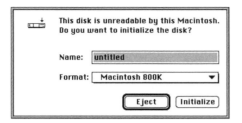

⊗<Caution> Be aware that initializing a disk erases any and all data that may have been on it. If you suspect a disk contains data that you'll want later, do not initialize it!

When you're asked to initialize a disk, the Mac will suggest the format it thinks is most appropriate for that type of disk. For instance, if you give Mac a high-density disk, it will suggest you initialize it at 1.4 MB—that disk's maximum capacity. It is possible to initialize high-density disks at a lower capacity (with an additional program), but that's only useful if you need to work with both a newer Mac and a much older Macintosh.

Notice in figure 7.5 that you can also name your disk. Type in up to 27 letters, numbers, or symbols (a colon will automatically change to a dash). You can always rename it later, the same way you rename any icon.

If you decide you don't want to initialize this disk, just click the Eject button (refer to fig. 7.5). The disk will pop back out of your drive and you can go about your business.

⊘Q&A *I have a disk that was created by MS-DOS. Why does Mac want to initialize it?*

You need special software for your Mac (included with System 7.5) to recognize MS-DOS formatted disks. See chapter 17, "Getting It All with Works Applications," for more information on working with DOS files and disks.

New icon! Opening a floppy disk

When you successfully place an initialized disk in the floppy drive, an icon appears on the Desktop that looks like a disk. This icon works like the Macintosh HD icon. Double-click on the icon and you've opened it (just like any other icon). Now you can organize your floppy disks just like your hard drive, if you'd like to. Create folders, save files, and arrange icons.

Getting a disk back from your Mac

There are two basic ways to get the disk back from Mac. If you've ever used another computer, you'll notice that, on the Mac, there's no button for ejecting the disk.

Let me say this again. There is no physical button to eject the Mac's disk! Some Macintosh "slimline" designs (like the Centris 610,660AV, Quadra 610,660AV, and Power Macintosh 6100) have the *power* button located very close to the floppy disk drive. Pushing this button will turn your Mac off, causing you to lose data and potentially damage system files by not shutting down correctly.

The first way to eject the disk is pretty straightforward. Select the disk by clicking once on its icon. Drag your mouse up to the Finder's menu bar, pull down the File menu, and select Put Away (see fig. 7.6). The disk pops right out. No questions asked.

The other way is easy enough to do, but I think it's a little counter-intuitive. You drag-and-drop the floppy disk's icon to the Trash. Yuck! That's throwing it all away, isn't it? Doesn't that delete all the files?

No, it doesn't. It ejects the disk. Go figure. It works every time (I promise) as long as you drag the floppy disk's icon to the trash...and not files from the floppy disk's window!

There's a third way to eject a disk: With the **Eject Disk** command in the Special menu. If you use this command, though, you'll still have to manually drag-and-drop the disk's icon to the Trash.

Fig. 7.6

Two ways to get the disk back. The logical way, and the, uh, strange way.

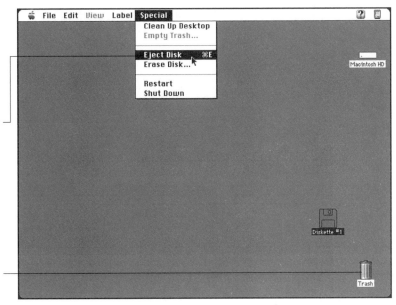

Use the Eject Disk command in the Special menu.

Drag the disk to the Trash.

?Q&A ⎡ **Why won't the disk eject when I drag its icon to the Trash?**

You can't throw away a disk that has files open, so if you still have documents open from the disk or you started an application from it, you'll need to quit those things before ejecting. If nothing's open, you may have dragged-and-dropped the disk's icon incorrectly onto the Trash icon. Try using the Put Away command in the File menu.

Finally, *this doesn't often happen, but...*the disk may just be stuck. Two ways to tell it's stuck: (1) the icon is no longer on the Desktop, or (2) the disk ejects part way and then jumps back in the drive. If all else fails, you can eject the disk manually by straightening a paper clip and pushing it (very carefully) into the small manual eject hole on the front of the drive.

When should I use a floppy disk?

There's one other difference between floppy disks and hard drives that we haven't really discussed. Floppy drives are a lot slower than hard drives. Loading and saving documents directly to a floppy disk is usually bearable, depending on how large the document is. Running an application from a disk (applications are often much larger than documents) can be annoying. So, you'll often want to copy files from your floppy disks to your hard drive so that things move a bit quicker.

Use a floppy for files you can't live without

Important files are vulnerable on your hard drive—if the drive fails or is damaged, you'll lose your data. Put a copy of files you "can't live without" on a floppy disk—preferably stored somewhere other than with your computer.

How do I copy a file from one disk to another?

How do you copy a file? It's just like moving files with drag-and-drop. Just pick up the icon and drop it in the window you want to use. If, for instance, I pick up the document Sales Presentation in the Stuff From Work window and drop it in Macintosh HD window, it will copy the file from the floppy to the hard drive (see fig. 7.7). I could also, if I wanted to, drop the Presentation File on the folder called Work Files and it would be placed in that folder on my hard drive.

So, why doesn't it just move the document? The Macintosh assumes that you want to copy files between different drives, instead of move them. If it was your intention to move them, you'll have to manually delete the files after you've copied them by dragging them to the Trash. If you drag-and-drop files to different folders on *the same drive*, the Macintosh will just move those files.

Fig. 7.7
Copying is as easy
as drag-and-drop.
I picked up the
Presentation File and
dropped it on the
Work Files folder in
the Macintosh HD
window.

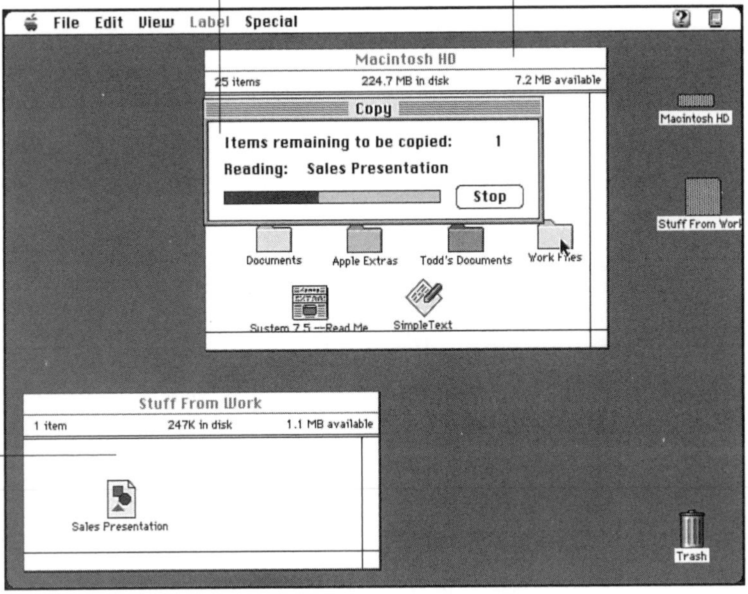

Mac reports copying in progress   *The Macintosh HD window*

The floppy disk window

②Q&A___ *I moved a file from my floppy disk to the Desktop. But when I eject the disk it disappears.*

The file leaves with the floppy because you never actually copied it to the hard drive. Hold down the Option key while you drag a file from your floppy to the Desktop. This tells your Mac that you want the file to stay on the Desktop. It will be copied to your hard drive and you can eject the disk.

Tips for managing your disks

While most copying and moving can be accomplished with drag-and-drop, you may occasionally want to do other things with your files. The Finder provides you with a few special commands that allow you to manage hard drives and floppy disks more easily.

When one copy just ain't enough

Since drag-and-drop simply moves files and folders on the same drive, the Finder gives you the option of **duplicating** a file or a folder, thus creating two copies (see fig. 7.8). Duplicating creates a clone of your file or folder that is a complete and exact copy of the original. It takes up the same amount of space on your drive or disk and it contains all the same data.

Fig. 7.8

The Duplicate command allows you to copy files and folders for use in different places on the same drive.

Choose Duplicate from the File menu

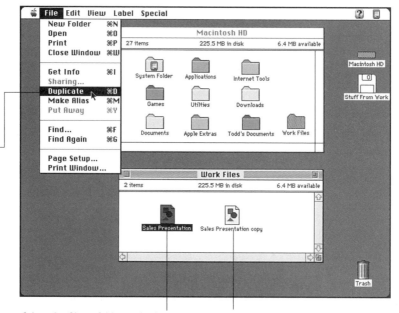

Select the file or folder to duplicate   And here's your copy

To duplicate, first select the file or folder you want to copy. Then, pull down the File menu and choose Duplicate. The command executes and up pops a new icon with the word "copy" added to your file or folder's name. You can now use this icon just as if it were the original document. Rename it, double-click to open it...anything you want.

 **{Note}**

The Mac renames a duplicate icon by adding "copy" because no two icons can share the same name while in the same folder. If you'd like to rename the copy to its original name, you'll need to move it first.

Creating an alias

In my living room there must be at least four different ways to turn on the ceiling fan! I can turn it on from just outside the kitchen, right next to the front door, right outside the bedroom, or by walking up to it and yanking its chain. That's a bunch of different ways to access the same thing.

Creating an alias on the Mac is a little like creating another switch for your ceiling fan. An **alias** gives you another way to access the same file or folder. When you create an alias, you don't duplicate the file, you just duplicate the file's icon. There's only one file, just like there's only one ceiling fan. The alias is just another switch for that file that you can put in a different place.

To create an alias, select the icon and pull down the Finder's File menu (see fig. 7.9). Select the **Make Alias** command. When that executes, you'll get a copy of the old icon with "alias" added to its name. It works just like the Duplicate command, except the alias isn't a copy of the document. It's just an icon that remembers where the document is. (It also takes up less disk space than a duplicate copy.) Click on this alias and you actually start the document. (For more on using aliases, see chapter 9, "Getting Organized with the Apple Menu and Aliases.")

Fig. 7.9
Creating an alias is like adding another light switch for your ceiling fan. It's just another way to access the old item.

Choose Make Alias from the File menu

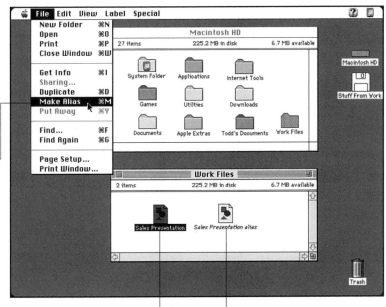

Select the file or folder to alias   *Here's your new alias to the same old file*

Notice how the alias' name is in italics? It always will be, even if you change the name. You can tell instantly than an icon is an alias for something else by the fact that its name is italicized.

Putting stuff away

The Finder offers one other unique capability that can be fun to play with. It's the **Put Away** command. Basically, the Put Away command takes the selected icon and puts it where it was before you moved it. For instance, if you drag an icon out onto the Desktop to work on it, you can use the Put Away command to return it to its original folder on the Macintosh HD when you're done.

Why would you do this? Two reasons. First, you might want to organize your work by projects. Whenever I'm working on something like a newsletter, for instance, I like to put all the files I'm using on my Desktop. Little notes I've written myself, graphics files, and any related research I've done. I just drop the icons on my Desktop so that I can see them all. When I'm done, I send them all back to their folders with the Put Away command.

You can also use the Put Away command to recover files from the Trash (before the Trash is emptied). This is a nice, quick way to send something back to its original folder (see fig. 7.10).

Fig. 7.10
The Put Away command is almost like a drag-and-drop "Undo" command. When you're done with your files, put them away!

After the Put Away command completes, they're back where they came from.

And, you can put away things you've decided not to throw out.

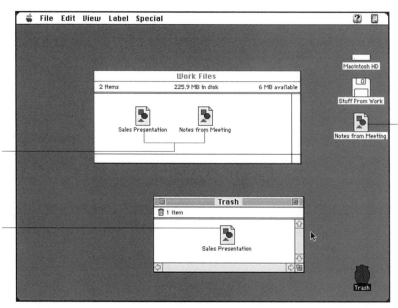

You can drop your work-in-progress here, and then put them away later.

To put something away, just select its icon. Then pull down the Finder's File menu and choose the Put Away command. It will disappear from the Desktop or Trash, and reappear in its original folder.

Sizing things up

Adding new files, documents, system programs, and applications to your hard drive is a lot like pouring water into a pitcher. Every time you add a new file, you're adding a little water. Keep adding water, and eventually that pitcher will overflow. Now, Mac won't let your data *overflow* the hard drive (and it's not wet...so, you won't be electrocuted), but running out of space on a disk *does* mean it can't hold any more new files.

What we need is some way of knowing how big files are, how much drive space we have, and how much is left. That way, if we ever fill our pitcher up to the rim, we'll know to toss out a couple of old files and applications (or save them onto floppy disks to store them away) to make room for the new ones.

We've talked a lot about how much drive space you need and how many megabytes are used by documents and applications. But how can you tell how much space your hard drive has and how much is being taken up?

Drive statistics

Drive and folder windows in the Finder are a great way to get information about your hard or floppy disk space. At the top of each window (when you use the By Icon or By Small Icon view) are statistics for how many items are in that window, how much space is used, and how much is left (see fig. 7.11). If you add these two numbers together, you'll get the total capacity of your drive.

Fig. 7.11
Your hard drive and floppy drive windows give you vital information about space being used and how much space is left. Add the two together for total disk capacity.

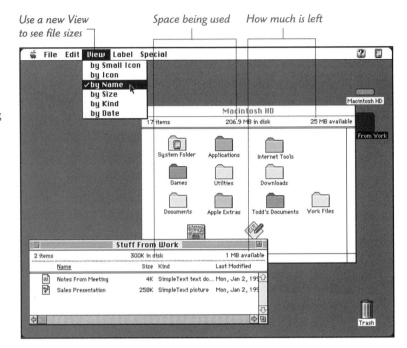

Use a new View to see file sizes

Space being used

How much is left

Also, changing the View on a Finder window can give you more information on your files. With a window selected, pull down the View menu and select **By Name**, **By Size**, **By Kind**, or **By Date**. Any of these views will give you a "listing" of your files (instead of an icon view) that includes information on file type and size. (See more on Views in chapter 10, "Banish the Bland Mac!")

By default, when you switch away from the By Icon or By Small Icon view, your drive information at the top of the window goes away. Want it back? Pull down the Apple menu and select Control Panels. Open the Views icon. Click the box next to Show Disk Info in Header. Now, click the Close box on the Views window. Now you've got your disk info in all Views!

Get info on applications, folders, and documents

The other way you can get information on your files is through the Get Info command on the Mac's File menu. Just select an icon, pull down the File menu, and select Get Info.... This brings up a dialog box that tells you things like how much disk space it consumes, where it's saved, and when it was created and last modified (see fig. 7.12).

Fig. 7.12

The Get Info window gives you all kinds of information about your files.

```
┌──────────────────────────────────────┐
│▤▥▦ Notes From Meeting Info ▦▥▤        │
├──────────────────────────────────────┤
│  ▤                                     │
│  ▤══  Notes From Meeting              │
│                                        │
│    Kind: SimpleText text document      │
│    Size: 4K on disk (3,270 bytes used) │
│                                        │
│   Where: Stuff From Work:              │
│                                        │
│                                        │
│  Created: Mon, Jan 2, 1995, 7:46 PM    │
│ Modified: Mon, Jan 2, 1995, 7:46 PM    │
│  Version: n/a                          │
│                                        │
│ Comments:                              │
│  ┌──────────────────────────────────┐ │
│  │                                  │ │
│  │                                  │ │
│  │                                  │ │
│  └──────────────────────────────────┘ │
│                                        │
│  ☐ Locked           ☐ Stationery pad   │
└──────────────────────────────────────┘
```

Getting Help When You Need It

If you're new to the Mac, you'll love Apple Guide. It's not only easy to use, but sometimes it does the steps for you. Now that's real help!

In this chapter:

- What kind of help can I get?

- Where should I start?

- I don't know what to do next

- I need help with an application

- How do I find help when I don't know the right terms?

For years the Macintosh has offered context-sensitive help for getting around the Desktop and applications. But in the most recent version of the system software (System 7.5), Mac's help is even more impressive. The latest system includes **Apple Guide**, which uses interactive graphics to show you how to do new things with your Mac. Sometimes, it will even do things for you!

What kind of help is available?

Along with Apple Guide, there are two other types of help you'll often encounter with the Macintosh. These are **Balloon Help** and **Application Help**.

Each type of help is more helpful in certain situations than others (see fig. 8.1). Apple Guide is almost a computer-based tutor. It's good for walking you through the processes required to get something done. Balloon Help, on the other hand, is very visual. Its main goal is to help you figure out what everything on your screen is for. Application Help is generally very specific to the application you're using. Microsoft Word's help, for instance, uses hypertext documents to delve deep into things like changing typefaces and centering text.

Fig. 8.1
Examples of the three different types of help.

Application Help gives you an in-depth look at your program

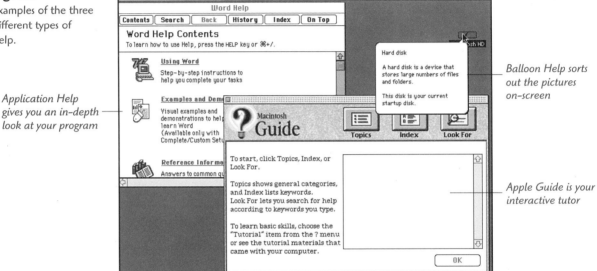

Balloon Help sorts out the pictures on-screen

Apple Guide is your interactive tutor

A little about the About box

Although not technically a help system, the About menu choice shows up with most applications, and it can occasionally be helpful. In the case of the Finder, the About box gives you information on memory usage, applications that are open, and the type of Macintosh you're using.

Other applications may not give you system-specific information, but the About box will tell you about that program. Generally it will show

you what version of the program it is, who wrote it, and what its copyright date is. Some About boxes also give you access to that program's help system.

If you're interested, pull down the Apple menu while your application's window is active. Then, select the **About "″** ... command, where the "″ is the name of your application. Then, learn all about it!

Plain English, please!

A **hypertext** document is a document with "links" built into it that move you from page to page based on context. For instance, on a page that talks about the menu bar, the words "menu bar" might be highlighted. Click your mouse on this link and a definition of the menu bar will appear. Click on something about "The Finder" and you might be moved to an entirely new page explaining the Finder.

Balloon Help is a good place to start

You know how comic books are generally pictures without a lot of substance? So is Balloon Help on your Macintosh. But, that's not necessarily bad. Balloon Help can be useful when you know what you're doing—you're just not sure how to do it. Maybe you know you want to center text in your word processor, but you're not sure how to do it (see fig. 8.2). Well, that's where Balloon Help comes in very handy.

Fig. 8.2
Here Balloon Help can show me what all these little buttons are for in Microsoft Word. Oh yeah, here's the Centering tool.

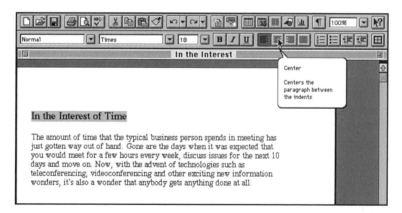

Clearly, Balloon Help is supposed to look like a comic book caption, too. That's probably our first indicator that it's not going to be the most in-depth help we can get. It's just Mac's way of giving you quick little descriptions of almost anything you see on the screen. If you're confused about something, turn on Balloon Help and point your mouse at it.

Showing balloons

All you have to do to start Balloon Help is put your mouse pointer on the Help menu (the question mark up on the menu bar, sometimes called the Apple Guide or Guide menu) and hold down the mouse button. The Help menu pulls down like any other menu on the menu bar. Then, highlight **Show Balloons** and release the mouse button (see fig. 8.3). Now, just about everything you point to will have something to say back.

Fig. 8.3
The Help menu pulls down like any other menu. Select Show Balloons and you're ready to go.

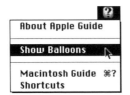

 Q&A _____

> ### I turned on Balloon Help, but I'm not getting any balloons!
>
> If you are working in an application, Balloon Help may not be available. Application programmers have to specifically support Balloon Help when they write their applications—and some don't. In that case, you just won't get much help. Balloon Help will still help you out with the standard items like windows, icons, and folders—just not the application-specific stuff.

Interpreting balloon speak

Basically, a balloon will tell you two things about something you point at. It will tell you what it is called and what you can do with it. It won't give you in-depth step-by-step instructions, it won't tell you where to find other things, and it doesn't interject witty little statements about life in its commentary. (So, I guess you still need this book.) But, at the same time, it does cut right to the chase, and can be very helpful (see fig. 8.4).

Fig. 8.4
Here are two examples. On the left is help on a standard window feature: the Zoom box. On the right is some application-specific help.

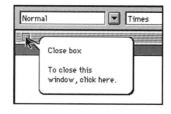 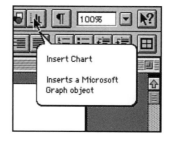

Stop showing these balloons

Although you can leave the balloons on all the time, it can get annoying. In fact, sometimes they just plain get in the way. When you're ready to turn off the balloons, it's easy. Just pull down the Help menu again, and select **Hide Balloons**. When you're ready for a little more help, you can show them again.

> I rarely leave Balloon Help turned on for any length of time, but I do find it to be a great way to get to know a new program. When you first start a program you're unfamiliar with, turn on the balloons and take a few moments to get a feel for what everything does. It could save you a lot of time later.

The Apple Guide holds your hand

For a while, Balloon Help was the only real built-in, Apple-designed way that the Macintosh had to give guidance. I suppose the thinking was that the Mac is so easy to use, the help system shouldn't have to be terribly complicated. The truth is, the Macintosh is even *easier* to use with a very sophisticated help system.

Enter Apple Guide. Apple Guide really is the "next frontier" of help systems (see fig. 8.5). It's an interactive tutor as well as a reference. It's designed to give you as much, or as little, help as you need and it has some amazing capabilities to make that happen.

> Apple Guide is only available on Macintosh machines running the System 7.5 or higher version of the Mac operating system.

Fig. 8.5

Here's Apple Guide in action: The Macintosh Guide. It's a nice way to learn the basics of using a Mac and the Finder.

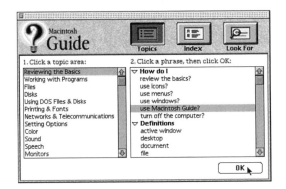

 **{Note}**

> Because Apple Guide is a relatively new addition to the System software, few, if any, older applications are going to support it. The Macintosh Guide, an implementation of Apple Guide that covers the Mac and the Finder, is a great start and a nice refresher course to use along with this book!

Where can I find Apple Guide?

Turning on the Apple Guide is about as easy as turning on Balloon Help. In the Finder, just pull down the Help menu and select **Macintosh Guide**. If you have another application that supports Apple Guide, its name entry will probably end in "Guide" as well. For now, we'll talk specifically about Macintosh Guide. Most everything we cover will be applicable in other Apple Guide systems.

How do I use Macintosh Guide?

The first thing you need to do to use Macintosh Guide is decide what you want to learn. There are a couple of different ways to get at your information, depending on how specific your question is (see fig. 8.6). You can either choose your lessons from a different list of topics, look things up in the alphabetical index, or have Macintosh Guide search for a specific word.

"Overview" Style Help   Search for Topics yourself

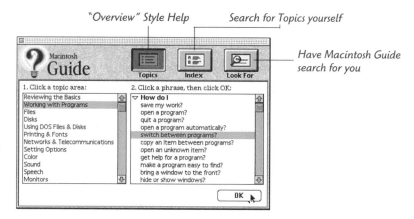

Fig. 8.6
The Macintosh Guide
gives you alternative
ways to get at its
lessons. We've got
Topics selected, and
we're ready to learn
how to switch between
programs.

Have Macintosh Guide
search for you

Using Topics

Click once on the Topics button and you get a list of topic areas to choose
from. Now, click on the topic area that interests you (refer to fig. 8.6). For
instance, we might click on Working with Programs. Next, double-click on
a phrase, like switch between programs under How Do I. That executes a
short Macintosh Guide lesson on how to use the Application menu to switch
between applications.

> The topic areas are probably the best choice if you are going to sit down for
> a while and learn how to use your Macintosh. The topic areas are organized
> logically and help to guide you smoothly through different Macintosh issues.

Using Index

The **Index** is for finding the answer to a more specific problem. It's organized
alphabetically, so you can go straight to the topic that you're concerned with.
To use the Index, first click on the **Index button** (see fig. 8.7). Next, you can
use the little slider to get the letter of the alphabet you're looking for. Either
drag the slider to your letter or click directly on the letter if it's showing (see
fig. 8.7). Next, choose your topic. For instance, I've chosen to look at the As,
and I've selected Application menu. Now, in the phrase box, I can double-
click on switch between programs to bring up the same lesson we got in
Topics.

Fig. 8.7
Using the Index entries requires you to know a bit more precisely what you're looking for.

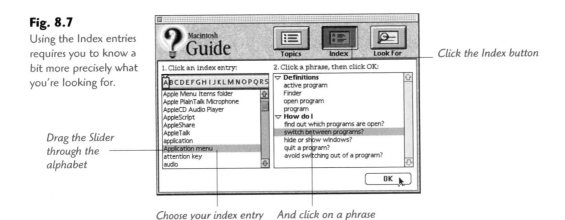

Click the Index button

Drag the Slider through the alphabet

Choose your index entry *And click on a phrase*

Using Look For

To search directly for a keyword in the Macintosh Guide index, click on the **Look For button**. This allows you to enter a word that has something to do with your problem. If I want to know how to switch between programs, I might type **Application menu** in the text box, and then click on **Search**. Then, I'll search for the relevant phrase. In this case, it's the same one we've seen before (see fig. 8.8).

Fig. 8.8
If you want to find a lesson by keyword, you use the Look For button.

Click here and start typing

Then click search

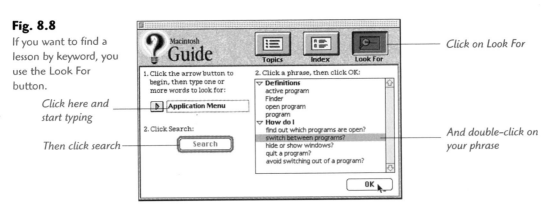

Click on Look For

And double-click on your phrase

It's like show-and-tell

Now we finally get to some of that interactivity I've been talking about. In a Macintosh Guide lesson, you get a couple different things. First, you'll get an answer to your question. Then, in many cases, the Guide will walk you through the steps it takes to complete the action you want to take (see fig. 8.9). This is the fun stuff.

Fig. 8.9
Help has arrived! After you read the answer, click on the right arrow and Macintosh Guide will show you the answer.

Click Huh? for more info. ────

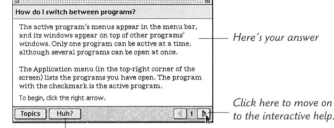

How do I switch between programs?

The active program's menus appear in the menu bar, and its windows appear on top of other programs' windows. Only one program can be active at a time, although several programs can be open at once.

The Application menu (in the top-right corner of the screen) lists the programs you have open. The program with the checkmark is the active program.

To begin, click the right arrow.

Topics   Huh?

──── *Here's your answer*

──── *Click here to move on to the interactive help.*

In this example, if you click on the right arrow, Macintosh Guide shows you again where the Application menu is with a bright red circle (see fig. 8.10). While it's showing that, it gives detailed step-by-step instructions on what we need to do to get something done. Follow these instructions and the Guide's marks and you've learned a new Mac skill.

(Tip) ──── If you come across something in the Guide's explanation that doesn't make sense, try clicking the Huh? button. This gives you context-sensitive definitions and explanations.

Fig. 8.10
Move on to the interactive help and the Guide will give you both text and visual cues for step-by-step learning.

Close box ────

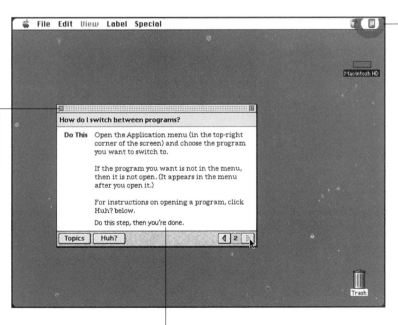

And some helpful markings!

File Edit View Label Special

Macintosh HD

How do I switch between programs?

Do This   Open the Application menu (in the top-right corner of the screen) and choose the program you want to switch to.

If the program you want is not in the menu, then it is not open. (It appears in the menu after you open it.)

For instructions on opening a program, click Huh? below.

Do this step, then you're done.

Topics   Huh?

Trash

The Guide's detailed instructions

Quitting the Guide

Learned everything you can? If you'd like to move back and learn something else, click on Topics and you'll get the original Guide window. When you're done, just click on the Guide window's Close box. You can head back to the Help menu if you need any further guidance.

Application Help: From the makers of...

Our third type of help system really isn't a system at all. Before Apple Guide, when Balloon Help wasn't enough, many application developers wrote their own help systems. Although some of this Help is similar from application to application, it's not under the control of the System software like Macintosh Guide. So it varies from developer to developer. The amount and kind of help you get is almost completely up to the individual application.

Figure 8.11 shows two different help systems side-by-side: Microsoft Word's and Lotus 1-2-3's. You can see where some of the concepts are similar, but the implementation is nowhere near as uniform as Balloon Help or Macintosh Guide. Both use an index view to allow you to search for topics and get help. Lotus 1-2-3 uses a "tab" system to get you to different types of questions, while Microsoft Word's help system is more outline-based.

Fig. 8.11
On the left: Microsoft Word 5.1's help system, with an outline-style index. On the right: Lotus 1-2-3 1.0's help includes index tabs for major topics.

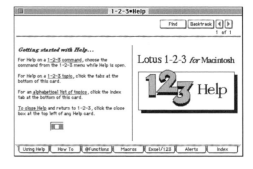

Hypertext helps you find the right path to help

A good deal of these application-specific help systems will use hypertext documents to help you get help. Hypertext is a little like the *Choose Your Adventure* books that were popular with children a few years back. These books allowed you to read a page or two of the story, and then asked you to make a decision. Based on that decision, you'd turn to a particular page to find out how the story continued.

That's a little like how hypertext works. You read along in a hypertext document until you get to what you're interested in. Then, if that topic is a "link," you can click on it and go to a page that explains that topic in more detail. Lotus 1-2-3's help system works like this, as shown in figure 8.12.

 **{Note}**

Sometimes the links will be the words themselves and sometimes they will be graphical elements (like in fig. 8.12). You'll just have to click around and find out!

Click one of these boxes to choose a different topic.

Use these buttons to move around.

Fig. 8.12
Lotus 1-2-3 's help system is an example of hypertext. You can jump around in the document by clicking on links.

Click this box for an example.

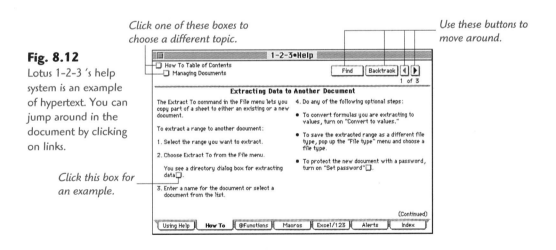

Perhaps what you need is a wizard!

Application developers want to help you use their products, so most provide help systems with some sort of index for you to look through to get help on a particular problem. Many also provide topic searching and hypertext to make things even easier.

Some programs even offer assistants. Microsoft Works, for example, has WorksWizards that step you through difficult tasks by asking you questions and then creating what you need. Other programs have full-fledged tutorials to get you started with the application. Whatever help you need, you'll probably find something in the program's help system that can point you in the right direction. Good luck!

Part III

This Mac is Mine!

Getting Organized with the Apple Menu and Aliases

With a few well-placed aliases and some additions to your Apple menu, finding everything you need will be fast and easy!

In this chapter:

• How can I make my folders and documents easier to find?

• I want to put everything I need for this project in one place

• What's on the Apple menu?

• I didn't know I could change options on the Apple menu

We talked a little in chapter 7 about creating aliases of applications and documents, and how these aliases work something like extra wall switches for a ceiling fan. An **alias** is just another way to access the same program or document—it's not a copy of the entire file, just a copy of the icon that you can put somewhere else.

To create an alias, click once on the icon you want to make an alias of, open the Finder's File menu, and choose the **Make Alias** command. Up pops a copy of the icon, with alias added to the original name. The alias can be renamed to anything you think is meaningful (see fig. 9.1). You can move the alias to just about anywhere in your Mac's organization of files and it will still open that original document or application when you click on it.

 **{Note}** ____ Throwing away an alias will not trash, delete, or otherwise harm the original file.

⊗<Caution> ____ Be careful about putting aliases on floppy disks. Because the alias just *points* to a file on your hard drive, it won't be useful with anyone's Mac but yours. Make sure you copy the actual file to your floppy if you're going to use it with another computer.

Fig. 9.1
You can rename an alias, group aliases for projects, or even put an alias on the Desktop—it will still open the original file.

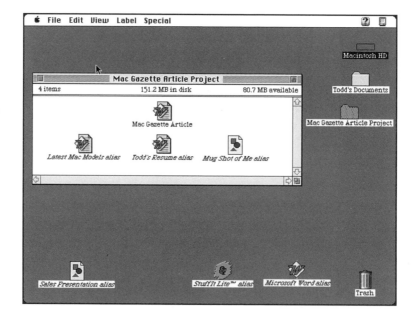

How will aliases help me?

If you've worked with your Mac for a while, you probably already noticed that it can be a pain to go searching through folder after folder to find the applications you use the most. Sure, it won't kill you to double-click three times before you finally get to Microsoft Word, but it would be nice to have it a little more conveniently placed. And the same goes for all the rest of the documents you use over and over again.

Aliases allow us to have icons for the same file in different places. Right off the top of my head, I can think of two places that can make life a little easier: the Desktop and project folders.

**(Tip)**

> In some versions of the System software, the quickest way to create an alias is to highlight the icon and press ⌘+M. The "M" stands for Make Alias.

Put stuff you use every day on the Desktop

For applications you use every day, just make an alias of the application icon and drop it on the Desktop (see fig. 9.2). Now all you have to do to start the application is double-click the alias on the Desktop!

Fig. 9.2
Just like your desk at work, you can put stuff you deal with everyday right on the Desktop.

A Microsoft Word alias on the Desktop

And here's where the real Word is, three folders deep!

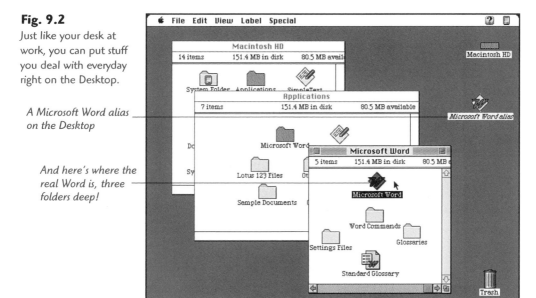

(!) (Tip) If you don't like having the "alias" appendage all over your desktop, edit the name back to the original. (You'll have to move the alias first, though, since you can't have two files of the same name in the same folder.) You can re-name an alias just like any other icon. You can still distinguish the alias from the original because the name on the alias icon appears in italic.

Using the Launcher for Desktop aliases

Although the **Launcher** has been something Performa users have known about for awhile, it first became available to all Mac owners with the release of System 7.5. What is it? It's a quick and easy way to organize application and document aliases you might otherwise just drop on the Desktop.

If the Launcher doesn't show up automatically on your Desktop, head to Control Panels (in the Apple menu) and select **Launcher**. The Launcher should pop on the screen. It already has a few entries. All you need to do is click once on the icon to start the application. If you'd like the Launcher to show up all the time, you can decide that in the General Controls Control Panel.

If you'd like to add your own applications, here's what you do. Create an alias of the application you want to add. Then, open the System Folder and look for the Launcher Items folder. Now, open the **Launcher Items** folder. Drag and drop your application alias into the Launcher Items window. You can edit the alias' name if you want to. Then, click on the Launcher and your new application will appear.

If you want to add your own "page" (like "Service/Support" in the figure), you just add a new folder in the Launcher Items folder. Rename the folder whatever you want, but remember to start the name with a bullet point ("o") by typing Option+8. Now, if you want to add aliases to this page, you'll need to drop them in this folder.

The System 7.5 Launcher organizes aliases of programs and documents on the Desktop.

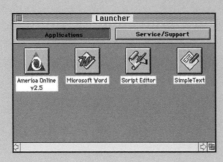

Set up project folders

If you find yourself working on projects that use the same files over and over again, create a **project folder** and drop aliases of the documents you need into that folder (see fig. 9.3).

Aliases for documents found elsewhere

Fig. 9.3

A project folder I created to help me write an article about the Mac. Latest Mac Models is an alias to some notes about Macintosh hardware, my Resume is for the author's bio, and the mug shot is a digital image.

The actual article document

Some of the files I aliased

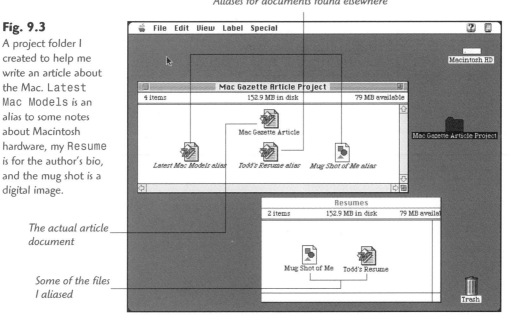

To create your own project folder, follow these steps:

1 Open the Finder's File menu and select New Folder.

A new folder appears with untitled folder highlighted.

2 Type a new name for the folder.

3 Find the folders and documents you want to include and make aliases by selecting the folder or document and choosing File, Make Alias.

4 Finally, drag each alias from its original folder and drop it on the project folder's icon.

(Tip)_____

> If you have a place on your Mac where you'd like to *permanently* store your projects, create your project folder there. Then, you can drag it from its permanent place to the Desktop when you're ready to work. When you're done, you can use the File, Put Away command (see chapter 7) to send it back.

What's special about the Apple menu?

In chapter 5, we talked about how the Apple menu is a little like the utility drawer in your kitchen; it can hold a lot of tidbits and utilities you can use with your Mac. But it can also hold just about anything else. If you want, you can add so many things to your Apple menu that you'll never have to double-click on the Macintosh HD icon again (see fig. 9.4). Sound good?

{Note}_____

> Some of the figures and suggestions in this section assume you are using System 7.5, which includes the new hierarchical menu options. If you haven't yet upgraded to System 7.5, you can still use the Apple menu for a lot of convenient functions, but some of these suggestions won't work. See chapter 13, "Develop Your Personal Filing System," for information on other companies' products that will add hierarchical menus.

Fig. 9.4
Here's my Apple menu, decked out with custom folders, hierarchical menus, and more. With this Apple menu, I can start any document or application I've got!

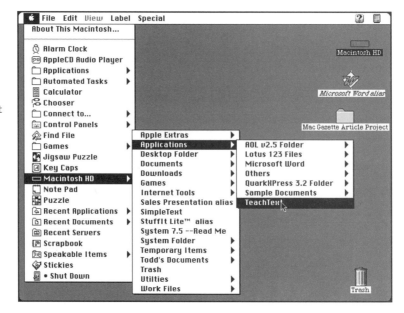

How does it work?

The Apple menu is a drop-down menu just like the typical File or Edit menus on any menu bar. But, unlike most of the other menus we've encountered, the entries on the Apple menu can be easily changed.

 **<Caution>** | Remember that the System folder contains important files that your Mac requires to operate. Throw away the wrong file and, at the very least, you're in for some major headaches. My advice: Think four times before moving or trashing any files in here!

Open the System folder and you'll find a folder called **Apple Menu Items** (see fig. 9.5). Here's where you can add or delete things from your Apple menu. What the Apple menu does is read all the items in this folder and turn them into menu items. If you drop an icon in here, it shows up as a standard menu item. If you drop a folder in here, it turns into a hierarchical menu item. Put a folder within a folder, and it adds a second level to the hierarchy. Get it?

Fig. 9.5
The Apple Menu folder in the System Folder is a mirror image of everything that shows up on the Apple menu. Adding icons and folders here is how you change the menu.

Open the System folder

Here's the Apple Menu Items folder

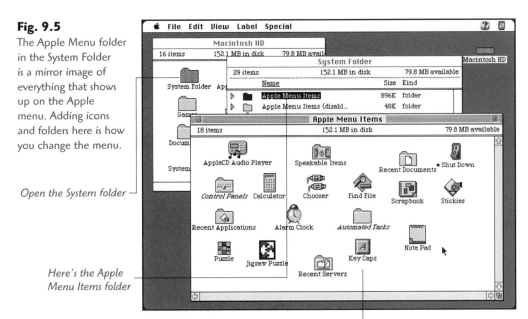

And here are the items that make up the Apple menu.

Q&A

> *I've got folders in my Apple Menu Items folder, but no hierarchical menus show up on the Apple menu. Why?*
>
> It could be a couple of things. If you don't have System 7.5 or some third-party product for hierarchical menus, selecting a folder in the Apple menu will just open that folder on the Desktop. If you do have System 7.5, the hierarchical menus may be turned off. Open the Apple menu and select Control Panels and Apple Menu Options. If there isn't a black dot in the circle next to On and the picture of hierarchical menus, click on that circle. Now you've got 'em.

What's on the Apple menu?

You'll notice that your Apple menu already has some stuff on it. These are the standard items that every Macintosh places on its Apple menu when the System software is first loaded. For the most part, you can decide whether or not you want to keep these things on the Apple menu or if you want to move them around.

Desk Accessories: Calculator, note pad, stickies, and more!

Every Macintosh comes with a few little **desk accessories** to get you started (see fig. 9.6). Some of these are just add-ons for fun, but some of them can come in very handy. To use one of the desk accessories, just pull down the Apple menu and select the desk accessory you want to use.

Fig. 9.6

Here are some of the things Mac put on its Apple menu to help you get started. It's up to you if they stay or go.

Chooser: Select your printer here

Control Panels: Use these to make changes to how your Mac operates

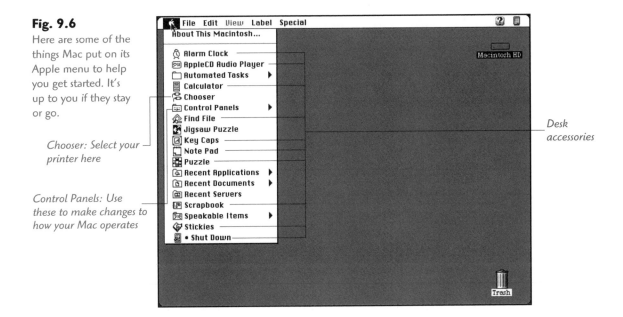

Desk accessories

Control Panels

The Apple menu is a quick and easy way to get at your Control Panels as well. What do they do? **Control Panels** are basically there to give you control over how the System software interacts with the hardware. For instance, you use Control Panels to tell your Mac how many colors you want to display on the screen, or how fast you want the mouse to move around the screen. See chapters 10, "Banish the Bland Mac!" and 28, "Inside the System Folder," for more information on Control Panels.

The Chooser

The Chooser is a small program you use to tell the computer which printer and network connections you want to use. In order for the Mac to print, it has to know a little something about your printer—like what port it's connected to and what type of printer it is. If you've got that set up correctly, the printer will appear here in the Chooser and you can choose it. See chapter 18, "Setting Up and Using Your Printer," for more on printing and using the Chooser.

Playing with the desk accessories

So, what are these desk accessories? If you'd like to get to know them better, go ahead and play with them a little bit. To start one of the desk accessories, pull down the Apple menu and select the desk accessory you want to run.

Each one has its own purpose, but some are a little more important to the System software than

others. Key Caps, for instance, is a great little program for showing you how to type special characters and symbols. Find File (System 7.5) is a convenient way to search for a file when the Finder isn't active.

Table 9.1 Breaking down the desk accessories

This Icon...	Is the...	Which...
	Alarm Clock	Adds an alarm clock to your Desktop (not in System 7.5).
	AppleCD Audio Player	Plays audio CDs through your Mac's built-in CD-ROM drive (if you have one).
	Calculator	Calculates (use the mouse or number pad on your keyboard)
	Find File	Is the same as the Find command on the Finder's File menu.
	Jigsaw Puzzle	Lets you put together the pieces.
	KeyCaps	Helps you find out what key combinations to use in order to create "special" and foreign language characters in your documents.
	Note Pad	Lets you jot down up to 8 pages of quick notes that you can print or refer back to later.
	Puzzle	Lets you slide puzzle pieces around for fun.
	Scrapbook	Lets you save and view graphics and text that you cut or copy out of documents.
	Stickies	Gives you the ability to create small "sticky" notes to leave on your Desktop as reminders.
	Shut Down	Is the same as the Shut Down command on the Finder's Special menu.

Things I did recently

Also new to System 7.5 are the **Recent folders**. In the Apple menu, these folders show second-level menus of the last few documents and applications you've used. It's a convenient way to start a document or application you've used in your last few sessions.

Automated tasks

Here's another new folder for System 7.5. This folder is full of scripts that allow you to perform some common tasks automatically. A **script** is simply a short program designed to perform one task, such as turning the sound off or finding the original of an alias.

 System 7.5 is the first version of the Mac's System software that features a "scriptable" Finder. Basically this just means that you can use an application called AppleScript to write small programs or scripts to automatically perform short file and icon management tasks.

What can I add to the Apple menu?

Now that we know a little more about what's already on the Apple menu, we can decide what we'd like to add. Once you get all your own stuff in the Apple menu, you'll see why it's such a convenient shortcut to have!

 By the way—if you ever want to take something *out* of the Apple menu, just drag it out of the Apple Menu Items folder. Or, if you're using aliases, you can just drag the alias to the Trash, since throwing away an alias does *not* delete the original program.

Add your applications

The first Apple menu enhancement you may want to try is adding an alias of one of your applications directly to the Apple menu.

1 Select the icon of the program you want to add.

2 Choose File, Make Alias.

3 Double click on the System Folder to open it and find the Apple Menu Items folder.

4 Drag and drop the alias on the Apple Menu Items folder.

That's all you have to do. You should see that application's name as one of the options on your Apple menu.

The Apple menu organizes its items alphabetically. If you want your alias to show up at the beginning of the list, rename the alias with a space at the beginning. If you want it to show up at the end, start the name with a bullet point (Option+8). Then type the rest of the name.

Add a new second-level menu

If you don't like the idea of adding all your applications directly to the Apple menu, here's a neater way to get things done.

To create a second-level menu for your applications, follow these steps:

1 Open the System Folder and then the Apple Menu Items folder.

2 Choose File, New Folder.

   A new folder appears with untitled folder highlighted.

3 Type the new folder name **Applications**.

4 Select the program icon of the application you want to add to the Apple menu.

5 Choose File, Make Alias.

6 Drag-and-drop the alias in your new Applications folder.

7 Repeat steps 4 through 6 to add more applications.

And that's it. Close your windows and check out the Apple menu. You should have a new Applications item (see fig. 9.7). Move your mouse pointer down to it, and out pops a second-level menu of your applications.

Fig. 9.7
Add a new applications
folder to the Apple
Menu Items and
you've got a new way
to access your favorite
applications.

*Start them from
the Apple menu*

*Create a new folder
for applications*

*Make a
few aliases*

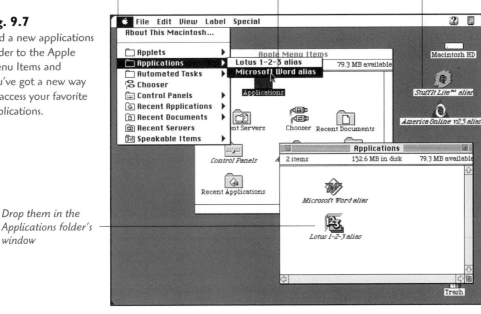

*Drop them in the
Applications folder's
window*

(Tip)

This doesn't just work for applications. You can make a second-level menu for
anything you can alias. You can even create a second-level menu for all your
desk accessories. Simply create a new folder called Desk Accessories inside the
Apple Menu Items window and drag the all the desk accessories to the new
folder.

Add your hard drive

So far we've talked about creating aliases for applications and documents.
What I haven't told you is that you can make aliases for disks as well. Why
would you want to do this? Well, with the Apple menu's hierarchical capabilities, you can move quickly through every single folder on your hard drive and
get at the folder or item you need very quickly. This one step alone can save
you from ever double-clicking on the hard drive icon again!

Start by making an alias of the hard drive icon. Just select it and choose File,
Make Alias. Next, open the System Folder and drag the alias to the Apple

Menu Items folder. Now close everything up and check out your Apple menu (see fig. 9.8). You've got your hard drive.

Fig. 9.8

Drop the hard drive alias on the Apple Menu Items folder and you've got a new way to get around all your folders and files!

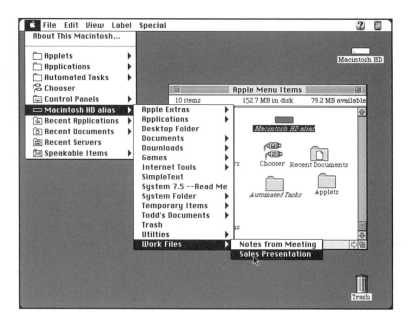

So how should you use this? When you place your mouse pointer over the hard drive menu item in your Apple menu, a menu of all your first-level folders and files will appear. If you move the pointer over a folder (still holding down the mouse button), another menu will appear. If you want to select an actual file, just let go of the mouse button.

 (Tip)

> You can also let go of the mouse button over a folder name, and that will open that specific folder on the Desktop.

So, we don't have to go clicking through the hard drive any more to get to any file or folder we want. We can open folder windows, execute applications, and start documents with the hierarchical menu feature of the Apple menu. Man, this is cool!

Banish the Bland Mac!

You can have a wild and crazy looking Mac, or something more subdued and business-like. It's your choice.

In this chapter:

- How do I change the colors and patterns on the Desktop?
- How do I change the way my Mac sounds?
- My Mac talks to me? That's cool!
- What else can I do to liven things up?

They said the Macintosh was going to be friendly. They said it was going to be easy to use, fun, and exciting. And then you get past the happy face, get welcomed to Macintosh, and up pops...the Bland Mac. What happened?

Well, this is just the starting point. From here you can customize how your Mac looks and sounds. Some changes you make will help you work more efficiently, others you'll make just for fun. But they'll all make that Mac feel a little more like *yours*.

⊛ {Note}

We'll be talking a lot more about Control Panels in this chapter. If you'd like an introduction to Control Panels, see chapter 9, "Getting Organized with the Apple Menu and Aliases." For an in-depth discussion on Control Panels, check out chapter 28, "Inside the System Folder."

How can I make my Mac look more interesting?

Control Panels let you adjust things about your Mac's System software. One of the things you can adjust, to varying degrees, is the appearance of your Macintosh Desktop and the elements of the interface. You can change colors, patterns, fonts, and other things about your Mac to make them work a little more like you want them to (see fig. 10.1). To open any Control Panel, first open the Apple menu and highlight Control Panels, and then highlight the name of the Control Panel from the second-level menu and release the mouse button.

Plain English, please!

Did I say **interface**? Interface is a catch-all word in the computer industry that means everything you see and use on the screen to accomplish tasks. Simply put, it's how you and your computer communicate with one another. The Mac's interface is a **GUI** (pronounced "gooey"), which stands for **Graphical User Interface**. What's GUI about it? Mac users get to move little pictures around in order to complete tasks.

Fig. 10.1
So, maybe I've gone a little nuts here. This Desktop is definitely all mine—'cause nobody else would want to look at it!

WindowShades keep window clutter down

Change the font

Change your Desktop pattern

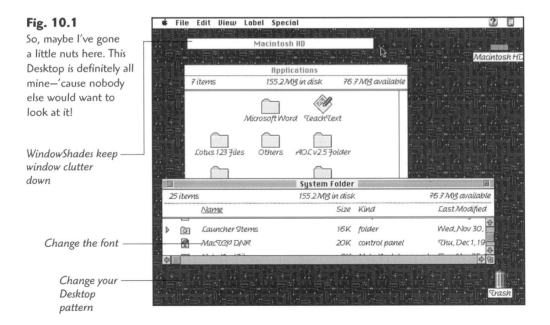

You can be as crazy or as sane as you want; it all depends on how you like things to look. In figure 10.1, for instance, some elements are functional and others are, well, less functional.

How do I add a little color?

Our first Control Panel is a quick way to give your Mac some life and add a personal touch. It's the Color Control Panel (see fig. 10.2). You can change the color of window elements (the title bar, scroll bars, close box, etc.) and change your highlight color—the color things turn when you select them (like text in your word processor).

Fig. 10.2
Here's the Color Control Panel. Just drag through the list until you find the color you want.

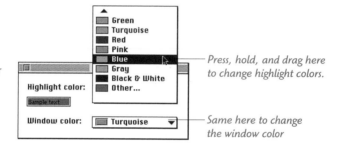

For the Highlight Color, you have the additional option of choosing Other... to choose a color that's not listed. If you choose Other..., you get a dialog box with Apple's color wheel. Just press and hold down the mouse button on the wheel while you drag around. When you find the color you want, let go of the mouse button and click on OK.

I hate this gray desktop

New with System 7.5 is the **Desktop Patterns Control Panel**, which enables you to choose from a number of different patterns for your Desktop. Adding a new Desktop pattern is like taking a roll of really obnoxious shelf paper and plastering it all over your fine mahogany desk at the office. The difference is, of course, you can change your Mac's Desktop pattern relatively easily. And it doesn't leave that annoying, sticky residue.

Fig. 10.3
It's the Desktop
Patterns dialog box.
Hey...I didn't create
the patterns, okay?

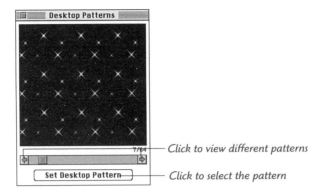

— *Click to view different patterns*

— *Click to select the pattern*

Hopefully you can scroll through and find something you like. Just click along the scroll bar until something meets your fancy, and then click **Set Desktop Pattern**.

If your System software is pre-System 7.5, you'll need a third-party utility to add Desktop patterns. You can, however, make some basic color changes to the Desktop with the General Controls Control Panel, which we'll discuss later in this chapter.

Interested in creating your own Desktop patterns?

If you're like me, it can be difficult to find one of those pre-made Desktop patterns that really expresses your "inner self." Wouldn't it be nice to be able to add your own patterns?

You can, with a little cut and paste. First, create a picture or pattern in a graphics application. Then, select that picture and from that application's

Edit menu choose Cut. Open the Apple menu and choose Control Panel, Desktop and from the Edit menu choose Paste. Now, with your pattern showing in the window, click on Set Desktop Pattern.

Your pattern gets *added* to the Control Panel—it doesn't delete any of the other ones that are already there. So, feel free to add a pattern that makes your Mac feel a little more like home.

How do I change the views?

Watch out here. What we're talking about now is the Views Control Panel, not the View menu in the Finder. What this Control Panel does is let us get at some of the settings for that View menu in the Finder menu bar, plus it lets us change the **font**, or typeface, that the Mac uses to show us the names of icons. It's pretty straightforward, as you can see in figure 10.4.

Fig. 10.4
This Control Panel lets you decide how some things will look in the Finder.

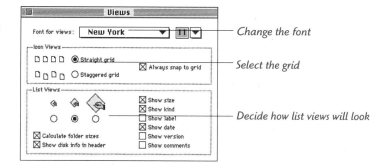

To make changes to fonts or other options in the View Control Panel, open the Apple menu and choose Control Panels, Views. At the top of the Views Control Panel is the font selector, which changes the font for every icon title that appears in the Finder or on the Desktop. Just choose according to your preference. I like New York because it's a fairly classy font that also lets you see an alias' italicized title pretty clearly.

The next section determines what type of **grid** the Mac will use, staggered or straight, when you select the Clean Up Window command in the Finder's Special menu. This command moves icons around in the active window (e.g. the Macintosh HD window) to make sure there are no overlapping icon titles.

 **{Note}** If no windows are selected, the Clean Up Window command changes to the Clean Up Desktop command, which will straighten your Desktop icons so that no icon titles overlap.

The third section has everything to do with list views. In the Finder, you can change how a folder's window will display files using the View menu. In a list view, you can see as much or as little about a file as you'd like (see fig. 10.5).

In the View Control Panel, these check boxes let you decide everything that will show up in that list view (more on the list views in chapter 13, "Develop Your Personal Filing System").

System Folder			
24 items	156.1 MB in disk		75.8 MB available
Name	**Size**	**Kind**	**Last Modified**
▷ Apple Menu Items	944K	folder	Thu, Dec 1, 1994, 2:11 PM
▷ Apple Menu Items (disabl...	4K	folder	Thu, Dec 1, 1994, 2:11 PM
Clipboard	4K	file	Thu, Dec 1, 1994, 6:53 PM
▷ Control Panels	2,312K	folder	Thu, Dec 1, 1994, 2:34 PM
▷ Control Panels (Disabled)	136K	folder	Wed, Nov 23, 1994, 12:10 AM
▷ Disabled Menu Items	zero K	folder	Fri, Nov 4, 1994, 12:23 AM
▷ Eudora Folder	32K	folder	Sun, Nov 6, 1994, 6:46 PM
▷ Extensions	14,064K	folder	Wed, Nov 30, 1994, 3:13 PM
▷ Extensions (disabled)	1,552K	folder	Tue, Nov 29, 1994, 8:56 AM
▷ Finder	444K	file	Tue, Aug 2, 1994, 12:00 PM

Changing things in general

What else can we change? Well, you can change a few basic Macintosh behaviors in the General Controls Control Panel (say that three times fast and see fig. 10.6). Here's where you can decide whether or not you'll use the Launcher (see chapter 9) full-time, whether you want to view the Desktop icons when you're working in another application, and if you'll protect some folders.

Make decisions about the Desktop and Launcher

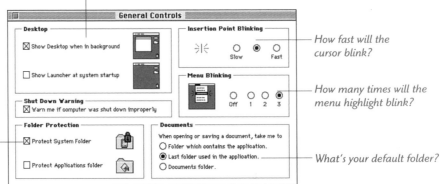

Protect these folders?

How fast will the cursor blink?

How many times will the menu highlight blink?

What's your default folder?

Most of these options are taster's choice, but there are some important system security issues here. Locking the System Folder and Applications Folder means, while they're locked, you can't delete any of the *first-level* folders inside those folders. So, for instance, if the System Folder is locked, you can't delete the Apple Menu Items folder we talked about in chapter 9. Go ahead and select those if you like the idea of limiting access to these folders.

✱ {Note} These folders cannot be locked using the General Controls when your Mac's File Sharing capability is turned on in the Sharing Setup Control Panel.

❶ (Tip) Got kids? Some of these security measures are designed to guard against the wanderings of little hands. Protect those System and Applications Folders to keep important programs from "disappearing."

Pulling up WindowShades

Here's another System 7.5 feature. Sick of all those annoying windows in your way? With a couple clicks on your title bar, you can roll that window up! Then only the title bar shows. Just head to Control Panels and select WindowShade. Then, choose the number of clicks you want to use and the modifier keys.

If you choose a modifier key, you'll have to hold it down while you click to get the WindowShade to work. I personally just use two mouse clicks with no modifiers. I also like the sound, which is just a neat little *whoosh* that couldn't hurt anyone. Right?

Should I use sounds, even at work?

I'd say yes. Sure, you can go overboard with sound, but the Mac uses alert sounds to let you know when your Mac needs you to do something special, or when you've done something wrong. Plus, alert sounds can tell you when something's happening on your Mac while you're not looking at the screen.

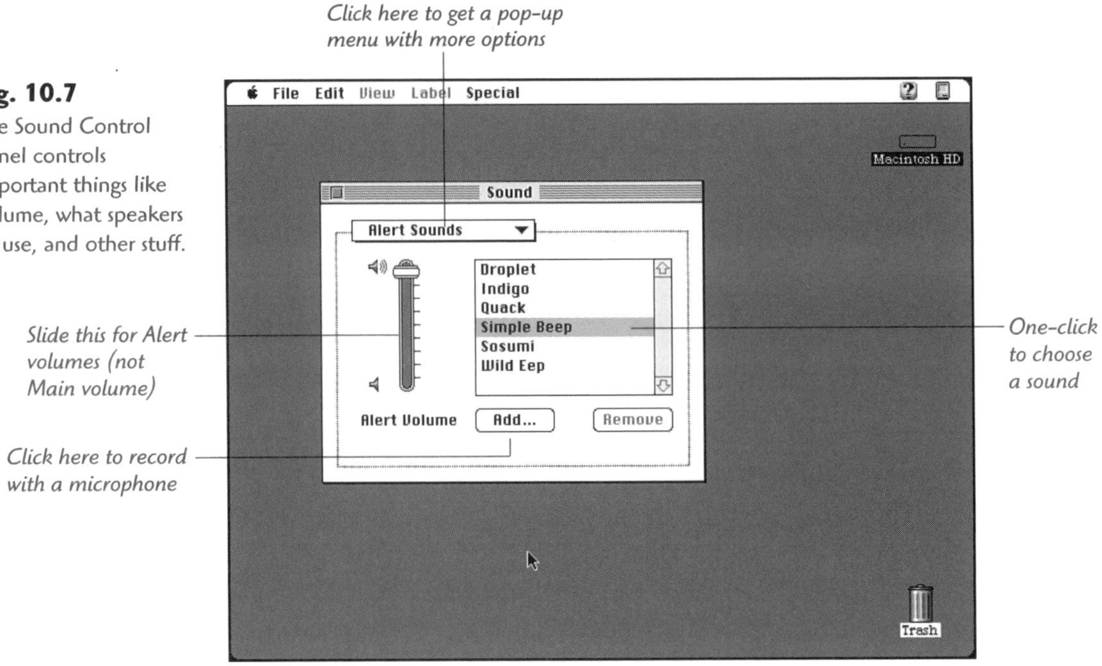

Fig. 10.7

The Sound Control Panel controls important things like volume, what speakers to use, and other stuff.

Click here to get a pop-up menu with more options

Slide this for Alert volumes (not Main volume)

Click here to record with a microphone

One-click to choose a sound

Changing your alert sound

At the top of the Sound Control Panel is a down arrow. Click on the down arrow and a pop-up menu appears with more selections for the various things you can change about your Mac's sound. **Alert Sounds** is where you change what sound Mac will use to alert you to something. Just click on the name of the sound you want to use; you'll get a sample of the sound through your Mac's speaker.

My Mac didn't make a sound. Why?

You've probably got the volume turned down. Try opening the Sound Control Panel and choosing Volumes from the selector box at the top of the Control Panel. Is the volume all the way down? If it is, drag the control up the slider bar to increase the volume. Now you should hear something.

With a microphone connected to or built into your Mac, you can also record sounds. If you click **Add...** in the Sound Control Panel, a dialog box pops up that looks a little like the controls for a cassette deck (refer to fig. 10.7). When you're ready to record your sound, click on Record. You have 10 seconds to tape your sound. Hit Stop when you're done. Now you can hit Play to listen to the sound. If you like it, click Save. Give it a name, and then select it under Alert Sounds. Now Mac sounds like you!

How do I get sound into Mac?

If you select **Sound In** from the pop-up menu, you can see what sources you have to choose from for recording sounds. Depending on the Mac model you have, you can record sound from a variety of sources, including a microphone, a CD-ROM drive, and others. We talk more about recording sounds in chapter 21, "The Multimedia Mac," and chapter 22, "The Mac as a Sound Machine."

Selecting your speakers

The **Sound Out** choices on the pop-up menu allow you to choose whether your Mac will send sounds to its internal speaker or to external powered speakers you've installed. It also lets you choose the sample rate for your sound output. **Sample rate** is simply the quality level of your sound. The higher the rate, the higher the quality. (CD-quality is around 48 kHz.) Your maximum sample rate will depend on your Mac model.

Only Macintosh AV and Power Macintosh computers feature true 16-bit digital sound. (That means that digital sounds created and played by your Macintosh would rival the quality of a professional audio CD.) Most other models offer 8-bit stereo or even mono sound. This does not, however, affect CD-ROM sounds and music played through your Mac—CD-ROM sound quality will only be hampered by the limitations of Mac's speaker.

How do I change the volume?

The last selection in the pop-up menu is **Volumes**. This volume control is different from the volume in Alert Sounds, as it effects everything that goes through the speaker—not just system sounds. Just drag the slider up and down on the slider bar to get the sound level you want.

Master your system sounds!

Your basic Macintosh setup gives you one whole choice for system sounds...you can choose which sound you want to use for Alerts. Want to go one better? Try SoundMaster!

SoundMaster is a shareware Control Panel available from many online services and BBSs around the country (see chapter 13 for more on shareware and chapter 26 for more about online services). Once you get SoundMaster, drag and drop the SoundMaster Control Panel to your

System Folder. Now you can add a sound to nearly any System event your Mac experiences!

What's a **System event**? Just about anything *you* do that Mac has to *react to*...like closing a Window, double-clicking an icon, or inserting a floppy disk in the floppy drive.

If you like SoundMaster, just send in $15.00 (or so) to a guy named Bruce in San Antonio, and you'll be a legal owner. That's shareware for you!

The SoundMaster Control Panel lets you add enough sounds to drive any sane person out of your office.

Using speech (on AV and Power Macintosh models)

If you have an AV or Power Macintosh model, you can use Apple's PlainTalk software for speech recognition and text-to-speech conversion. **Speech recognition** allows you to give your Mac vocal commands. **Text-to-speech conversion** allows certain applications (including SimpleText and TeachText) to read selections of text aloud. Either of these can be fun, and, depending on your circumstances, useful.

Getting Mac to recognize speech

To use speech recognition, open Control Panels and select Speech Setup (see fig. 10.8). This Panel lets you turn on speech recognition and change the appearance, voice, and other options of the character who represents your Mac. When you turn recognition on by clicking the On button in the Recognition section, a little window with your character should pop up on-screen.

Fig. 10.8

Set up speech recognition and then experiment to see what works.

Turn recognition on

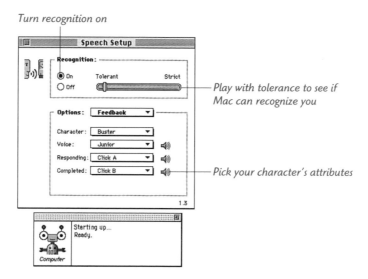

Play with tolerance to see if Mac can recognize you

Pick your character's attributes

Once you have recognition set up correctly, try saying something. Usually, you start by saying the computer's name (default is "Computer") and then give a command.

Your Mac can understand a number of different phrases, including things like "close window" and "switch to the Finder." You'll have to experiment a little to find out what your computer does and doesn't know.

**(Tip)**

> Aside from the standard phrases, a few phrases have been included with the Speech Recognition software to get you started. If you want to see what these are, pull down the Apple menu and select Speakable Items. The computer understands how to open anything in the list.

Getting TeachText to read things out loud

In certain applications, you can use your AV or Power Macintosh to read selections of text out loud. It's just another menu choice, like Print or Save (see fig. 10.9). You might find this feature useful for kids, for proofreading documents, or just for fun.

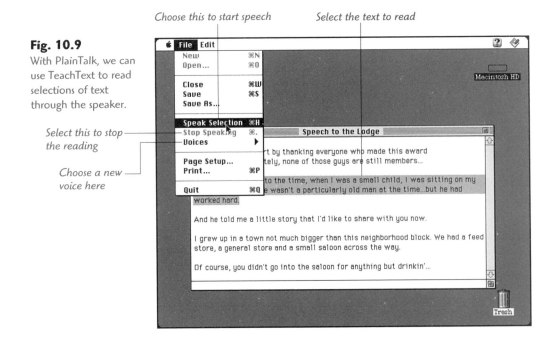

Fig. 10.9
With PlainTalk, we can use TeachText to read selections of text through the speaker.

 | SimpleText also offers this capability under its Sound menu.

In TeachText, highlight the text you'd like to hear Macintosh say aloud by placing your mouse pointer at the beginning of the text and dragging the pointer to the end of the text, and then release the mouse button. Now, from the File menu, select Speak Selection. Your Mac should start reading to you. If you want it to stop, choose Stop Speaking from the File menu. You can also use the Voices command in the File menu to change the way the speech sounds.

 | Don't change your Mac's voice while it's reading something. Choose Stop Speaking first, and then change the voice and choose the Speak Selection or Speak All command again. Changing voices while Mac is speaking may cause your computer to "freeze up," forcing you to throw the power switch and potentially lose data.

My desktop still looks empty. What else is there?

How about a couple more customizing tidbits? We'll see a couple of ways to put a clock on your Desktop. Then, I'll show you how to change almost any item's icon!

Put an alarm clock on your desk

In pre-System 7.5 (System 7.5 doesn't have an alarm clock), open the Apple menu and select Alarm Clock, and it'll pop right up on the Desktop. It's a great way to keep track of time while you're working—and you can even set an alarm to ring as well.

To set the alarm clock, click once on the time to make it active. Then, click the little "spinner" so that it points down (see fig. 10.10). Now you can click on the clock to set time, the calendar page to set the date, or the alarm clock to set the alarm.

Fig. 10.10

The alarm clock desk accessory. Click the "spinner" to set the time, date, or alarm.

 (Tip)

Want to start the alarm clock every time you start your Mac? Open the System Folder and look for a folder called Startup Items. Make an alias of *any* program and drop it in Startup Items and it will start automatically when you power up your Mac. It can be anything from the alarm clock to stickies to your favorite word processing application!

Put a clock on the menu bar

New to System 7.5 is a handy little feature that lets you add a clock to your menu bar (see fig. 10.11). Go to Control Panels and select Date and Time. In the bottom right corner of this Panel is a setting for the menu bar clock. Click the On button if it's not already selected. The next time you power up you'll have a handy little clock up next to the Help menu.

Fig. 10.11

Click the icon picture and a box appears around it. Now, pull down the Edit menu and Paste your new picture.

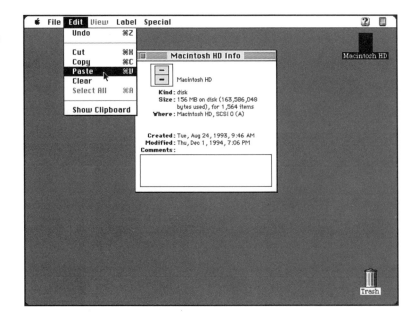

Change the look of your icons

If you think of your hard disk as a filing cabinet where you file all your folders and documents, maybe it should look like one. It's easy to change any icon, whether it's for a folder, program, or document. You just use the Get Info box.

First, you need to draw or acquire a new picture. Remember that a very detailed picture will get messy at icon size. (In fact, you'll get best results if you draw a picture that's about the same size as a standard icon.) Select that picture and from the drawing application's Edit menu choose Copy. Next, select the icon you want to change and in the Finder choose File, Get Info. Click once on the icon's picture in the Get Info box, and then select Edit, Paste. There you are...a brand new icon picture!

The Macintosh Memory Tune Up

In this chapter:

- How can I make my Mac run faster?
- I need more memory to run my applications
- I've got more than enough memory. What can I do with it?

Getting the best possible performance from your Mac may take a little tinkering under the hood.

RAM (a.k.a memory) works a little like a human's short-term memory in that it holds information that's current to the task at hand and not much else. Turn off your computer off and it loses everything it had in memory unless it "jotted things down" to a disk.

So, we jot things down a lot. The problem is, jotting things down to a disk is slow. In order for the Mac to perform at its best, it's important to properly balance how much information we keep in memory versus how often we have to read or write to a disk. This takes a little tinkering under the hood, so to speak.

Sounds good, but what's the cache?

One of the ways that Mac makes things move more quickly is by **caching** (pronounced "cashing") information from the hard disk into memory. It's the same basic concept that squirrels use when they gather nuts for the winter.

They could go out into the forest every single day and get some nuts. But it's cold, they've got better things to do, and winter nut-gathering is a slow process.

Same thing with caching hard drive data. Mac just stores the most recently used data in RAM, which is faster (warmer? drier?) than the hard drive. If it needs to use that data again, it can quickly grab it out of RAM instead of venturing out onto the dark, cold, ugly hard drive.

 Plain English, please!

On your Mac, the **disk cache** is just a portion of RAM that's set aside for quick access to recently used data. Why? It's designed to speed up your Mac when it uses the same data over and over.

How much cache should I have?

So what do we need to do? Decide how large our cache will be. The general rule is 32 kilobytes (KB) of cache for every megabyte of RAM you have in your system. The minimum cache is 32 KB, and each click on the up arrow will increase the amount of RAM set aside for cache (see fig. 11.1).

Fig. 11.1
Using the Memory Control Panel we can decide how much information to store for this session.

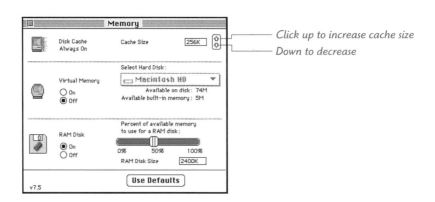

Click up to increase cache size
Down to decrease

But, with most Macs, the rule falls down if you have much more than 8 MB of RAM. In general, you don't want to set your cache memory over about 256 KB ($8 \times 32 = 256$), because, for some reason, it actually begins to slow down the

Mac. Plus, we encounter a point of diminishing returns here, where it's probably best to use that RAM for something else (like running applications).

 **<Caution>** | Be aware that some high-end graphics applications (like Adobe Photoshop, for instance) have their own caching schemes that require you to turn your Mac's built-in cache down to the minimum setting in order to perform correctly.

What if I don't have enough memory?

Here's the other side of the spectrum. What happens when the squirrels fill their tree with nuts? They have to start storing them outside of the tree, out in the forest. Sound counterproductive? Well, when you don't have much tree space, you've got to keep shuffling things around.

If you don't have much RAM, you can use **virtual memory** as a RAM substitute. What Mac does is send data that should be in RAM—but is currently not in use—to the hard drive. The trade-off is that the hard drive is slow. As a result, virtual memory slows down your Macintosh .

How do I turn virtual memory on?

You can turn virtual memory on and off in the Memory Control Panel (see fig. 11.2). You'll have to restart your Mac every time you make a change. You can also choose which hard drive to use (if you have more than one) and how much hard drive space to dedicate to virtual memory.

Fig. 11.2
You use the Memory Control Panel to decide how much virtual memory you want.

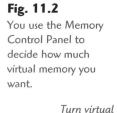

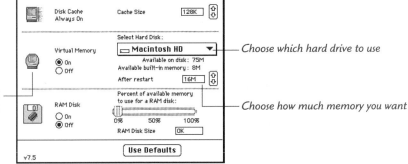

Turn virtual memory on or off

Choose which hard drive to use

Choose how much memory you want

Should I use virtual memory?

Unless you have a Power Macintosh or other PowerPC processor-based Mac, then no...*not if you can help it.* Virtual memory is a serious trade-off—it can make up for a lack of RAM, but at a substantial hit to performance. Every once in a while virtual memory isn't an awful idea, but, it is not a long-term solution.

> Frankly, the best solution for a lack of RAM is to buy more RAM. Nearly every Macintosh model is designed to accommodate extra RAM, and, in many cases, it's an upgrade you can do yourself with a little guidance.

PowerPC-based Macs are the exception to the rule. In nearly all cases it's a good idea to leave virtual memory on with a Power Mac. The PowerPC processor deals with data a little differently than the older Mac's processors, so Power Macs work well with virtual memory turned on. Plus, Power Macs generally require more RAM (all things being equal) than do older Macs. So, virtual memory can be a nice cost saver, too.

I've used this program hundreds of times but suddenly it won't open. What's wrong?

Have you opened and closed several programs since the last time you turned your Mac on (or restarted)? Sometimes, after working with a bunch of different programs, your Mac's memory can become fragmented. It's nothing to worry about, but it can keep you from running programs. Just quit all open programs and restart from the Finder's Special menu.

How much virtual memory should I use?

There's no hard and fast rule here, because virtual memory depends on how much hard drive space you have free. On older-technology Macs, you probably don't want to set virtual memory any higher than double your actual RAM. (If you have 4 MB, set virtual memory at 8 MB.) Any more than that and you're probably slowing your system to a crawl. A Power Macintosh can handle more virtual memory, but just make sure you leave yourself some room on your hard drive for actual files.

I don't have as much memory as my program says it requires. Will virtual memory help?

No. If a program requires more RAM than your system has installed (it requires 4 MB, and you only have 2 MB), virtual memory won't help, even though your About the Macintosh box suggests you've got enough RAM free. Virtual memory is best used for running a few smaller programs in limited RAM. If you can't load the entire program in "built-in" memory, you probably need to get another program or add RAM to your Mac.

The Macintosh paradox—RAM disks

Okay, so we've got these squirrels, right? Let's say they've moved to a slightly more upscale tree and now they've got some room to play with (RAM). Instead of storing their nuts in the forest (hard drive), they store all the nuts they want in their tree (RAM again). Then, they figure out they can put some other things in their tree—like rocks for sitting on and a nutcracker (bear with me) for opening nuts. Now they're in business.

Somehow this relates to a RAM disk. A **RAM disk** allows you to set aside a certain amount of memory for holding data or application files. It looks like a disk and acts (for the most part) like a disk (see fig. 11.3), except it's really, really fast.

What's the difference between a RAM disk and other disks?

The difference is that the RAM disk is still RAM, and it's still volatile. Turn off your Mac's power or get hit by a blackout or power surge, and the stuff on that RAM disk is gone. Forever.

Fig. 11.3

Looks like a disk, acts like a disk. But it's volatile and dangerous like RAM.

A RAM Disk icon...

...and its window

Otherwise, a RAM disk acts like nearly any other disk. You can drag things to it, copy things from it, and start applications that are on it. You can even save data files to it.

 **<Caution>** | Do you want to save documents to your RAM disk? **DON'T!** Still want to? You can...but it's very risky. Make sure you copy those files to disk often. Any power interruption and you will lose your hard work.

When should I use a RAM disk?

I use a RAM disk whenever I want a particular application to run very quickly—and I'm not overwhelmingly afraid of losing data. For instance, I often put games on a RAM disk, since there's nothing about the game files that I'm likely to change. When the game needs me to save a file, I just specify a folder on the hard drive instead of a folder on the RAM disk.

How do I create and use a RAM disk?

You can create a RAM disk by using the Memory Control Panel. Just open the Panel and turn the RAM disk option on (see fig. 11.4). Then select the size for your RAM disk. Keep in mind that you still need RAM left over to actually *run* your applications. It's probably not a good idea to use more than half of your available RAM for the disk. When you're done, you'll have to restart your Mac in order to get the RAM disk to show up.

Fig. 11.4
Create your RAM disk, but don't use more than half the available RAM.

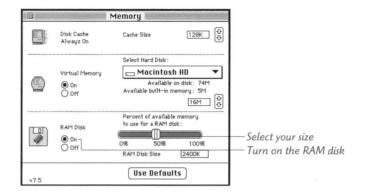

Select your size
Turn on the RAM disk

With your RAM disk created, you can drag-and-drop copy files to and from your hard drive just like any other disk. You can open files there, too, by double-clicking them. You can even create folders.

 Q&A

> ### My Mac is frozen! How can I save the data on my RAM disk?
>
> I've said that a RAM disk is volatile. But, unlike regular RAM, a RAM disk can survive a restart. If you can, use the Restart command in the Finder.
>
> If you can't, use your Mac's Restart button (see chapter 2 for information on restarting). If your Mac doesn't have a restart button, try pressing Control+⌘+Power key.

How do I get rid of this RAM disk?

You can't just toss a RAM disk in the Trash. First, start by saving any files you need to keep to a folder on your hard drive. Then, drag-and-drop everything on your RAM drive to the Trash. Empty the Trash. Now you can go back into the Memory Control Panel and turn the RAM disk off. It should disappear from the Desktop.

12

Cool Customizing Software

In this chapter:

- How can customizing software help?
- What programs can I get?
- What can these programs do for me?

Fuzzy dice and sheep-skin covers for your Mac? Make your Mac yours with cool customizing software.

Macs, like cars, come off an assembly line looking just about the same. But the way you customize your car—where your put your cassettes and CDs, even how you tilt the steering wheel and seat—make it yours. The way you arrange your Mac's Desktop, the software programs you add, and how you work with your Macintosh make it yours, too.

What's customizing software?

Some programs are fuzzy dice and sheepskin steering wheel covers. They make your Mac look better (or, uh...different) and they help make things easier to work with. Other customizing programs are more like adding a turbocharger to your car's engine. They make your Mac move faster and help you organize your work for more productive sessions.

Most customizing programs make changes fairly deep down in the System software, adding Control Panels, changing elements on the Desktop, or enhancing the way the menu bar works. Most of them are short programs designed to get into the guts of your Mac's System software and enhance it. This can be great fun, but it can also be a big problem if something doesn't work.

 **<Caution>** | Before adding customizing software, check the documentation and any "Read Me" files that come with the software for incompatibilities. Not every Mac works the same as every other, and some programs can be incompatible with your Mac or with other software you use.

What can I do with Now Utilities?

Now Utilities is basically a packet of really neat trinkets in the form of Control Panels and System software enhancements that are designed to help you get around on the Desktop more easily. There are also some great tools for improving your applications and extras added in to make opening and saving things easier. In all, Now Utilities offers some great help for organizing stuff.

What does it include?

Table 12.1 points out all the different enhancements included in Now Utilities 5.0. If you are using System 7.5, you'll notice that some of these features have been incorporated into the latest version of Apple's operating system.

Table 12.1 A quick look at Now Utilities 5.0

The feature...	What it does...
Super Boomerang	Adds an entry to the Apple menu that keeps track of the most recent applications and documents. Also adds a menu bar for opening and saving dialog boxes.
Now Menus	Enhances the hierarchical capabilities of the Apple menu (or adds them for pre-System 7.5). Also lets you add new menu items to the Finder's menu bar.
WYSIWYG Menus	Allows the Font menu of most applications to show you a sample of the font's appearance, instead of just the name.
Now Startup Manager	Allows you to determine which Extensions and Control Panels will load every time you turn on your Mac. Also helps you troubleshoot any conflicts between your extensions and Control Panels.

The feature...	What it does...
Now Save	Gives you the ability to automatically save your work in most applications. Reminds you to save at intervals or actually does the auto-saving.
Now Scrapbook	Replaces the Mac's Scrapbook with enhanced features for viewing and editing.
Now Profile	Checks your Mac and helps you troubleshoot problems.
Now FolderMenus	Allows you to click and hold the mouse on any folder, thus generating a hierarchical menu of that folder's contents.
Now QuickFiler	Allows you to quickly find, move, copy, alias, and print items. Also lets you compress and decompress files to save drive space.

The good stuff

WYSIWYG menus are one of the main reasons I like Now Utilities. What this does is let you see the fonts in your Font menu without forcing you to keep trying them out until you find one you like (see fig. 12.1).

Fig. 12.1
The WYSIWYG menu in action. Now I instantly know what my fonts look like!

Now Save is also a worthwhile addition. I'm actually a bit surprised that the Mac System software doesn't incorporate this function. In most applications, anything I'm working on is automatically saved at certain intervals (I like 15 minutes). This can be an incredible help if you ever lose power to your computer.

(Tip)

> If you have Now Save enabled, make it a habit to Save or Save As... your documents under their correct names the moment you have them open (even if they don't have anything typed in yet). That way, you'll never accidentally overwrite a file with an auto-save.

Super Boomerang is also a welcome addition. What's really helpful is the hierarchical menu it adds to the Open command in your File menus (see fig. 12.2). You might never need to use the Open dialog again...just move the mouse over to open recent folders and documents.

Fig. 12.2
Get to your most recent files more quickly with Super Boomerang's features.

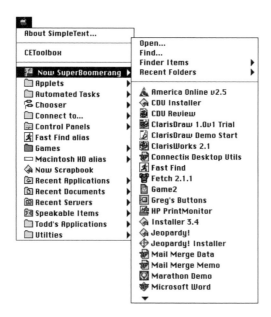

There's one last feature that I find amazing. If you pull down a menu, continue to hold the mouse button on an item, and then hit a key sequence (like Ctrl+Alt+T), you can assign a new keyboard shortcut to anything in a menu. That includes items like fonts. So, instead of heading up to my Font menu anytime I want to select Times, I can just hit Ctrl+Alt+T and my font changes.

(Tip)

These shortcuts can get very confusing, so I like to use a system. For instance, I like the idea of using Ctrl+Alt+(a letter) to pick my fonts. If I'm consistent, I won't forget.

Is Now Utilities worth it?

If you use your Macintosh a lot, or if you don't have System 7.5, Now Utilities will be your Mac's best friend. It adds great functions that make your work sessions a little easier to cope with. If you do have System 7.5, it's worth a little thought. You'll definitely see some benefit, but frankly, it won't be quite as dramatic.

 Q&A

I got Now Utilities for my Power Mac, and I think everything slowed down. Why?

This doesn't just happen with Now Utilities, it happens with any program not written specifically for the Power Macintosh. You need a new version of Now Utilities. Version 5.0 supports your Power Mac.

Will Connectix Desktop Utilities do more?

Connectix Desktop Utilities (CDU) is another customizing package that enhances your Mac's ability to move around in menus and control the characteristics of your Desktop (things like fonts, background pictures, and the menu bar).

Connectix also makes a program called Connectix PowerBook Utilities, which offers a lot of the same functions that CDU does. The reason I mention this now is CDU has a "keyboard-orientation" that makes it very functional for a portable notebook computer like the PowerBook, but not quite so for a desktop Mac. I'll show you what I mean.

What's cool about CDU?

There are two things you notice almost immediately after you've installed CDU and restarted. All the menu bar items in the Finder and your programs have little lines under one of their letters. Why is this? CDU lets you access these menus using keyboard combinations (see fig. 12.3).

Fig. 12.3
Holding down
Shift+Ctrl+F pulls
down the File menu
in the Finder. Now
I can access menus
without a mouse.

File	
New Folder	⌘N
Open	⌘O
Print	⌘P
Close Window	⌘W
Get Info	⌘I
Sharing...	
Duplicate	⌘D
Make Alias	⌘M
Put Away	⌘Y
Find...	⌘F
Find Again	⌘G
Page Setup...	
Print Desktop...	

CDU also lets you change the way menus on the menu bar work with the mouse. Right now, if you head up to your menu bar to pull down a menu, you have to hold down the mouse button or the menu disappears. CDU can be configured so that one click on the menu item pulls down the menu and leaves it on the screen. Then, the next click lets you select the item.

(Tip)

> Both of these features make a Mac's menu bar behave a lot like Microsoft Windows. If you're a seasoned MS Windows user, you may appreciate CDU.

The third interesting offering from CDU is its ability to dim your monitor after a specified period of time. You may have heard of "screensavers" or even used one. CDU's Power Saver is similar, except that, instead of displaying pictures or cartoons, it simply dims the brightness of your monitor. It's not terribly exciting, but it supposedly does save a little energy.

Plain English, please!

A **screensaver** is just a program that waits for your computer to become idle (for you to stop typing or using the mouse). After a specified number of idle minutes, the screensaver begins displaying pictures or cartoons. This is supposed to prevent monitor "burn-in" that causes ghosted images on your monitor (you may have seen burn-in on ATM screens). Incidentally, on nearly all Mac-compatible monitors, burn-in is next to impossible. For the most part, it's best to think of screensavers as entertainment.

The best of the rest

CDU offers about 13 other capabilities, but they range in usefulness. You can change the look of your Desktop and make people enter a password to use your Macintosh. You can also add a display on your menu bar that can show the time, date, and your available hard drive space. CDU also lets you config-ure special keyboard shortcuts for opening specific Control Panels, opening the Chooser, or changing Sound levels.

Is CDU worth it?

My advice here is pretty similar to my advice for Now Utilities. CDU is worthwhile and a lot of fun if you don't already use System 7.5. It adds a number of features that earlier System software doesn't have, like the Desktop patterns, menu bar clock, and more.

If you own System 7.5, you get a lot of these features, and I'd suggest shop-ping elsewhere for any other abilities, like screensaving or password security. My only qualification is this: CDU does a really nice job of adding the key-board shortcut abilities found in Microsoft Windows. If you're a Windows user, and you're uncomfortable with the Mac, CDU may go a long way to solve this.

What is RAM Doubler?

RAM Doubler, unlike our other utility packages, has one function only. As the name implies, RAM Doubler doubles the amount of available memory you have for opening applications. Install RAM Doubler and check the About This Macintosh... command in the Apple menu (see fig. 12.4). You've now got twice as much memory available as you have physically installed in your machine.

Fig. 12.4
With RAM Doubler installed, I've got twice as much RAM showing as before!

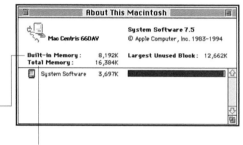

My actual, physical RAM.

My available RAM, thanks to RAM Doubler.

How does RAM Doubler work?

I know this sounds kinda crazy—but RAM Doubler uses things like virtual memory and other little memory tricks to load more applications into memory than you otherwise could. By shuffling your open applications around a little bit, it makes your Mac think it's got more memory than it does.

 <*Caution*> | Some applications hate RAM Doubler. Check the documentation for RAM Doubler and your application before using it.

The problem with RAM Doubler

RAM Doubler is a good idea, but it has its limits. The biggest one is this: RAM Doubler doesn't let you run any application that requires more memory than you've *actually got*.

RAM Doubler will let you load *more*, but not *bigger* applications. If I want to run a program that requires 8 MB of memory and I only have 4 *physical* MB of memory, RAM Doubler won't help. If, on the other hand, I have 4 MB of *physical* memory, and I want to run two programs that each require 4 MB, RAM Doubler can handle that.

Some other really cool programs

There's another way to get some great customizing software for your Mac, without heading to your computer store and blowing your paycheck. How? Shareware and freeware.

 Plain English, please!

Shareware describes a program or application that you "try before you buy." If you like it, you send a check to the author of the program, and then you're a legal owner. **Freeware** is software that the author doesn't want any money for...they presumably just wrote it for fun or to be helpful.

Where do you get this stuff? Most people use their modems to call up an online service like America Online or eWorld, and download these programs (see chapters 25–27 for info on modems and online services). Then, they try them out to see what they like and what they don't.

So what's good?

Here are a few shareware and freeware titles you might want to own.

- MenuChoice (Kerry Clendinning) offers hierarchical menus for pre-System 7.5 Macs. $15 shareware.

- StuffIt Lite (Aladdin Systems) compression utility offers compatibility with the very popular StuffIt format. $15 shareware.

- Disinfectant (John Norstad) antivirus software is updated regularly to combat computer viruses. Freeware.

- SuperClock! (Steve Christensen) adds a menu bar clock for pre-System 7.5 Macs. Freeware.

- Desktop Patterns (Howard Wright) adds different patterns to the Desktop for pre-System 7.5 Macs. Freeware.

- Greg's Buttons (Greg Landweber) customizes your System 7 or higher user interface. Change colors, menu bar font, buttons, and others. $15 shareware.

Some of these programs are designed to help you keep your Mac healthy, others are just for fun. Also, this is by no means a comprehensive list—there are thousands of shareware and freeware programs available to Macintosh users—whether through the mail, at your local computer store, or via an online service. And most of them don't cost much more than a good set of fuzzy dice!

Develop Your Personal Filing System

In this chapter:

- How should I organize my folders?
- How do I make things stand out?
- How do I find things?
- A little advice on cleaning

One day you'll wake up and realize that you'd better organize your files or you'll never find your stuff again!

I used to know every program and every document on my hard drive. Then, one day the realization hit me that I actually had to start organizing things or I'd never find them again. How did I do this? It's not tough—all the tools are built right into the Finder.

How should I organize my folders?

You can do whatever you want to organize your folders. Just pick a system and stick to it. I personally use a combination system—I group documents by project and applications by type. I put all the productivity applications in one place, all the utility applications in another, and games in a third. Then, I organize my documents by project type and then project (see fig. 13.1).

I'm a writer, so I use folders like "Magazine Articles" and then "Computer Universe 2/94." If you're in business, you might use folders like "Budget Presentation" and then "Fourth Quarter, 1995."

Fig. 13.1

Here's how I like to organize my hard drive.

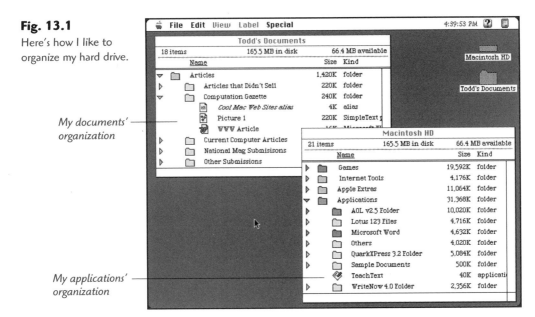

My documents' organization

My applications' organization

Now, I have a tendency to want to send applications and programs pretty deep into my folders because I start most of my programs using aliases on the Apple menu. If you'd prefer to have the actual icons for your programs "higher" in the organization, more power to you. It's up to you—just follow a system.

(Tip)

> If you're worried about novice users or kids, you might want to organize all your applications using the Applications folder in System 7.5. That's one of the folders you can lock, as we saw in chapter 11.

Manage projects with aliases

I mentioned using aliases to create project folders, and I really think that's one of the strengths of the alias concept. But, it depends on how much you re-use certain documents in your work. If you have a few particular documents you have to use on a regular basis, aliases work well.

Because an alias points back to the original copy of a document, any changes you make when working with the alias will change the original document. So, let's say you often work with a draft of your company's annual report (see fig. 13.2). If you have a project that is dealing with the financials of the report, and another that deals with the text, you can drop an alias of the actual report in both folders. That way, you won't have to search to find the one place you've stored the actual annual report document.

Fig. 13.2

If your projects often involve the same files, use aliases.

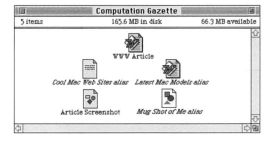

Try filing documents by project, not type

I see a lot of people who file their documents according to type, like spreadsheets, Word documents, and graphics files. But I recommend against doing this. Why? Because it isn't the way most people work. You wouldn't file things by letter, chart, and picture in a physical file—you'd file them by project or subject.

Instead, organize by the different reasons you create documents (articles, lists, newsletters, annual report) and then by projects. If you create a lot of sales presentations, put all the letters, memos, figures, and graphics for those presentations in the same folder (or better yet, use aliases).

When two people share one Mac

Sure, maybe the two of you can share a home, a kitchen, or even a closet. But a Mac? Impossible, right? No—not really. Especially with liberal use of friendly names, aliases, and conveniences like the Apple menu.

How does dividing things help? Well, with aliases, we can both see exactly what we want to, and we don't have to sift through stuff we don't care about. Plus, if we do want to find something that's not in our own folders, the original icons are still out on the hard drive.

You can probably tell I'm a fan of the new Apple menu. But look at what we can do with hierarchical menus and aliases! There's all my stuff, with no clicking required! I can avoid opening and closing windows every time I want to get to something.

Some of the fun of organizing your Mac is deciding how many ways you can do things. Take advantage of Mac's capabilities for your sharing.

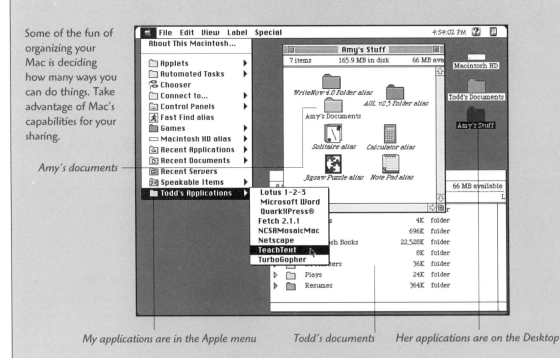

Amy's documents

My applications are in the Apple menu   *Todd's documents*   *Her applications are on the Desktop*

How do I make things stand out?

Did somebody once say that perception is nine-tenths of reality? Maybe not, but, on your Mac, the way you look at things can make a big difference. There are a couple of tricks you can use to make things stand out, and they all take advantage of the graphical nature of the Macintosh.

Use descriptive icon names

Folders and documents can have up to 31 characters in their names, *so why not use them?!* (Check out fig. 13.3.) Believe it or not, this is one of the features that makes the Macintosh stand out from many other personal computers. Every name you give a folder or document can—and should—be meaningful. This one step will go a long way toward making your files easier to manage.

Fig. 13.3
I personally am completely taken with Mac's capability to handle long file names. I recommend you take advantage of them, too.

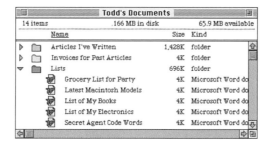

Choose the right view in the Finder

The **View menu** allows you to see things in basically three different ways (see fig. 13.4). You can view things by regular icon, by small icon, and in a list. Which view you should use depends almost completely on what it is you're looking at.

Fig. 13.4

Here are the different ways you can view files, and some examples of when they're useful.

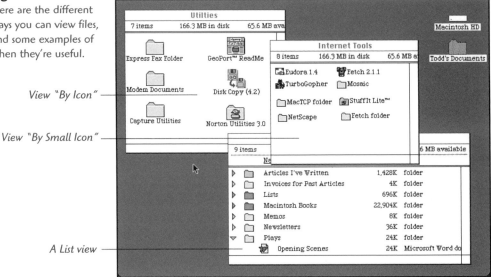

View "By Icon"

View "By Small Icon"

A List view

When should you use each? Here's my system. I like to see the regular icons almost any time I can. They're prettier, they look better on the screen, and they're easier to recognize. So, I use those for many of my application and utility folders. If you hold down the Option key while choosing the Special menu, the option **Clean Up By Name** becomes available so that you can view the regular icons in alphabetical order.

 Q&A

I held down the Option key and selected Special but the first menu option was Clean Up by Date not Clean Up by Name. Did I do something wrong?

No, the first menu option in the Special menu changes depending on which list view you selected the last time. You need to open the View menu and select By Name and then open the View menu again and select By Icon. Now when you hold down the Option key and select Special, the first menu option will be Clean Up by Name.

I almost never use the small icon view, but they can be really useful if you need to see a lot of files at once. A notable exception, though, is the System Folder. Using the small icon view makes it easier to see all the folders (Apple menu items, Launcher, Control Panels) that I often drag-and-drop stuff to when I'm adding new features to my Mac. Plus, with small icons the System folder's window takes up less space on my screen.

⊛ *{Note}* | When I say the list view, I'm talking about all four of these options in the Finder's View menu: by Size, by Name, by Kind, and by Date. These simply tell you how the list view will be organized initially.

Get serious about list views

If you've got a lot of levels of folders and files to manage, list views can be a lifesaver. Why? The list view's capability to see more than one level of folder at a time is a very powerful way to manage documents.

There are three distinct advantages that list views have over the other types of folder views. You can change how your list is organized, you can see more than one level of folder at one time, and you get more information.

How do you do this stuff? Open the Apple menu and choose Control Panels, Views. Here you can choose what file information (size, kind, date, etc.) shows up in a list view.

While in a list view, click on the arrow next to a folder's name. It will turn down, letting you see what folders and documents are inside. (See how it looks like a written outline?)

To sort the information you're viewing, click on the headings at the top of the window. These headings are the same as the options that are available to you in the Finder's View menu.

All the different things you can do to your list view.

Click to drop down to the next folder level

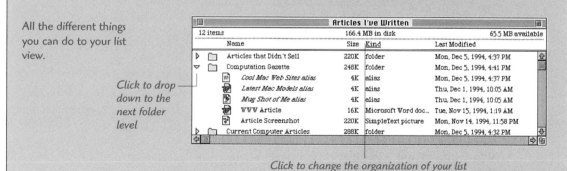

Click to change the organization of your list

I end up using ssome type of list view in almost all my document folders. List views are by far the most flexible, and they have the added advantage of allowing you to easily see more information about your files. I like to know how much space I'm taking up, and I like having the ability to lookat more than one hierarchy of folder at a time.

Go nuts with labels and colors

Do you use colored file tabs on your physical file folders at work or in your home office? If you do, check out the Label menu in the Finder. Here's where you can decide how to define your colors for filing excellence.

To change the label for a folder, just select that folder in the Finder, pull down the **Label menu**, and choose your color. That's it.

But, those colors and labels can't possibly suit everyone. If you'd like to make them more descriptive and personal, that's easy, too.

1 Open the Apple menu and choose Control Panels, Labels (see fig. 13.5).

Fig. 13.5
Change your filing colors and labels with the Label Control Panel.

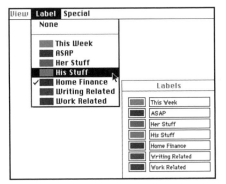

2 Click on the color of the label you want to change.

The color selection dialog box opens. If the color wheel is not showing, you may need to click on More Choices to get an options panel with Apple HSL or Apple RGB on the left side of the dialog box. Once you have this panel, click on Apple HSL to get the color wheel.

3 Click anywhere in the color wheel to select a new color. The selected color will appear in the box labeled New on the right.

4 If this is the color you want, click OK.

If you want to change a label description, click on the word (such as "Essential") and type your new label name. It's that easy. Now, when you pull down the Label menu, you'll have your own custom color scheme!

Black-and-white monitor? If you can't see the colors, you can still see the label names in any folder window you've set to a list view. Just make sure the Show Label box is checked in your Views control panel.

How do I find things on my Mac?

It's important to organize your files, if only because a little forethought can go a long way toward avoiding the repetitive clicking of opening folder after folder. But, if you ever get in a real bind, there are some other tools you can fall back on.

Use the basic Find File dialog box

To find a file, you can pull down the Finder's File menu and select the **Find...** command. This brings up the Find File dialog box (see fig. 13.6). Here, all you do is tell your Mac what you know about the file. Each of the selection boxes lets you limit the search further. For instance, you can choose to search only a certain disk, only local (i.e. not another computer connected via a network) drives, or even certain folders.

Fig. 13.6

Here's the basic Find File dialog box. It's only limited by what you know about the file you're searching for.

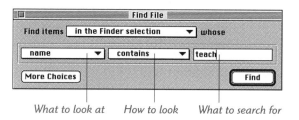

What to look at   How to look   What to search for

If you know what folder a file is in (you know, for instance, it's in the Documents folder on the Macintosh HD, but you don't know how many folders deep it is), select that folder in the Finder. Now, in the Find File document box, tell it to search "in the Finder selection." It will limit its search to the folder you selected and all its subfolders.

Plus, in System 7.5, you can use up to 10 different phrases to help you find a file. Just click on the **More Choices** button in the dialog. Now you can create two search phrases by changing the selection bars to show what you know (see fig. 13.7). This is particularly helpful if you have a large hard disk or have a number of computers connected together—or, if you just happen to have thousands of documents filed away and you've lost one.

Fig. 13.7

I told it everything I know. And it found the file I was looking for!

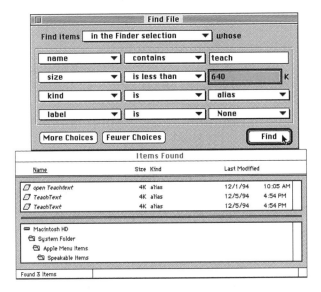

A little advice on cleaning

Look, I don't want to tell you how to run your Mac. Work with it any way you like. But, please, consider just a little advice. *Back things up and throw things away!* Unless you have a completely unlimited budget, you probably have a limited amount of hard drive storage space. Even if you don't have many files now, it won't take long before you've filled up that space. And, chances are you'll have filled it with more than you need to get by.

> ❝ *Plain English, please!*
>
> In computerese, **backing up** is the process of copying files from the disk you use most of the time (your system's hard disk) to a disk you can store elsewhere for safekeeping (like a floppy disk or a magnetic tape cartridge). Anyone who owns a computer should back up their files on a regular basis. ❞

What files can I throw away?

Some file types take up a lot of room, so if you have one or two of these that you can delete, you can free up a big chunk of space. What kind of files take up a lot of room? You may already know that most applications take up many megabytes of disk space. Some other culprits are

- *Games.* This especially includes games with a lot of graphics. Your average multimedia adventure game can take 10 to 20 MB of disk space.

- *Graphics files.* Especially "photo-realistic" graphics files. Many of these can be compressed, however, with third-party tools.

- *Sound clips.* You may get sound files from software you buy in the computer store or from online services. Add enough sound files for your system's sounds and you may be losing a lot of disk space.

- *Digital movies.* We'll talk about these later in chapter 23. If you have any sitting around now, though, look and see how much space they're taking. It's quite a bit.

What files should I keep?

Document files that you create in word processing, spreadsheet, and paint programs are usually quite small. If you're likely to need these files again, there's nothing wrong with keeping them on your hard disk, as long as you remember to copy them to disk or tape regularly, just to keep them safe in case your Mac's hard disk gets damaged.

If you use your Mac for serious work (either for business or for important home tasks), it's a good idea to create a regular backup schedule. You might even look for retail software that helps you set this schedule.

An example? Back up new documents (and any documents you've changed) at least once a week—maybe even every 3 or 4 days. Also, make sure you back up using *different* disks or cartridges from week to week, so that you don't lose months worth of work if that disk goes bad. Finally, store your backups somewhere away from your computer (preferably, off-site). This will keep your data safe even if your desk, home, or building meets with disaster.

Here's another good reason to keep your files well organized. If you organize by project, you can back up by project. It's a lot easier to drag one folder to a floppy drive than it is to sift through all your files trying to find the most recent ones.

Lock your files to keep them out of the Trash

Of course, there are some files you never want to throw away. If you'd keep the paper equivalent of these files in a locked filing cabinet or a safe, you might want some protection from accidental trashing. You can do this by **locking** document files (see fig. 13.8). If you throw a locked file in the Trash, Mac won't let you empty the Trash until you unlock the file.

Fig. 13.8
Click the Locked box to keep files out of the dumpster.

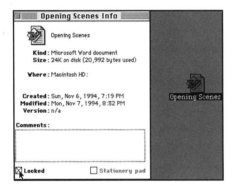

To lock a document file, select that file in the Finder and choose File, Get Info. In the Get Info dialog, click on the Locked box to lock the file. Now you can't empty the Trash if this file is in there.

This thing isn't exactly in Fort Knox. A locked file can easily be unlocked or thrown away, especially by someone with Mac experience. If you need real security for sensitive files, you'll probably need to look into a retail program.

All you have to do to unlock the file is click on Locked again in the Get Info dialog. You can throw away locked files in the Trash by holding down the Option key when you select Empty Trash from the Special menu in the Finder.

If you're looking for more security, there are a number of retail packages that will allow you to password protect or even encrypt sensitive documents. If you just want to keep the kids out of trouble, At Ease from Apple Computer is a great way to let them work while keeping your stuff safe. And, it comes with most Performa model Macs!

Part IV

Getting a Little Work Done

14

All It Takes Is an Application

Applications are like tools, screwdrivers, hammers, cordless drills, and so on. And like tools, you need the right one for the job.

In this chapter:

- What are applications and why are there so many?
- What can I do with these applications?
- How do I install an application on my Mac?
- How do I get rid of an application I don't want?

W hy are there so many different applications? The easy answer is: *There's a lot to do!* Computers have come a long way since the time that they were considered substitutes for typewriters—or even high-end calculators. Sure, you can use a computer to write. But you can also use a computer to manage. Or to consult. Or to communicate. How? With applications.

Plain English, please!

A **computer program** is computer code tells your Mac how to do something; an **application** is a specific kind of computer program. Applications are programs that are designed to *apply* computer technology to a real world problem, like creating printed pages or calculating finances. Microsoft Excel, WordPerfect, and ClarisWorks are all applications.

What can I do with applications?

Here's a brief introduction to some of the things you can do with applications. In the following chapters, we'll discuss each function in more detail.

Write and create documents

There are two very general categories for applications that help you create the printed word (see fig. 14.1). These are word processors and desktop publishing.

Fig. 14.1
Creating written documents, especially desktop publishing, is one of the Mac's strong points.

What is word processing?

Word processing applications are probably the most familiar of all computer tools. Most computer owners use a word processing application. Popular titles include Microsoft Word, WordPerfect, and WriteNow. These programs let you type, edit, and perform basic layout design. Word processing applications give you the freedom to edit and replace sections of text, to automate the management of text and typefaces, and to generally make a document more readable. They can also help to make repetitive tasks, like creating form letters or mass mailings, easier to accomplish.

Plain English, please!

Layout design is basically the electronic version of "cutting and pasting" printed documents like newsletters and magazine pages. Word processing and desktop publishing applications let you move text around, decide what will be centered on the page, how the typefaces will appear, and where you will insert graphics or tables.

What is desktop publishing?

Desktop publishing applications (refer to fig. 14.1) are more specialized than word processing programs, in that they are most useful in the *design* of printed pages. Where word processors get your thoughts on the page, desktop publishing programs help you make that page look better.

In fact, many desktop publishing applications can **import** the files from word processing programs so that you can change the appearance and placement of the text on the page. Some popular desktop publishing applications are Adobe PageMaker, QuarkXpress, and FrameMaker.

In some areas, the gap between word processing and desktop publishing has shrunk. Many word processors now have the capability to generate well-designed newsletters, tables, charts, and graphics. Desktop publishing programs now generally have more word processing features to make creating an entire document easier.

Crunch numbers

Here's the second reason most people buy computers: to manage numbers. Of course, that often means money. The Macintosh has a number of applications designed for doing a good deal of accounting. From standard checkbook applications to full-blown payroll and payables/receivables programs. And, of course, there are a number of spreadsheet applications written to run on your Macintosh.

What's a spreadsheet?

A **spreadsheet application** is designed to act something like a smart ledger-book (see fig. 14.2). It allows you to enter numbers and formulas in rows and columns, and then generate totals, produce reports on that data, or represent the data graphically. The spreadsheet offers amazing flexibility for money management. Once you've set up your spreadsheet and entered the formulas for the calculations, you can change any number and all the calculations in the spreadsheet that use that number will update automatically. You can build "what-if" scenarios and play out different decisions. And, spreadsheets are very convenient for creating charts, graphs, and other graphical elements. Common spreadsheet applications include Lotus 1-2-3 and Microsoft Excel.

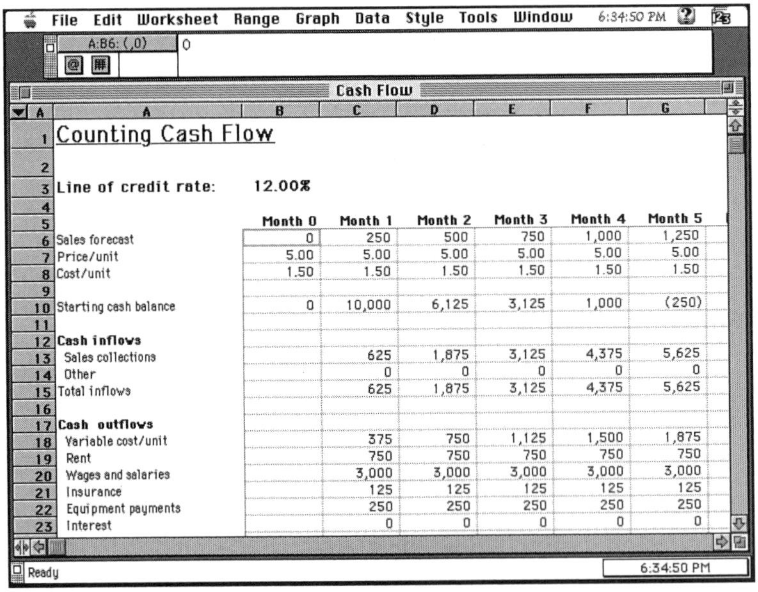

Fig. 14.2
A Lotus 1-2-3
spreadsheet in action.

File Edit Worksheet Range Graph Data Style Tools Window						6:34:50 PM

A:B6: (,0)   0

Cash Flow

	A	B	C	D	E	F	G
1	Counting Cash Flow						
2							
3	Line of credit rate:	12.00%					
4							
5			Month 0	Month 1	Month 2	Month 3	Month 4	Month 5
6	Sales forecast		0	250	500	750	1,000	1,250
7	Price/unit		5.00	5.00	5.00	5.00	5.00	5.00
8	Cost/unit		1.50	1.50	1.50	1.50	1.50	1.50
9								
10	Starting cash balance		0	10,000	6,125	3,125	1,000	(250)
11								
12	Cash inflows							
13	Sales collections			625	1,875	3,125	4,375	5,625
14	Other			0	0	0	0	0
15	Total inflows			625	1,875	3,125	4,375	5,625
16								
17	Cash outflows							
18	Variable cost/unit			375	750	1,125	1,500	1,875
19	Rent			750	750	750	750	750
20	Wages and salaries			3,000	3,000	3,000	3,000	3,000
21	Insurance			125	125	125	125	125
22	Equipment payments			250	250	250	250	250
23	Interest			0	0	0	0	0

Ready   6:34:50 PM

What other numbers can I crunch?

There are many other more specific finance applications available for the Macintosh as well. For the home you can use checkbook management and home finance applications to keep track of your bills, investments, taxes, and savings. Some will even allow you to manage home inventories for insurance and other purposes. Examples of these include Intuit's Quicken (see fig. 14.3) and Meca's Managing Your Money. Some of these programs can even help you manage a small business.

Fig. 14.3

Quicken's checkbook metaphor makes home finance a breeze.

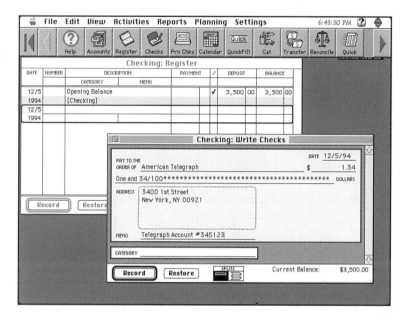

Organize data

Database applications vary widely in their scope and audience, and they are generally as flexible as you need them to be for managing your data. What kind of data? Anything from your record collection to your company's inventories to your high-school reunion address list.

What is a database application?

Database applications are generally very far reaching in their capabilities, but they require a lot of input from the user. You create the way a database stores information by giving it categories and the types of data (words, numbers, dates) that you want to store. Is this complicated? It can be.

Some advanced database applications require a certain amount of programming to work, others just require some time getting used to their style of information storage. For home-based projects, many people use the database modules included with their works programs—like ClarisWorks or Microsoft Works. For higher-level tasks, some popular database programs include Claris Filemaker Pro, Microsoft FoxPro, and ACI's 4D.

⊕ (Tip)

If you're just starting out with databases, I'd recommend trying out the database module in ClarisWorks or a similar application. If you decide you need more capabilities than they offer (like the ability to cross-reference data in different databases), look into the more advanced applications.

What is personal information management (PIM)?

PIM applications are similar to databases in that they store information. They tend, however, to be more specialized in what they organize. Most are set up as the computer equivalent of your Franklin or DayTimer planner (see fig. 14.4). They allow you to store the names of friends or clients, track your schedule, and generate to-do lists. Many are sold as "contact managers" geared toward the businessperson or sales professional. Popular PIMs include FIT Software's Full Contact, Attain's In Control, and Now Contact from Now Software.

Fig. 14.4

Personal information managers are popular and useful ways to manage your contacts, appointments, and schedule.

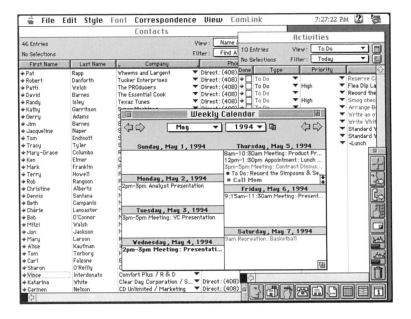

Paint and draw

The graphical nature of the Macintosh has made **painting and drawing applications** very popular since Mac's introduction. Some of these applications are geared toward professionals and are very expensive—especially those that are designed to support high-end desktop publishing, such as Adobe Photoshop and Illustrator. Others outside the bane of graphic artists are more suited for other business and home uses.

What's the difference between painting applications and drawing applications?

Usually it's the tools offered by the application. Paint programs tend to allow you to be freer with your illustrations, giving you electronic tools that mirror real world paintbrushes, colors, and textures of the palette. Popular paint programs include Claris' MacPaint and Fractal Design's Painter and Dabbler applications.

Drawing applications, with exceptions, are designed more for the precision of the drawing, and less for the art. Drawing programs tend to suggest more professional applications like 3D renderings, architectural designs, and other graphic arts. The market is rich with this type of application if only because they are used so often in the printing and publishing worlds. Drawing applications include Adobe Illustrator, Aldus FreeHand, and Deneba Software's Canvas.

Communicate with other computers

Your Mac isn't the only computer in the world, and there are some amazing tools out there for dealing with those other computers. Through **communications software** you can hook up with other computers, and emulation software will let you run applications designed for other computers.

What is communications software?

Applications designed for communications come in a few different flavors—but they all have one thing in common: They're designed to help you use your modem to connect to the outside world over a phone line. You can use these programs to dial into your office computers from home, online services, or local bulletin board services. Popular programs include Software Venture's MicroPhone Pro, FreeSoft's White Knight, and Timbuktu Pro from Farallon Computing.

Plain English, please!

Often called **BBSs, bulletin board services** are similar to online services like eWorld or America Online, but they're usually smaller and more local in scope. Generally, BBSs are run by private computer owners or organizations who allow other computer owners to call their computer using a modem. Then, software on the BBS computer allows callers to leave messages for one another, participate in discussions, and trade software programs.

What is emulation software?

Sometimes you need to do more than talk to other computers—you need your Mac to behave like them, too. That's where emulation comes in handy. Emulation applications offer a range of capabilities, from the capability to read different computers' disks to actually running many DOS and Windows-based applications (see fig. 14.5). Most of these programs are written by either Apple or Insignia Solutions, like Insignia's SoftWindows and SoftPC applications.

Fig. 14.5

Windows programs on a Mac? With Insignia's SoftWindows, you can run many Microsoft Windows applications without needing another computer.

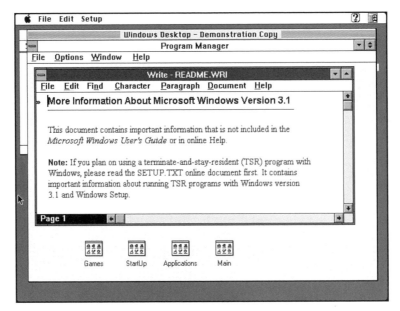

Can you really have it all?

You can buy a single application that combines all the basic functions we've discussed so far. Often called **works applications**, these packages are great for the home user or for business people who see all the bells and whistles of the professional applications as overkill. Most include the basic business programs, but they're scaled-down in breadth of function. These applications include word processing, paint and drawing, database, communications, spreadsheet, and presentation abilities (see fig. 14.6).

Fig. 14.6

Works applications give you scaled down tools for many different business needs, including word processing, graphics, and number crunching.

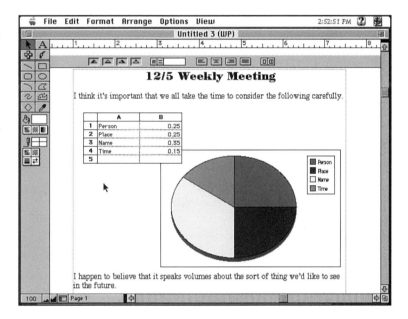

Generally speaking, works packages can fit the needs of many home or home/office users. The big names, like ClarisWorks, Microsoft Works, and WordPerfect Works, don't really skimp on details. Plus, most of these works packages offer a high level of integration between their programs, making it easier to combine graphics, text, and numbers in a single document.

⊛ {Note}

Works packages and application suites (like Microsoft Office) are two different animals. Works packages tend to be smaller in scope and size, giving you the basic functionality of popular business applications without all the extras. Suites, on the other hand, are usually bundles of the high-end business applications (like Microsoft Word, Excel, and PowerPoint) sold together in one box.

How do I get applications on my Mac?

Many Macintosh models come preloaded with certain applications—all you have to do to get these fired up is find their icon and double-click. If you have an application still on the original floppy disks, though, you need to **install** those applications so that all the right files can be put in all the right places.

Installing from floppy disks

Most applications will have numbered disks. Generally, the disk you insert first will either be called the "Install" or "Installation" disk. If you don't have one of these, just start with the disk labeled "1."

When you insert this disk into the floppy drive, you should get an icon and an open window. (If there's no window, double-click the floppy's icon.) See a program called *Installer*? Most Macintosh applications use this or something like it (see fig. 14.7). If you see anything that says "Installer," "Install Me," or some derivation of such, then double-click away.

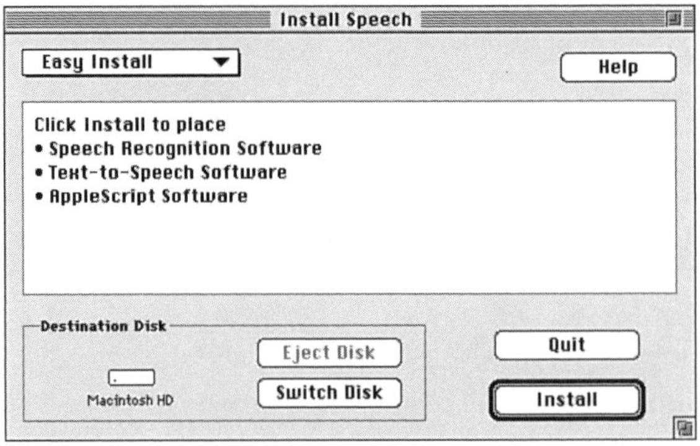

Fig. 14.7

Apple's Installer program. Just follow the instructions and switch disks when asked.

```
                      Install Speech
  ┌─────────────────┐                         ┌──────────┐
  │ Easy Install  ▼ │                         │   Help   │
  └─────────────────┘                         └──────────┘

    Click Install to place
    • Speech Recognition Software
    • Text-to-Speech Software
    • AppleScript Software



  ┌─Destination Disk──────────────────┐   ┌──────────┐
  │              ┌───────────────┐     │   │   Quit   │
  │   [___]      │  Eject Disk   │     │   └──────────┘
  │ Macintosh HD └───────────────┘     │   ┌──────────┐
  │              │  Switch Disk  │     │   │ Install  │
  └──────────────└───────────────┘─────┘   └──────────┘
```

Many applications use a standard installer program to help you install programs. Double-click on the installer program and it will walk you through the rest of your installation. Don't forget that you'll have to switch disks as the installation progresses, so stay somewhere close while it installs.

Q&A

I'm trying to install an application but nothing says "Installer!" What should I do?

In some cases an application doesn't require special installation. Try creating a folder on your hard drive and drag-and-drop all the files from your floppy to that folder. Then look for the application's icon and double-click. If the application starts, you've done the right thing. If not, you may need to look harder on the disk for an Installer. It may be inside another folder or named something else, like "Setup."

Installing from CD-ROM

If your application came on a CD-ROM disc and you have a CD-ROM drive, great! Just put the CD-ROM in its drive (don't forget the caddy if needed) and up pops the CD-ROM icon. If you don't already have a window open, double-click the CD-ROM icon.

Now the rules are basically the same as installing from a floppy, except you won't have to switch disks. The CD-ROM will automatically install the entire application for you.

Moving your files around

If you didn't install the application where you want it in your organization, or if you reorganize, you may want to move your newly installed files around. This is fine, if you keep two things in mind. First, you can always use an alias to keep an icon of a program handy. Second, many applications need you to keep their folders intact for proper operation.

**<Caution>**

Avoid breaking up the files in an application's folder. If possible, keep everything intact just as the installer program left them. Not all programs mind, but some programs rely on other files in the folder to work correctly. You can, however, move the entire application folder if you desire.

I hate it! How do I get applications off my Mac?

Sometimes your tools just don't work for you. If you've got an application you need to get off your Mac, it's a fairly easy process. You just need to make sure you look in all the right places. But, before you trash everything, step back for a moment and consider the consequences.

Things to think about before throwing it all away

Here's the $64,000 question. *Did you do any important work in this application?* If you did, you need to make sure you saved it in the right place and you've done any importing or exporting you need to do.

Plain English, please!

What are **importing** and **exporting**? Different applications, even if they offer the same basic functions (e.g. they're both word processors), usually save files in different file formats. WordPerfect, for instance, can't automatically read Microsoft Word document files. But, many applications will import another application's documents, making the appropriate translations. Some applications will also export documents by translating the document from its own file format to one it thinks is compatible with the other application.

Converting your older documents

Say, for instance, you're going to get rid of your word processing application. If you're moving to another application, the first thing you should do is make sure that new application can import your old files.

How? Usually it's through the new application's Open dialog box. Pull-down the File menu from the new application's menu bar and select the Open... command. Then, using the Open dialog box, find the folder that contains the document you want to import. Select the document you want to open, and then tell the new application what application created the document. Now you should be able to open the old document.

Fig. 14.8
Here's the Open
dialog from WriteNow.
Shown are some of the
files it can import.

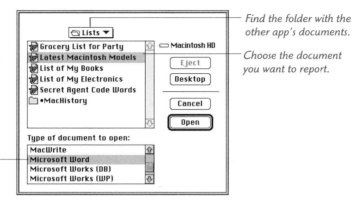

Find the folder with the
other app's documents.

Choose the document
you want to report.

Choose the application
that created the
documents.

⊛ **{Note}**

Not all applications import the same. Take a moment and make sure your new
application not only imports your document, but that it imports it with all the
styles, formatting, and elements you had in the original. You might want to
print the document from both applications and check them visually for
differences.

🛈 **(Tip)**

If your new application won't directly import your old application's files, try
to find a happy medium. Use your old application to Save As... files in a more
universal file format (like standard Mac text), and then load this stripped-down
document into your new application.

Don't throw your documents away!

The other thing we need to consider is whether or not you've stored any
documents in the folders you are about to throw away. Some applications
create document folders within their application folders. Make sure you've
moved these documents somewhere else on your hard drive before you trash
everything. Even if they've been properly converted, they won't do you any
good if you toss them out!

Deleting that application

Now it's pretty straightforward. Pick up the application folder and drag it to
the Trash. Empty the Trash and the application's gone! That's it, right? Well,
almost. We still have some minor cleaning to do.

What about aliases?

First, you'll probably want to get rid of any aliases you've created for that program. Do you have any on the Desktop, in project folders in the Apple Menu Items folder? Better go get 'em. Don't forget to delete the aliases out of the Launcher and Startup Folders too, if you used them. Just drag any aliases out to the Trash.

(Tip)

> You can use the Find File command to find every instance of the application's name. Plus, if you type just the first few characters of the name, you can hopefully get any combination you may have used when you renamed aliases.

Where else should I look?

There are two other places we haven't checked yet where you might want to Trash some files. Some programs like to drop data files in the System Folder, so check there and see if anything looks like it belongs to your trashed application. Another place you're likely to find a trashable file is in the Preferences Folder in the System Folder (see fig. 14.9). Open this folder and look for the Preferences file that's related to your trashed application. This file can go too—just toss it out.

⊗<Caution>

> If you're not sure that a file belongs to the application you've trashed, don't delete it! For instance, if you have more than one Microsoft program on your Mac (like Word *and* Excel), it might be difficult to tell if a file belongs to one or the other. You're better off just leaving it, even if it wastes a little disk space.

Fig. 14.9
The Preferences Folder. If I want to get rid of WriteNow, I'd go here to throw away its preferences file.

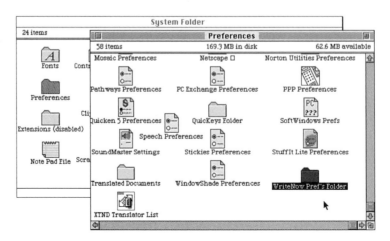

15

The Printed Page and Applications that Create Them

It's easy to add special effects with a word processor that make your documents more professional and interesting.

In this chapter:

- What's so great about word processing?

- If a word processor does all that, why do I need a desktop publishing application?

- Drawing and painting sounds fun. What do I need?

A lot of people get their first computer to help them to write. In fact, word processing is probably the most popular reason for buying a computer. So let's talk about the different ways you can create printed pages, and what application is best for what you want to print. We may even come across some things you didn't know you could do with your Mac!

Why is word processing so great?

Because it's easy. Once you get the hang of word processing, you'll have the ability to create a document, edit it, change the fonts, check the spelling, and have the computer look over the grammar. A word processor allows you to generate high-quality documents fast.

Plain English, please!

Technically, a **font** is a collection of letters and characters with the same typeface and size, such as Courier 12. **Font families** are sets of fonts in several sizes and weights. Some people get mad if you say typefaces and fonts are the same thing, but the term font is often used to refer to typefaces or font families.

Of course, word processors vary in their capabilities. Different word processors have different talents that set them apart from the others. But, just like cars, word processors all have a core set of functions in common. Nearly all cars "go," "stop," and "turn." All word processors allow you to enter text, arrange it on the page, and print it out.

Getting text on the page

The first and most important thing a word processor can help you do is get text on the page. Not just tossed out there, but in the right order, spelled correctly, grammar-checked, and with all the t's crossed and i's dotted.

The place to start is **Page Setup,** usually in the File menu, which is where you can choose the right size and orientation of paper you're using for what you plan to create. Also, if you can find it, head to **Document Setup** and set your margins (1" for most correspondence, 2.75" for late-night college term papers...). In any word processor, you start out with a blank page, pick the first font you want to use, and start typing. You might want to **boldface** some things, *italicize* other things, or even <u>underline</u> a really good point or two (see fig. 15.1). Otherwise, just type.

Plain English, please!

It's the world-famous dogcow! That animal (whatever it is) is there to help you determine what **orientation** your paper will be in when it prints. The standard setting is **portrait**, which means the paper is normal—that is, longer than it is wide. **Landscape** means you're using the paper sideways—wider than it is long.

Fig. 15.1

The word processor helps you get your ideas down on the page quickly, correctly, and cleanly.

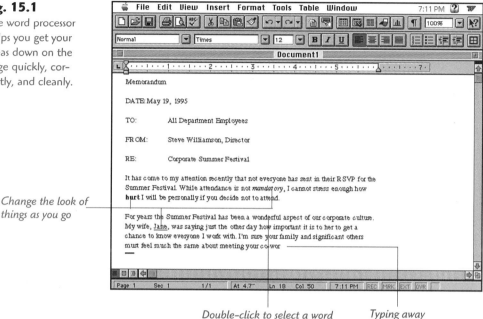

Change the look of things as you go

Double-click to select a word　　*Typing away*

①(Tip)

Remember keyboard shortcuts in chapter 4? That's ⌘+B for bold, ⌘+I for italics, and ⌘+U for underline.

If you look at the Untitled window in figure 15.2, you can see that I've started a short memo as an example of what you can do in a word processor like Microsoft Word. It's just like a typewriter, with one small difference: When I get to the end of a line, I don't have to hit Return to get to the next line. Word (and most other Macintosh text and word processing programs) automatically "wraps" the text from one line to the next. This makes it easier to reformat text later.

❋{Note}

You do, however, still need to hit the Return key whenever you want a new line or new paragraph. Notice in figure 15.2 that I've hit Return whenever I wanted a new line, like right after I typed the "To" and "From" lines.

Fig. 15.2

Typing in Word isn't much different than using a typewriter. Just watch your Returns!

Hit Return on a blank line to create these spaces.

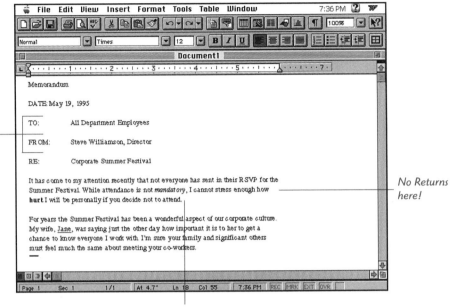

No Returns here!

But there is a Return to end this paragraph.

If you make a mistake and mistype something, there are two ways to fix it. You can hit the Delete key on your keyboard (usually two rows above the Return key) to back up and delete everything you've typed. Or, you can use the cursor keys to place your cursor next to the word you've mistyped and then use the Delete key to back up over just the mistake. It's up to you.

You use this same concept for entering letters you've omitted. Just move the cursor to where you want to insert the letters and then type. You won't type over any other letters—your word processing will automatically make space for your new letters.

 **(Tip)**

Want to see where you've typed returns, spaces, and even tabs? In Word, there's a command in the View menu that's called Show ¶. Choosing this command will let you see these "hidden" characters.

Cut, copy, and paste

So far, using the Mac to type a memo isn't much better than using a typewriter. But, the **cut**, **copy**, and **paste** functions are what makes word processing really shine. What we can do, if we like, is pick up entire blocks of text and put them somewhere else in the document. Some people find this offers amazing freedom over writing things by hand or using a typewriter. It allows you to toss all your ideas down on the page and then arrange them in whatever way makes the most sense.

To move text in my document, I simply place the mouse pointer at the beginning of the text I want to move and hold down the mouse button. Next, I drag to the end of the selection and release the mouse button. That highlights the text (see fig. 15.3). Then, I pull down the Edit menu and choose Cut. The text will disappear.

Fig. 15.3

Cut, copy, and paste are ways to apply Mac's power to editing your documents.

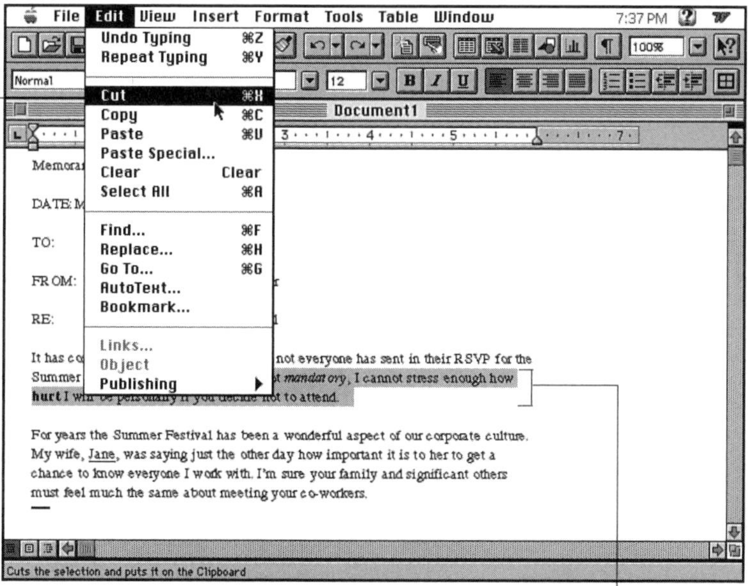

Choose Cut from the Edit menu.

(a)

I want to cut this section and put it at the beginning of the next paragraph.

And choose Paste to drop it in.

Now, I position the cursor where I want to paste the text.

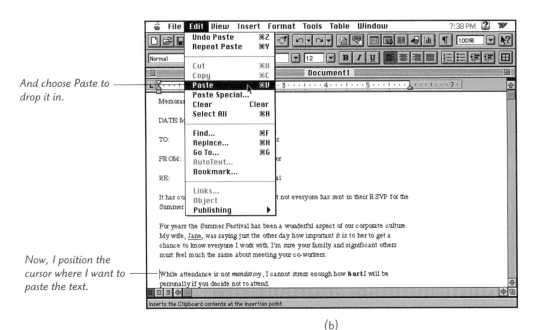

(b)

{Note}

Notice that when you put the mouse pointer over text, the mouse pointer changes to a cursor that looks like the capital letter I. This is to let you know that it's acting as a text selection tool, which enables you to highlight text in a document. You'll hear this referred to as an **I-beam**.

The next step is to move the mouse pointer to the place you want to paste your text. Click once and the cursor appears in the document. Head up to the Edit menu and select **Paste**. The cut text drops back into the document, just as if you'd typed it again.

The Copy command works the same as Cut, except that it leaves the text in the document and allows you to add a copy of that text somewhere else. Basically, it duplicates the selected text and allows you to paste as many copies of that text into the document as you desire.

Saving your creation

When your document is the way you like it, it's very important to **save** that document. Remember, just because something is on your screen doesn't means it's safe. Things you create on the screen are in the Mac's memory—but that memory is only good as long as the computer is turned on. Turn the computer off (or lose power in your building) and that data will be erased from memory. So, you have to tell Mac to "write stuff down" by saving to the hard drive.

To save, you'll need to pull down the File menu. Then, select Save. The Save dialog box will appear, asking you what you'd like to name the file and where you want to put it. I'll call my document "Festival Memo" and save it in Todd's Documents. After you enter that information (see fig. 15.4), click Save to save the document to that location, under its new name. If you're successful, your Word window will change names, too, as shown in figure 15.5.

Where does it go when you cut?

One of the reasons that cut, copy, and paste show up on nearly every application's menu bar is that the Macintosh system software provides a universal "Clipboard" for sharing text and graphics between applications. This means you can, for instance, cut text out of a Microsoft Word document and paste it into an Excel document.

When you cut or copy text or a graphic out of your document, it's placed temporarily on the Mac's Clipboard. When you paste, it's copied from the Clipboard and put back in your document at the point where you've placed the cursor.

There are two things you should know about the Clipboard. First, items stay on the Clipboard until you cut or copy something different. So, you can paste the same item more than once if you need to. Second, you can view the Clipboard without pasting. Just open the System Folder and double-click on the icon named Clipboard.

Fig. 15.4
Decide where you're going to file your document, and then save often.

The Save command   *Click and hold to change folders*

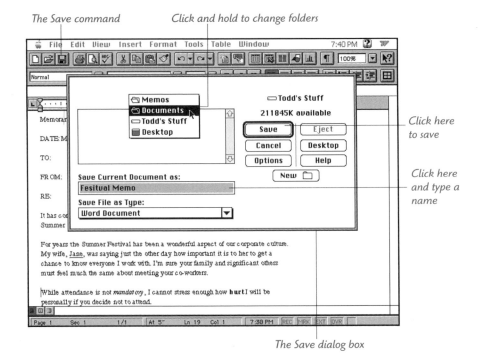

Click here to save

Click here and type a name

The Save dialog box

Fig. 15.5
With a successful save, my document window has changed.

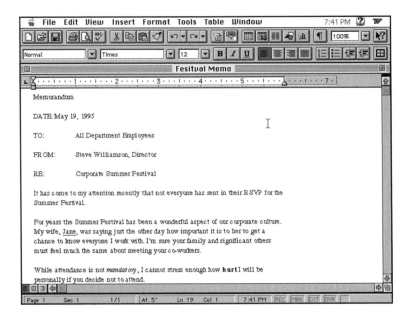

Now, if I make changes and again select Save from the File menu, the document automatically updates this file in the same location.

Save As...

But, what if I want to save this file with another name or to a different location? Since Save will now default to my original file name and folder, I'll need to use another command. Under the File menu, I select the Save As... command. This lets me save another copy of the file, either by changing the name, the folder, or both.

 **<Caution>** Remember that with the Save As command you are saving a new copy of your document—not just changing the name or moving it to a new folder. Any changes you make in the new copy will no longer show up in the original.

I can also use the Save As command to create a **template**. I'll change the name to "Festival Memo Template" and save it in the same folder, choosing Stationery from the selector menu (see fig. 15.6). Now, whenever I want to write another festival memo, I'll just open "Festival Memo Template," change a few things, and save a new copy. When I choose Save, Word will ask me to give a new name to what I'm working on. That way, my new work won't be saved over Festival Memo Template. It's almost like making a photocopy, "whiting-out" the dates and names, and rewriting them (except it's much cleaner and easier).

 Plain English, please!

In the computer world, the word **template** (or Stationery, depending on the program) is used to describe any file you use as a standard for creating other files more easily. For instance, in my example, I've created my own template to make generating future "festival memos" nearly effortless. Many applications use templates of some form or another to make things easier. Depending on the application, that can be anything from creating newsletters to figuring loan payments or generating payroll checks.

Fig. 15.6
I'll use the Save As...
command to save a
copy of this document
with a new name. I
also could have moved
the copy to a new
folder.

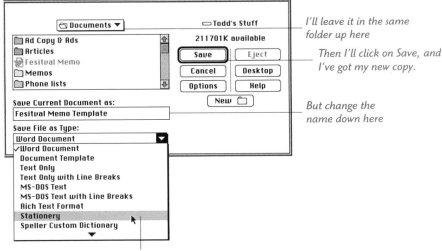

*I'll leave it in the same
folder up here*

*Then I'll click on Save, and
I've got my new copy.*

*But change the
name down here*

Change file type to Stationery

When you're done typing, you can go back and clean things up a little bit. Run
the spell checker and grammar checker if you like to do that sort of thing, or
go through and look everything over on your own.

You already know that clicking once on a word will move the cursor up to that
word. But did you know that double-clicking a word selects the entire word?
Now you can just start typing and replace the word—no deleting required.
Triple-clicking, by the way, selects an entire line or paragraph, depending on
the program.

Making the text pretty

Once you get your text on the screen, you'll need to start thinking about
formatting. This is where your Mac blows away anything a typewriter could
do. In my example, I'd like to jazz a few things up. I think it's important to
have the word "Memorandum" in really big, cool-looking letters across the
center of the page (see fig. 15.7).

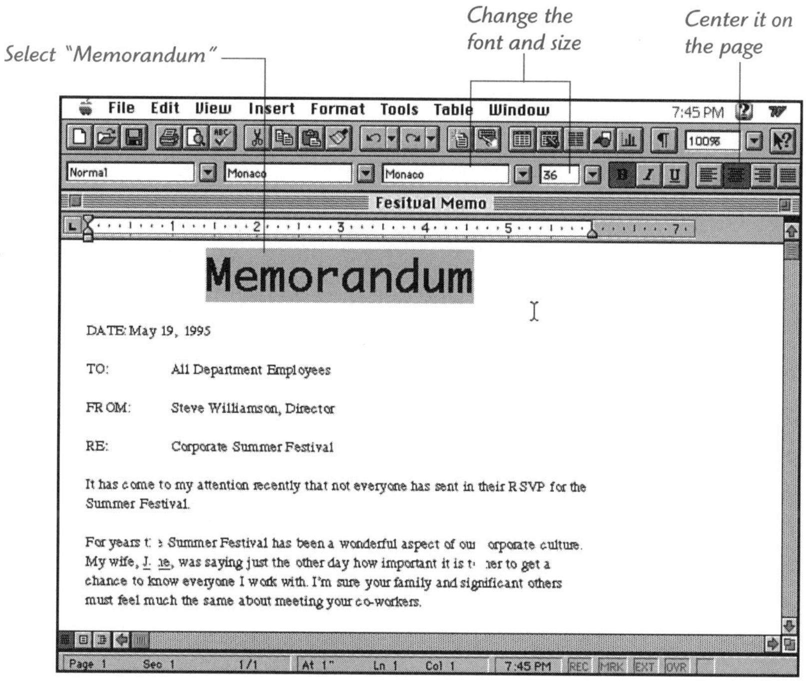

Select "Memorandum"

Change the
font and size

Center it on
the page

Fig. 15.7

Even a few special
formatting elements
can improve the
appearance and
communicate better
than plain old text.

Memorandum

DATE: May 19, 1995

TO: All Department Employees

FROM: Steve Williamson, Director

RE: Corporate Summer Festival

It has come to my attention recently that not everyone has sent in their RSVP for the
Summer Festival.

For years the Summer Festival has been a wonderful aspect of our corporate culture.
My wife, June, was saying just the other day how important it is to her to get a
chance to know everyone I work with. I'm sure your family and significant others
must feel much the same about meeting your co-workers.

I start by selecting the word "Memorandum" and changing its **alignment** to
centered. Then, I pull down my Font menu and change the appearance of the
word to something a little cooler. Finally, I'll beef it up a little bit with my
Size menu. 36 points oughta do it.

Plain English, please!

Alignment refers to how you arrange the text on the page—you can arrange it
so that all the lines start at the left margin or so that all the lines end exactly at
the right margin; or, you can justify the text (like a newspaper column) or you
can place the text in the middle of the page. **Point size** refers to a character's
size on the page. 72 points is about an inch tall—or about the size a reputable
newspaper would print the headline "We Are at War!"

What else can a word processor do?

To a certain degree, it depends on the features your word processor offers. Do you want page numbers, footnotes, or your name at the top of every page? You'll do those things in **headers** or **footers**—sections at the top and bottom of every page. Want to add borders, lines, or graphics? You can probably do that too, depending on the application you have.

The last thing I want to do to my sample document is create a simple mail merge. I'm going to merge two documents, a main document and a data document. Why do this? It's how you create a personalized form letter, by creating and printing multiple copies of this one memo with different names in the TO: spot. The main document has the text and format of the memo I want to distribute around the office. The data document contains the names of people I want to send this to (see fig. 15.8).

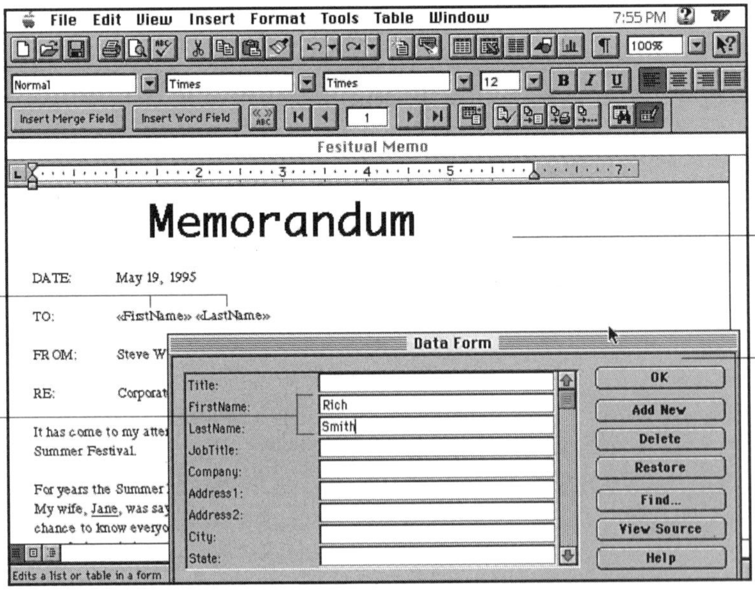

Fig. 15.8
My mail merge takes only moments to set up, yet it has the power to create un-limited personalized memos.

My variables

Names that will replace the variables

The main document

The data document

The key here is to create a document with a **variable** in it. That is, the name of the person I'm sending this memo to will vary every time I print. So, I'll tell my word processor that, instead of printing this word, I'll be inserting another word from my data document.

Be aware that different programs will create mail merges in slightly different ways. In general, however, you'll need a data document containing the information that will replace the variable and a main document, usually a memo, a letter, or a form.

Since my word processor understands this idea, it's a pretty simple task. Once I have the variable name in place, I just tell it what data document contains the names it's supposed to insert. Since there are two variables (Firstname and Lastname), the word processor takes the matching data (Rich and Smith) out of the data document and prints it in the new memo.

How many memos would I have typed or photocopied by now? Now consider how easy it would be to send a personalized letter to every member of your alumni association!

A variable can be anything—not just a name or address. And, I can have more than one variable in the main document. What about a variable for spouse's name, type of pet, or date they last donated to your organization? If you're clever, you can easily create a form letter that *sounds* truly personal!

Which word processor is right for me?

There are three big issues you need to concern yourself with here: compatibility, features, and price. Let's look at a few of the offerings out there and see how they stack up.

Microsoft Word ($300)

Microsoft Word is the industry standard for the business Mac and most home users, too. If you own a word processor, you probably own Microsoft Word. Does this mean it's the best? Well, it's highly compatible simply because most other Mac users have it. It's also full of great features, like mail merge, voice annotation, graphics, embedding, and more.

It's also very expensive, and Version 6.0 is annoyingly slow on older-technology Macs. But, if you can afford it, or if you desperately need it to share your documents with others, go ahead and get Word—especially if you own a Power Macintosh.

WordPerfect ($100)

WordPerfect, the company, is well known for its word processing prowess, and it really makes a good product for the Macintosh. Why isn't it more successful? Probably because there aren't many other WordPerfect-created programs for the Macintosh. Generally, people and companies are interested in buying all their big applications like word processing, spreadsheets, and databases from one company so that they'll all work together.

WordPerfect's word processor may be the best available for the Mac. You can do almost anything with it. It's feature rich, requires a little less RAM to run than Microsoft Word, and is Power Macintosh accelerated. It's highly customizable, including features like button bars, ruler bars, tables, and an equation editor. It's a great value with lots of features, and a good choice if you need to share documents with WordPerfect for Windows or WordPerfect for DOS.

WriteNow ($45)

Here's an interesting entry. WriteNow is from WordStar, WordPerfect's biggest competitor in the DOS market about half a decade ago. It's designed to be sleek, can be optimized for PowerBooks, and includes some high-end features you might not expect in an application under $50.

WriteNow creates and edits tables, imports and manipulates some graphics, and includes a 135,000-word spell checker. And, it only requires about 600 KB of RAM! The downside? It's not yet Power Macintosh accelerated and it does leave out some of the features and Windows/DOS compatibility you'd find in Word or WordPerfect. Can you live without that stuff? Maybe—especially in your home office or on your PowerBook.

The Macintosh as a printing press

If word processing is the electronic equivalent of a manual typewriter (with some improvements), **desktop publishing** is roughly analogous to typesetting and paste-up. A desktop publishing application lets you take text from your word processor and arrange it on the page in almost any way you please, almost as if you were cutting the text into strips and pasting it down on a board.

Do I need a desktop publishing application?

You may be able to live without one. Many desktop publishing programs for the Macintosh are targeted for professional designers and agencies, and they really can take a long time to learn to use correctly. There is some middle ground, though. Some "home" publishing software is aimed at the casual

A question of compatibility

Here's one of the biggest complaints you'll hear about business applications: *It's not compatible!* It doesn't matter if it has the neatest gizmo features in the whole world—it's gotta work with your other documents and applications. Eventually you'll need to be able to move files around in the office, take them home, or take them with you on business trips.

What do I mean by **compatible**? Two things, really. First, can you work with files you bring home from work or get from someone else? Make sure your program can work with other file formats. Second, is it compatible with your other applications? Some applications work well

together, some don't. Make sure you're using programs that like to talk to one another.

Compatible doesn't necessarily mean the same application. If you have WordPerfect at work, you don't have to have WordPerfect at home—just make sure your home software can translate WordPerfect documents.

But, applications from the same company do tend to work better together. If you want a spreadsheet that works well with Microsoft Word, Microsoft Excel is an excellent choice. This isn't a rule...but it's a pretty decent pointer.

newsletter creator or someone who would like a little more freedom to create greeting cards, stationery, and so on.

Realize that recent word processors can do a lot of this. It is possible to create a three-column newsletter with tables and graphics completely within Word, WordPerfect, or WriteNow. Desktop publishing, however, gives you many more tools to work with the details. If you've already got a works application, like ClarisWorks, it might be the best place to do your desktop publishing. In fact, works applications sometimes do a better job of desktop publishing than the expensive word processors!

What can a desktop publishing application do?

Let's see. I'm going to take the memo I created with my word processor and turn it into a company newsletter (see fig. 15.9). That shouldn't be too tough, right?

The first thing I do is import the memo from its word processing document. I do that by "placing" the text on my desktop publishing page. Next, I go in and edit this thing a little bit. I need to take out some of the text that suggests this is a memo. What else? Add a masthead, a company logo, and a nice little graphic to spruce things up. Oh, and I'll put the text in columns and "wrap" it nicely around the graphic.

You can see that I've made good use of the tools floating in the upper-left corner of figure 15.9. That's where I decide if I'm working with text, graphics, boxes, lines, or whatever. Is this different from word processing? It depends on the user and the word processor. We could probably manage all this in a high-end word processor, but not much more—and it'd take a whole lot longer.

Fig. 15.9
Desktop publishing is a bit like the real thing—cutting and pasting text to fit on a paste-up board.

The different tools for placing and drawing

Used the Text tool to create a new masthead

Placed a logo I created in my graphics program

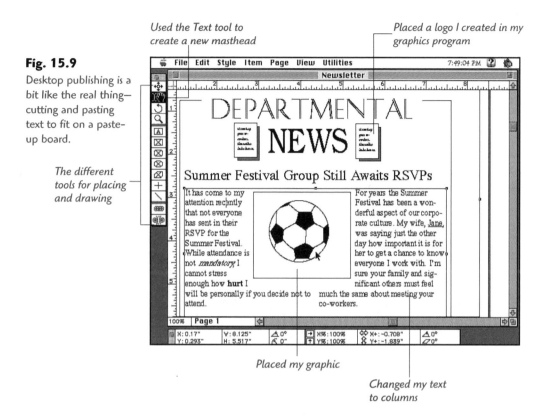

Placed my graphic

Changed my text to columns

Which desktop publishing application should I buy?

Buying a desktop publishing application is a little different from buying a word processor. Everybody can make good use of a high-end word processor after some time—some people will never need the power of high-end desktop publishing. If you're a graphic artist, designer, advertising professional, or some other such animal, however, you'll look at QuarkXpress ($600), PageMaker ($600), FrameMaker ($800), or other similar products.

For the home and home/office user, there are a few interesting alternatives. If you're serious about your sales newsletter, take a look at Aldus Home Publisher ($50), a scaled-down offering from the makers of PageMaker. Also available are a number of "Print Shop" style programs (like Print Shop Deluxe, $50) designed to help you easily create smaller projects, like greeting cards, posters, and signs. This may be all you need—and all you want to mess with.

The Mac as an easel

Where's the power in creating a printed page with your Macintosh without graphics? That's been the point for the last decade or more. The Macintosh has given the average computer owner unprecedented tools for the creation of effective graphics for use in business, education, or just for fun.

These tools are found in the paint and drawing applications available for the Macintosh. There are a great deal of them, if for no other reason than the Mac is the premiere computer tool for artists. Lucky for me you don't have to be an artist to create some great stuff in the bulk of these programs.

What's the real difference between drawing and painting?

In general, drawing programs just give you different tools than paint programs. We talked about that in chapter 14. In computer terms, however, drawing and painting are altogether different tasks.

In a drawing application, you use its tools to create **vector** graphics. What does that mean? When you draw a line in a drawing program, the computer remembers a mathematical equation describing that line, not the line itself. That's why you end up using mostly geometrical shapes (circles, squares, lines) in drawing programs.

Paint programs take a different approach. When you draw a line in a paint program, you're dealing with **bitmap** graphics. The computer

divides the screen into thousands of little dots. When you change the color of a dot it remembers that dot's position and its color. So, it doesn't care what shape things are in. It just changes each dot as you "paint" it.

Why is this significant? Two reasons. In a drawing program, you can pick up geometrical shapes and rearrange them while you work. In a paint program, once it's changed, it's changed (for the most part). All you can do is paint over it.

Secondly, bitmap graphics files are much larger than vector graphics. It takes a lot of space on your hard drive to store all those little dots. Mathematical equations, on the other hand, are a bit more efficient.

What can I do with these programs?

Paint and draw applications are designed to help you quickly and easily create graphic elements, generally so that you can use them for presentations, newsletters, or letterhead. I'll assume you're not creating "art for art's sake" (although I'm sure Art would be pleased), but there are some great programs for doing that, too.

Drawing with your Mac

Chances are you'll end up drawing more than painting if you use your graphics program for business, so let's create a quick drawing. I'm going to give my new company, ExtraInfo, a new logo that I can drop into my word processor as letterhead.

Remember when you're drawing that you're generally using geometric shapes. Each of these shapes is an independent "object," which means I can pick it up and drag it around on the screen if I want to. I start my logo by creating a box object as in figure 15.10.

Fig. 15.10

Using the Square tool, I press the mouse button to "anchor" one corner of the box, then I drag out to where I want its opposite corner. Let go of the button and there's my box.

My drawing tools

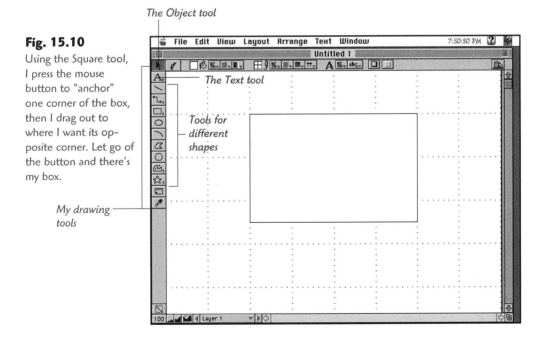

The Object tool

The Text tool

Tools for different shapes

The Drawing tools

Most drawing programs feature a few common tools, like an Object tool for moving things around, a Text tool for adding text, and Shape tools for creating different geometric shapes. To change tools, just click once on the picture of the tool you want to use. Then head out to your "page" and start drawing.

After creating my box, I use the Fill tool to fill it in with color. I've chosen a gradient pattern for my fill color, which gives its background a blended look, like it's moving from one color to another in a rainbow (see fig. 15.11).

 (Tip)

> Most drawing programs let you use the Object tool (usually shaped like a mouse pointer) to **resize** objects on the screen. If you've drawn a square that you now want a little smaller, use the Object tool to click once and select the square. Then, just click on one of its corners and drag to resize it.

Move it to the front   *A gradient background*

Fig. 15.11
After I get my text positioned correctly, I just add a few circles at the top and I'm done!

Then select the black text

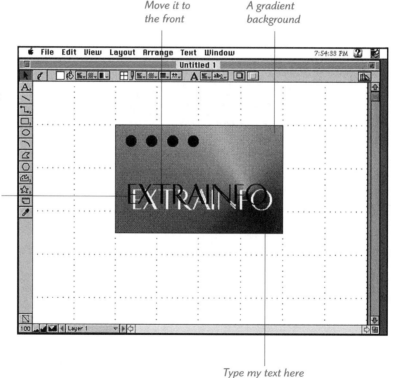

Type my text here and color it white

Then I add the text. I just click on the Text tool and head out to my page and click. I pick my font, style, and size from the Font menu on the menu bar, and then type my company's name. To create a shadow effect, I use the Text tool to type the name again, only this time in white. Now I select the original text and use the **Arrange** menu and select **Move To Front**. Now my black text is on top.

Saving your graphics

When I've completed my logo, I have two choices for saving. I could save a document in my drawing program just like any other document and then work on it later. The other option is that I could export the logo in a "standard" graphics format for other programs to use.

The most common of these is the PICT format on the Macintosh. Nearly any Macintosh program can read a PICT file, and if it's my intention to use this logo in a newsletter or letterhead, I'll need it in a common file format so that I can use it with my word processor or desktop publishing application.

Nearly all the figures in this book were saved as PICT files and then placed in a desktop publishing program to give it a finished look. So, PICT is pretty powerful!

What graphics application should I get?

Like desktop publishing, there are tons of graphics applications available for the Macintosh. My suggestion is to get one designed for the type of user you are. Power users will need something like Aldus Freehand ($500) or Adobe Illustrator ($500) for high-end needs. For business graphics like the logo I created, a less expensive program like ClarisDraw ($200), Expert Draw ($40), or something similar will probably serve the purpose nicely.

For painting, look into programs like Adobe SuperPaint ($50) or Dabbler ($100) by Fractal Design. These and other similar programs are great for the home or home/office user interested in generating great graphics for their printed pages.

16

Number Crunching and Managing Lists

In this chapter:

- What can I do with a spreadsheet?

- I don't have time to set up spreadsheets; I just want to pay bills

- Can I do the books for my business on my Mac? Even payroll?

- How can I keep track of appointments, phone numbers, and to-do lists?

With the electronic equivalent of Scrooge's ledger books, your Mac can do incredible things with numbers.

A **spreadsheet** is essentially a computerized version of the same ledger books that Scrooge used, but with amazing power and flexibility in the ways it can report information. Set up your bank account in a spreadsheet, for instance, and display that data as a chart or graph that shows you relative spending levels. Generate a monthly budget summary and instantly compare the categories where you overspent.

The most powerful feature of a spreadsheet, however, is its capability to generate **what-if scenarios**. Say, for instance, you set up a family budget. If you build your spreadsheet correctly, you can change one figure, such as your income, and see how that will affect your finances (see fig. 16.1). Then you can figure how much you could lower your credit card debt or how buying a new car would change things.

Fig. 16.1
A spreadsheet lets me
link, for instance, my
Total Expenses and my
Income together so
that changing my in-
come level affects my
Savings totals at the
bottom.

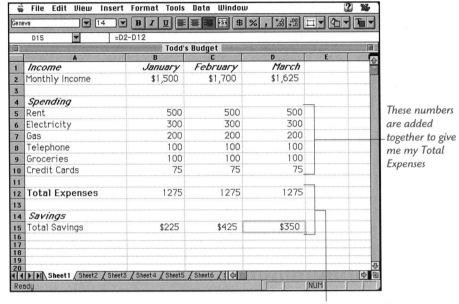

These numbers
are added
together to give
me my Total
Expenses

Total Expenses subtracted from Monthly Income gives me Total Savings

Crunch numbers with a spreadsheet

You can see in figure 16.1 that a spreadsheet is a pretty plain-looking tool. Its
ledger-book roots are pretty clear—it's basically just rows and columns of
numbers. But beyond that, a spreadsheet can be pretty powerful. You can put
different types of numbers in each cell of a spreadsheet. In a ledger book, you
can enter either a word or a number. In a spreadsheet, you can use words,
numbers, references to other cells, and even formulas for mathematical
calculations.

 Plain English, please!

A **cell** is just one of the boxes on a spreadsheet where you enter your numbers
or formulas. Each cell has an address, which is simply the column letter and row
number. Cell E3 stands for the cell in the E column in the third row. 🙷

Getting the numbers in

The first thing you have to do to make a spreadsheet useful at all is enter
something into it. You generally do this by using your mouse cursor to select

a particular cell and typing away. You'll probably start by entering some text for headings and description (see fig. 16.2). Sometimes this can be the most important part—it's how you'll organize your data.

(Tip)

> When you enter text, each cell is almost like a tiny word processing page—you can center or left- or right-justify text and change its font and size.

Fig. 16.2
I start by setting up meaningful names for my columns and rows. Now I'm ready to enter some data for calculating.

...And here in the cell once I'm done

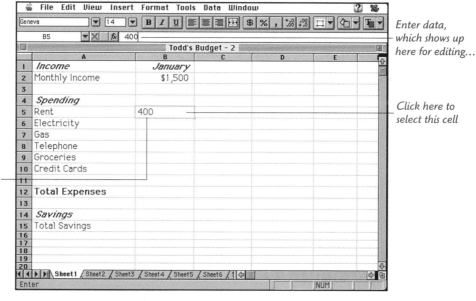

Enter data, which shows up here for editing...

Click here to select this cell

Moving around in spreadsheets

Getting your cursor where you want it in spreadsheets can take a little getting used to, especially for folks who do a lot of word processing.

Hitting Return in most spreadsheets moves you *down* to the next row—but this isn't always the best way to enter your data. For movement, it may be best to concentrate on the cursor keys. Move up, down, left, or right from one cell to

another. Generally, you don't ever even need to hit Return. Just hit a cursor key to go on to the next cell.

Often, pressing **Tab** will move you to the next cell to the right, and **Shift+Tab** will move you back to the left. Also, experiment with the **Home** key. In Microsoft Excel, Home moves you to the first cell of a row. If you're entering your data from left to right, hitting Home and the down arrow will get you to the beginning of the next line.

⊛{*Note*}——— Notice in figure 16.2 that you can use different parts of the spreadsheet for different elements. At the top of my spreadsheet I've put an entry for my income, then I've created a table for my monthly budget expenses.

Next, I'll enter some numbers. What I'm concerned about here is budgeting, so I'll create two columns for each month, one for my budget numbers and one for my actual spending. I enter numbers in exactly the same way I entered text, by selecting the cell I want to use for data and then typing the number.

Notice in figure 16.3 how some of my numbers have dollar amounts and some don't? The spreadsheet doesn't really care if these are dollars or widgets, so it lets me format them any way I please. So, I've formatted the number cell next to my income for dollar amounts, but the rest I've left blank. (Not for any good reason—I just don't like having the page full of dollar signs.)

⊛{*Note*}——— There are some number formats, like date and time, that are important to have correctly formatted. Your spreadsheet will interpret 3/16 as a fraction (0.1825), not March 16th, if you don't correctly format the cell.

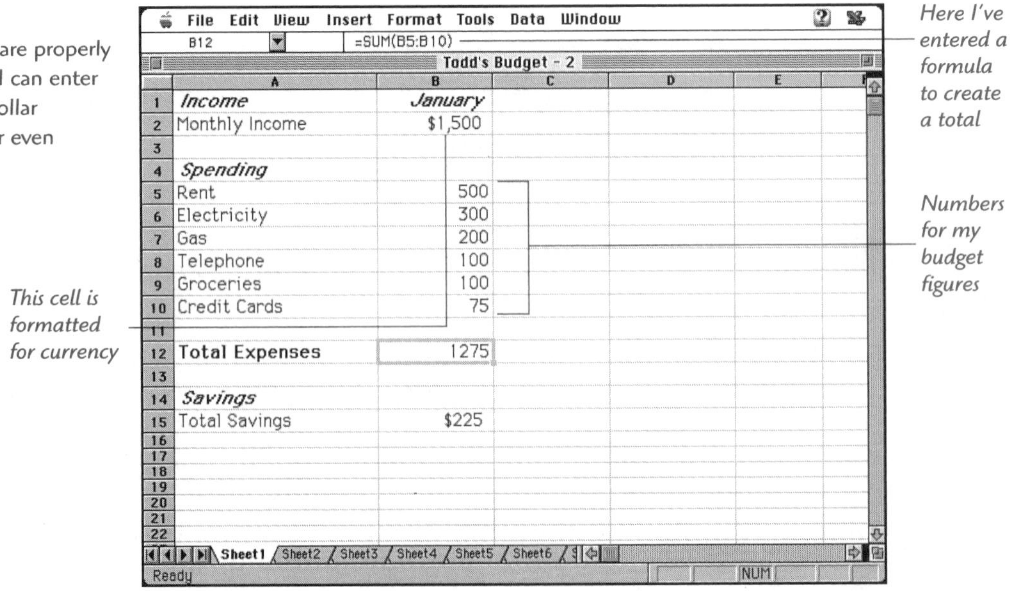

Fig. 16.3
When cells are properly formatted, I can enter numbers, dollar amounts, or even formulas.

This cell is formatted for currency

Here I've entered a formula to create a total

Numbers for my budget figures

	A	B	C	D	E	
1	*Income*	*January*				
2	Monthly Income	$1,500				
3						
4	*Spending*					
5	Rent	500				
6	Electricity	300				
7	Gas	200				
8	Telephone	100				
9	Groceries	100				
10	Credit Cards	75				
11						
12	Total Expenses	1275				
13						
14	*Savings*					
15	Total Savings	$225				

Getting answers

With my numbers entered, I can start creating some formulas for adding and subtracting things (refer to fig. 16.3). Formulas are generally created by choosing a function (like Sum) and telling the spreadsheet what cells you want to use for that formula. For example, "SUM(B7:B17)" will come back with the sum of the numbers in B7, B17, and all cells between the two in the B column.

{Note}

In almost every spreadsheet application there's a particular symbol that lets the program know that what you're entering is a formula. In Microsoft Excel, for instance, it's the equal sign (=), so that a formula looks like "=SUM(B7..B17)".

I could also use a fixed number in a formula, such as "SUM(B7,4)", which would add the value of cell B7 to the number 4. For the most part, formulas are only limited by the spreadsheet application's capabilities. Among its hundreds of formulas, Microsoft Excel lets me enter formulas for SUM, AVERAGE, and even STDEV (standard deviation of a sample). Clearly, there's a good deal you can do with a spreadsheet.

(Tip)

You don't always have to enter a formula for math, as long as you remember some algebra. In Excel, "=E2+E4" is a perfectly legitimate formula.

Getting the big picture

Now that I've got everything entered, I want to create a graph to visually show how well I've done this month. I start by selecting all the data I want to graph. With the mouse, I click and hold on one cell and then drag the mouse over all the other cells that concern me (see fig. 16.4).

{Note}

It's okay to select text for graphing—it'll be used as the axis labels for your chart.

Then I simply select the Charting tool. In Excel, I pull down the Insert menu and select Chart, and then select On this Sheet. Next, I choose the style of chart I want, how I want text arranged, and so on. Once I've made all my choices, I end up with something that looks like figure 16.4. Now can I see exactly where I'm overspending!

Fig. 16.4

After a few quick mouse clicks, I've got my entire financial life laid out in a nice little bar graph.

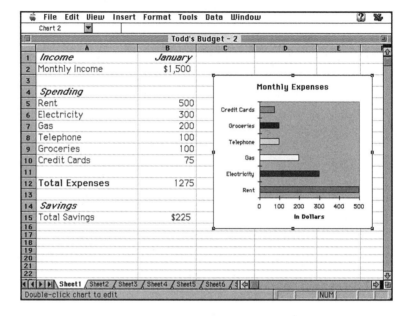

Which spreadsheet program should I use?

Here's what I'll do for you. I'll give you a list of every Macintosh spreadsheet program you're likely to find in your local computer store. Ready? *Microsoft Excel* ($300). That wasn't tough, was it?

If you're not interested in shelling out the big bucks for Excel, there are some alternatives. Although Lotus 1-2-3 is no longer supported on the Mac, you may be able to find a cheap copy. If you own a "works" application, as discussed in chapter 17, "Getting It All with Works Applications," the included spreadsheet module is perfect for home budgeting and creating simple charts. If your main interest is in graphing, there are a number of graphics applications available for creating business graphics, performing statistical analysis, or generating high-end scientific visuals.

Manage your money

While spreadsheets may be designed with accountants in mind, there are also a number of applications on the market today designed for managing your home or business finances without an accountant (sorry, Dad). Some of these are full-blown accounting packages for business. Others, like Quicken ($45), are designed for managing your personal finances on a day-to-day basis (see fig. 16.5).

Just click on a button to print checks, reconcile your accounts, or get Help

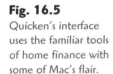

Fig. 16.5
Quicken's interface uses the familiar tools of home finance with some of Mac's flair.

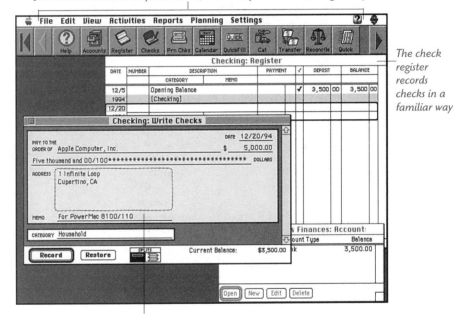

The check register records checks in a familiar way

Write actual checks and then print them

I need to write checks and balance the budget

Home finance programs actually do a lot of the things you can accomplish with a spreadsheet—they just make it much easier. In fact, for any type of bookkeeping, I'd definitely recommend you get financial software that meets your needs. Using a spreadsheet for budgeting and playing "what-if" is definitely a worthwhile pursuit. Financial management software provides conveniences like a register for managing your accounts, a check-writing interface for entering and printing checks, and tables for tracking your monthly budget (see fig. 16.6).

These programs also often include functions for estimating taxes, categorizing expenses, graphing expenses, and paying recurring bills. Most also feature a number of "calculators" for figuring loan payments, retirement savings, college expenses, and the like.

Fig. 16.6
You might be able to do all this in a spreadsheet, but personal finance software is cheap compared to the time and pain you'll save when tracking accounts and planning for the future.

You can create a budget in Quicken

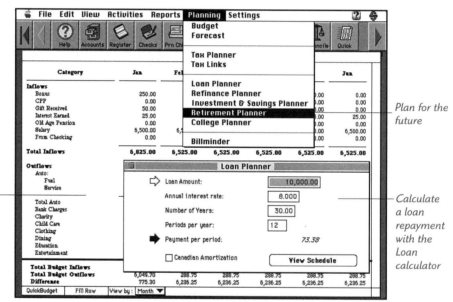

Plan for the future

Calculate a loan repayment with the Loan calculator

What's the best financial software?

Quicken is easily the industry standard for personal finance, and it is the application that is most easily linked up with other programs—including tax preparation packages. Another good purchase is Meca's Managing Your Money ($35), especially if you're heavy on savings and investment planning. It also features financial advice from Andrew Tobias, which may be of value to followers of this financial guru.

But I have customers and employees

For high-end accounting, a number of packages offer features like general ledger, accounts payable and receivable, invoicing, payroll, and management reports. In the $100 and up range are programs like M.Y.O.B. Accounting (Mind Your Own Business—$100) and Peachtree Accounting ($125).

Manage information with a database

If a spreadsheet is like a ledger book but more flexible, the same analogy holds true for a database program and a card file. For instance, in the public library, one finds card files dedicated to books. In one section you could search for cards organized by author, in another by title, and in a third by subject. A computer database, however, can easily hold all these records— and allow you to search by more specific criteria. By, say, author's name and subject. Or by publisher or date of publication—anything.

Design your records

With nearly any database program, you start by creating a form for your records. This is where you decide what your electronic "card" will look like for each entry. You do this by determining what fields you'll use for the entry screen, and which of those fields you'll use for indexing your data (see fig. 16.7).

 Plain English, please!

A database **field** is just space in each database record for data. If each database record was a library card, one field would store the book's title, another would store the date of publication, and so on. Each field holds a particular type of data (text, numbers, dates), which can then be sorted into an **index** for searching and reporting on your data.

Fig. 16.7
I start by creating various fields for data entry. Later, I'll use these fields to search for certain records.

Create a new field for my "card"

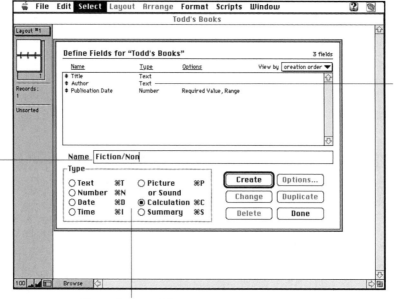

Add it to the list of fields

Choose the type of data

Enter your information

With my fields created, I'm ready for data entry. Here's the part of the process where you generally want to hire someone else—it's dull. In fact, it may be this daunting task alone that's keeping some local libraries from switching their card system over to computers!

> When you create a database, think through your fields carefully, considering what you'd like to use as an index. If you create a database with one name field, for example, you'll have a lot of trouble indexing by last name later!

Get reports

Once you've entered your records, you can generate reports. This is where the power of database software usually shines. A database program provides you the flexibility to sort your data by any of the fields and then create reports that can easily tell you what you want to know (see fig. 16.8).

Fig. 16.8
Here's a report of all my paperback books. Notice that I've been able to change fonts and organization so that things are easy to read and more understandable.

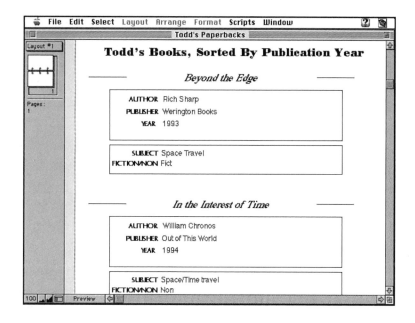

Which database should I buy?

Like spreadsheet programs, there are relatively few dedicated database programs for the Macintosh. Two of the more popular programs for home and small business are Claris FileMaker Pro ($275) and ACI's 4D First ($300). Programs like Microsoft's FoxPro ($470) and ACI's Fourth Dimension ($740) offer "big-business" features and more breathing room for programmers and serious computer types.

If your database needs are light, you might find everything you need in a works application. ClarisWorks, for instance, offers a database program that is basically a scaled-down version of FileMaker Pro that also happens to work well with the included word processor for tasks like mail merge and generating reports.

Stay on track with PIMs

Over the last few years, **Personal Information Management** (**PIM**) software has become very popular. These are basically the "virtual secretaries" of the computer world—very specialized database programs designed to manage your appointment schedule, to-do lists, and phone/address lists.

For most of these programs, entering data is similar to entering data for a database program (see fig. 16.9). You have fields for names, addresses, phone numbers, and fax numbers. The difference is that most of these are pre-defined, and are designed to work with other fields in the program.

Fig. 16.9
A PIM is a great way to get the power of a database for tasks like managing to-do lists and business contacts.

Enter data here

Here's a field name

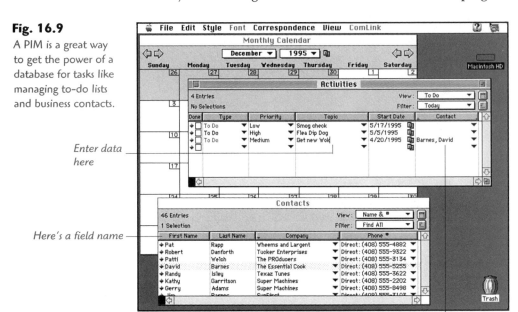

It links to other parts of the program

What PIM should I buy?

There are a large number of PIMs available, and they vary widely in price. Realize, however, that not all PIMs are alike. My suggestion is to take into account *what* exactly you want to organize. Are you more worried about your appointment calendar or organizing sales phone calls? Are you trying to keep up with a large client base or just worried about project management within your department?

Under the broad umbrella of Personal Information Management are some sub-categories. **Contact managers** are designed for salespeople and others who deal with a lot of people. These programs, like Now Contact ($50), Fit's Full Contact ($50), and Aldus TouchBase Pro ($50), tend to worry more about your calls and letters than your appointments or grocery lists.

Also available are what I call **organizer** programs that are a lot like the paper-based organizers (Franklin, DayRunner, or whatever) that many professionals use. These programs have less of a sales orientation and more of an appointment schedule orientation. These programs include Aldus DateBook Pro ($50), Now Up-to-Date ($65), and Attain's In Control ($85).

Getting It All with Works Applications

In this chapter:

- What can I do with a works application?
- I want to write letters and include graphics and tables
- I need to set up mailing lists and send out flyers
- Which works application is right for me?

Works applications are the Swiss army knives of Mac applications. They're light, well-built tools that do a little bit of everything!

Welcome to works applications—the Swiss army knives of Macintosh software. Works applications usually include a word processor and spreadsheet, database, drawing, painting, and communications applications all in one box. It might not be the sharpest 6" hunting word processor you can buy, and the spreadsheet may not fell a redwood, but for many people, their works application is all they ever need.

Can you really have it all?

Frankly, those "business" applications, like WordPerfect and Microsoft Excel, are huge. They have amazing functions for working together in groups, they are good for high-end presentations, and they do things like mail merges and database queries very well. Does your backroom travel agency or freelance writing business need this? What about your kid's homework assignments and your letters to the editor?

Fig. 17.1

Microsoft Word's versus Microsoft Works. MS Works may be no frills, but it may get the job done more easily.

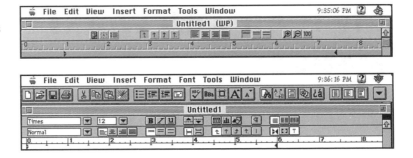

Your Swiss army knife doesn't offer you the biggest, meanest hunting-style blade for doing something like taking out a buffalo by hand. Same goes for works applications. They do away with some of the high-end stuff and instead offer smaller application modules that are designed to work well together. If you can do without some of the whiz-bang of the business applications, a works application is probably your best choice.

Is it a works application or a suite?

It's not unheard of for people to confuse works applications and suites. After all, both offer an "all-in-one-box" solution for your Macintosh. They do so, however, in completely different ways.

An **application suite**, like Microsoft Office, is ultimately just a collection of high-end productivity applications offered in the same box. Office includes the full versions of Microsoft Word, Excel, PowerPoint, and some other tidbits. In some ways, Office is just a convenient way to buy these popular business applications at a slight discount.

A **works application**, on the other hand, might offer similar types of abilities, but in a much more basic package. Microsoft Works, for instance, includes a word processing module, a spreadsheet module, a drawing module, and more. Individually, however, none of these modules approaches the features of their higher-end relatives Word, Excel, and PowerPoint.

The other difference? Price. Microsoft Office costs somewhere around $500. Microsoft Works—about $90.

Plain English, please!

For the most part, a works application is really *one* application, even though it offers you different tools, like word processing, drawing, database, etc. Within the works application then, each of these different sets of tools is a **module**, or a sort of mini-application. If you're working in the word processing module and decide to create a pie chart, you'd switch to the spreadsheet module.

Make sure the works package you choose offers strength in the areas you need it most, whether that's word processing, spreadsheet analysis, or graphics. The other functions will be icing on the cake.

What can I do with a works application?

Actually, a better question might be, "what *can't* a works application do?" First, you get most of the really important functions of the big applications for word processing, spreadsheets, and so on. Second, you get a level of integration that's difficult for those business applications to match. Pick up a graphic from your paint module and drop it in your word processing module and it will work every time.

Start with word processing

Let's take, for example, ClarisWorks. In most things you'll do with ClarisWorks, you'll start with the word processor (see fig. 17.2). That's not a golden rule, just an observation. The power of ClarisWorks and many other integrated packages is that you can usually start wherever you want to. If you need to use another module, just start a new document.

The spreadsheet tool

Fig. 17.2

Starting in the word processor, you can build a document using tools from all the different modules.

Draw and paint tools ——

Word processing tools

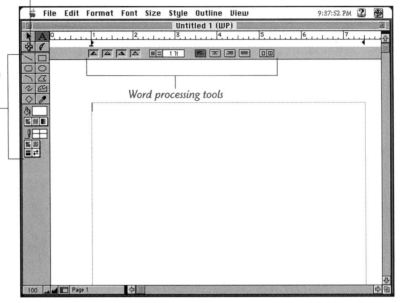

ClarisWorks' word processor has most of the standard features, like the capability to change your text, center text, spell check, and change margins. Plus, it gives you the added capability of switching back and forth between some of the different "tools" ClarisWorks offers for getting work done. This is the magic of ClarisWorks. In some cases, you don't even have to change modules to use new tools!

If your tools aren't showing, head up to View on the menu bar and choose Show Tools. Now things should look more like figure 17.3.

Put graphics in a document

For this example, I'm going to create an invoice for a hypothetical photo studio. I start out by loading the draw module and drawing a graphic for my logo. ClarisWorks' draw module works much like the draw programs we talked about in chapter 15. After I finish my logo, I choose Edit, Copy in the drawing module to place the logo on the Clipboard. Then, in the word processor, I click in the document to select a place for the logo and choose Edit, Paste (see fig. 17.3). Quick and easy!

Fig. 17.3
Now I can put the graphic anywhere I want on the page by dragging with the mouse pointer.

Make sure I'm using the Object tool

Then I paste the graphic

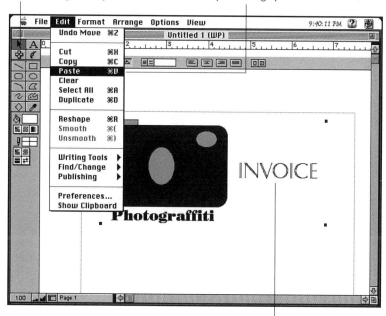

And I can move it when it's selected

?Q&A

Why can't I move my graphic object around on the screen?

You need to have the Object tool selected when you paste your graphic. Otherwise, ClarisWorks assumes you're pasting the graphic "inline" with the text, almost as if the graphic were just more words. Since the graphic will now move when you edit the text, ClarisWorks won't let you drag the graphic to another part of the page.

Add tables with the Spreadsheet tool

Next, I'm going to create a spreadsheet table (in ClarisWorks lingo, this is an "object") that can automatically generate a subtotal, tax, and grand total for my billing. How do I do that?

1 Begin by clicking once on the Spreadsheet tool.

2 Next, click in the document to select the top left corner of the spreadsheet table, hold down the mouse button, and drag diagonally to create the table.

3 Now, still using the Spreadsheet tool, enter numbers and calculations for the tax and total (see fig. 17.4).

I'm still using the Spreadsheet tool

Fig. 17.4

Now all I have to do is change to the Spreadsheet tool, change a few numbers, and instantly I've got a new, totaled invoice.

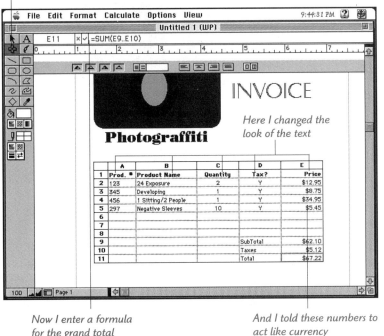

Here I changed the look of the text

Now I enter a formula for the grand total

And I told these numbers to act like currency

Create a flyer using mail merge

Now suppose I need an easy way to send out a sale flyer to all my customers. I don't want to type each one, I want to generate a bunch from my database. I've already put together a quick sales flyer in the word processor. Now I'll create a simple customer database in ClarisWorks' database module.

1 Pull down the File menu in the word processor and select the New... command. I selected a Database file.

2 When asked to define the fields, I tell the computer what type of data to store, like text, numbers, or a date, for example (see fig. 17.5).

3 Then I enter data in the database form for all my customers.

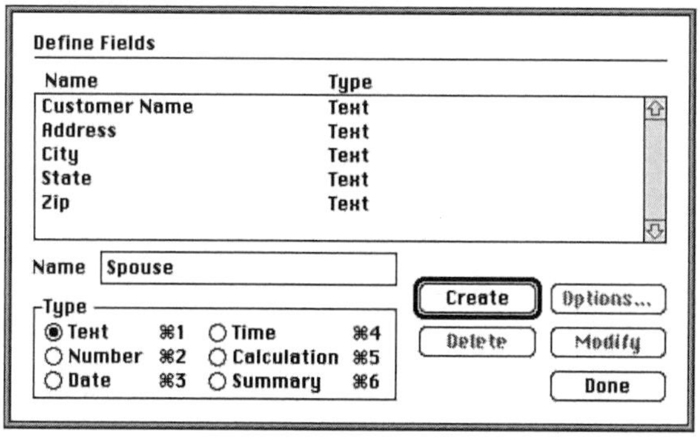

Fig. 17.5

Here I tell ClarisWorks what kind of data I want to store in the database. I give these meaningful names, because they'll be used later in the word processing document for the mail merge.

```
┌──────────────────────────────────────────────────────┐
│  Define Fields                                         │
│  ──────────────────────────────────────────────────── │
│   Name                    Type                    ▲    │
│   Customer Name           Text                         │
│   Address                 Text                         │
│   City                    Text                         │
│   State                   Text                         │
│   Zip                     Text                    ▼    │
│                                                        │
│   Name  [ Spouse                    ]                  │
│   ┌Type─────────────────────┐  ┌─────────┐ ┌────────┐ │
│   │ ⦿ Text      ⌘1  ○ Time      ⌘4 │ Create │ │Options…│ │
│   │ ○ Number    ⌘2  ○ Calculation ⌘5 └────────┘        │
│   │ ○ Date      ⌘3  ○ Summary    ⌘6 │ Delete │ │ Modify │ │
│   └─────────────────────────┘               ┌────────┐ │
│                                              │  Done  │ │
│                                              └────────┘ │
└──────────────────────────────────────────────────────┘
```

4 When I'm done entering the customer data, I head back to the word processing document. Using the Text tool, I entered some headings for the address section of my flyer.

5 Now I just have to create some mail merge variables in the word processing document. I head up to the word processor's File menu, and select the Mail Merge... command.

(Tip)

Notice that, in my database, I stored a spouse's name along with the customer's. With the power of a database, it's easy to store and reuse personal information that might get someone's attention. Now, I add it to my mail merge and it feels a little less like a form letter.

6 A dialog box appears that lets me drop variable names into the word processor direct from the database module. They're the same names we used in the database module (see fig. 17.6). Now, with our variable names in place, we can set the mail merge printing.

⊗<Caution>

Remember that a mail merge with a big database file can create a lot of printouts and waste a lot of paper! Make sure you have everything set up right before you start the merge. Then, check the first few pages. If things look bad, try clicking Cancel or hitting ⌘+.(period) to stop your printer.

Fig. 17.6

With my database filled in, I quickly put the variables in my flyer document and set it printing. When the printer finally quits, I'll have a stack of flyers, ready to mail!

Here are the matching variable names

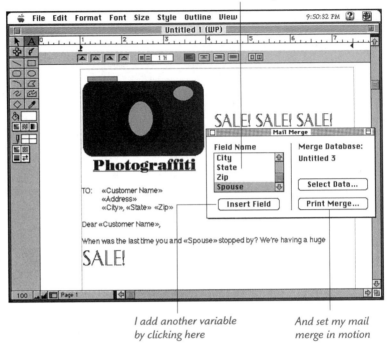

I add another variable by clicking here

And set my mail merge in motion

Connect to other computers

In the last example, I used the word processing, spreadsheet, database, draw, and paint modules, but there's one module I haven't mentioned yet—the communications module. The communications module lets you use a modem to call over phone lines and access other computers. Commercial services like CompuServe (see fig. 17.7) and Delphi will let you use a program like ClarisWorks' communications to call up and exchange information. You can send and receive electronic mail, transfer shareware files, or even check stock quotes (see more on communications software in chapter 25, "The Online Essentials").

Fig. 17.7
The ClarisWorks communications module is a handy little program for calling out with your modem. Here I've used it to connect to a local online system.

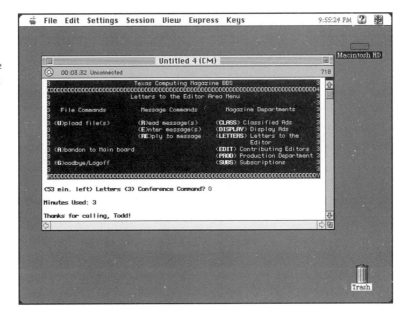

Which works application should I buy?

In general, any works application you get will allow you to easily and effectively get some great work done on your Mac. When you make your decision, determine what module is most important to you. We'll discuss the strengths of the three leaders, ClarisWorks, Microsoft Works, and WordPerfect Works.

ClarisWorks ($125)

There are two reasons that I've harped a good deal on ClarisWorks in this chapter. First, it's an innovative application that has changed the way a lot of people work with computers. Its integrated nature gives it amazing flexibility for the home or even the business user.

Second, it comes with nearly every Performa, and is available at huge discounts to many other Macintosh users. If you've already got ClarisWorks, I don't see any reason not to stick with it. It may just be the best all-around works application, and its ability to create integrated documents is very impressive.

WordPerfect Works ($75)

WordPerfect concentrates on its strength—word processing. The word processing module in WordPerfect is one of the most powerful you can find in works applications. It has advanced features that are usually reserved for the more expensive word processors that make it very capable of layout design. Things like newsletters and brochures are a snap.

The other modules in WordPerfect Works leave a little more to be desired. Its database and graphics modules are great for small tasks, but the more complex the task, the more trouble you'll have. And frankly, the spreadsheet module leaves a lot to be desired. Should that stop you? Not if you want the best word processing this side of $100!

Microsoft Works ($90)

Microsoft Works offers a little bit of everything, with many of the same strengths as ClarisWorks. It has good functionality all around, with a nice word processor and a decent spreadsheet. It does offer one of the best communications modules in the line up, and has some great features for beginning users.

The real strength in Microsoft Works is its compatibility with Microsoft Word and Microsoft Excel. Microsoft Works deals well with files created in these programs, and features the ability to include objects (like charts and tables) created in other Microsoft applications that support object linking and embedding. (The current Microsoft Works—version 4.0—cannot create OLE objects, however.) This offering alone may make it attractive to folks who use other Microsoft applications in the office, but don't want to spend the big money for their Mac at home.

Plain English, please!

Object Linking and Embedding (**OLE**) is a technology that Microsoft uses to share objects, like a chart or logo, with other programs. You can, for instance, pick up a pie chart created in Excel and drop it into Microsoft Works' word processor module. If you want to edit that chart, just double-click on it and Microsoft Excel will load automatically.

The Wizards of Microsoft!

Many Microsoft products geared toward the home user, like Microsoft Works, include little features called **Wizards** that help beginning users perform advanced functions more easily.

Some folks find these Wizards a big help. Depending on what you're doing, a Wizard will step you through a pre-determined layout, insert text and graphics, and show you how to make changes.

Microsoft Works 4.0 features Wizards to help you create greeting cards, invitations, certificates, newsletters, and presentations. If you don't think you could do those on your own, maybe you should ask for the guidance of a Wizard!

Here's the MS Works Newsletter WorksWizard, walking us step-by-step through creating our document.

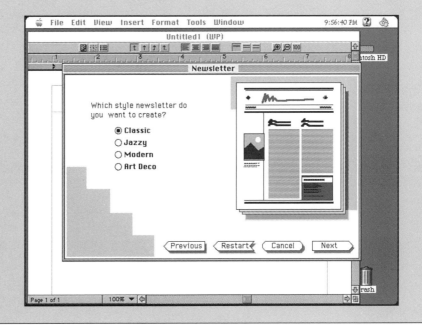

Part V

Getting Your Stuff in Print

18

Setting Up and Using Your Printer

Not only do you need a printer in the "paperless" society, but you should buy the best you can afford!

In this chapter:

- What kind of printer do I need?
- How do I connect the printer?
- What are printer drivers?
- Finally, you can print!
- Why not share a printer and save money?

E ver heard of the "paperless office"? It's this grand idea that a computer can replace paper in the workplace. But it hasn't happened yet. Most of us still need to buy a printer with our Macintoshes because there's a lot of stuff to print. The printed page is still the best way to share ideas, mull over topics, and get people to look at your work. Maybe paper will go by the wayside in the future, but right now, getting the right printer is important.

What kind of printer should I buy?

The best you can possibly afford. A printer can be the most luxurious item in your computer setup—or the biggest hassle. For the most part, you need to buy a printer that gives you the best speed and quality for your budget. There are actually some great deals out there, but you've got to know where to look.

Laser: The top-notch solution

I guess it'd be nice if everyone could have a laser printer on their desk. It's actually not completely outside of the possible, because laser printer prices have finally dipped under $1,000 and continue to point lower. Laser printers generally offer the best quality of printing at the fastest speed. Even the low-end printers spit out around four pages per minute and offer print quality of 300 dots-per-inch or better. The higher you go in price, the faster and more crisp your output.

Plain English, please!

A printer creates text and graphics by placing dots on a piece of paper. The **dots per inch (dpi)** rating of a printer tells you how crisp and tight a printed character will look—more dots per inch means the less "jagged" the image. For instance, 300 dpi is the standard laser-quality number, while 600 dpi is the first level where printed photos start to look pretty good. True 1200 dpi is close to camera-ready for professionally printed material, and magazines usually print their photos at thousands of dots per inch.

If you decide that a laser printer is something you can afford, make sure it has as much RAM memory as possible. A laser printer generally accepts an entire "image" of a page from your Mac before printing, so it needs enough RAM to handle big pages with lots of graphics and fonts. Most laser printers use PostScript as their "page description language," which is also very RAM hungry. Two megabytes is a *minimum* for a laser printer, 4 MB is closer to ideal.

> You also want to make sure your laser printer offers the capability to print on the types of paper you intend to use. Some printers offer only a limited capacity to print to, say, legal paper as opposed to letter-sized. Ask your salesperson about expansion options for your laser printer's paper feeder.

Inkjets: Fast and affordable

If price immediately takes you out of the laser market, there's nothing wrong with an inkjet printer. Inkjets often offer laser-quality dots-per-inch ratings, and they're getting faster all the time, with many able to offer up 3 pages per minute or faster.

What you do sacrifice is a certain amount of print quality. Inkjets offer the same dots-per-inch as low-end lasers, but that's theoretical. The fact is that the ink that most inkjets use can't be put on the page quite as precisely as a laser's toner. So, characters and graphics tend to look just a little fuzzier than they would with a laser printer (see fig. 18.1).

Fig. 18.1

On the top: inkjet output comes in a bit fuzzier. On the bottom: the crispness of laser.

It was a dark and stormy evening when Nancy slammed the car door shut and headed up the walkway.

It was a dark and stormy evening when Nancy slammed the car door shut and headed up the walkway.

Is it worth it? Could be. Inkjet printers are considerably less expensive than lasers, coming in well below $500. And inkjets can offer a few options that are very expensive on laser printers—like color printing. In some printers, you just swap out the cartridges in certain inkjet printers and you're printing color documents. In others, you just print!

 **{Note}**

While inkjet printers are generally cheaper than lasers, they also tend to have a higher cost per page. Inkjet cartridges usually cost between $20 and $30 dollars and can print 500–1,000 pages. Toner cartridges range from $50 to $150 dollars and average 3,000–5,000 pages or more.

Is there still room for dot matrix?

Dot matrix printers used to be the most common printers around. They print on a page by striking a ribbon with a certain number of hard pins, hence the name dot matrix. Given the output of today's inkjet and laser printers, though, I'd be hard pressed to recommend that you go out and buy a new dot matrix printer for your Mac (if you can find one). The only advantage a dot matrix printer has is the cost per page to keep it running. Ink ribbons for dot matrix printers are very cheap when compared to the ink cartridges for inkjets and the toner cartridges for lasers.

How do I hook up my printer?

We talked a little in chapter 2 about the basics of setting up a printer. All you really have to do is plug your printer cable into the printer and then into the printer port on the back of your Mac. Then, plug the printer's power cord into the wall. If you need to, you can also plug your printer into the modem port. The only really good reason to do this, though, is if you have another printer or a LocalTalk network connected to your printer port.

 **<Caution>**

I'm assuming your printer has a Macintosh serial connection that will allow it to connect directly to the printer port (check your documentation). If your printer has a LocalTalk connection, see the special instructions at the end of this chapter.

Why does my printer need a driver?

Once everything's hooked up, you'll probably need to turn on your Mac and run the installation program that came on a disk with your printer. If your disk doesn't have an Installer program, you may have to manually install the correct printer driver for your printer.

 Plain English, please!

Printer drivers are just small programs that tell your Mac special things about your particular printer. Every printer is slightly unique, with special features that other printers don't have. So the printer manufacturer writes a small program that tells the Mac how to "drive" its printer.

If you bought an Apple printer or ran the Installer program that came with your printer, chances are your driver is already installed. You can find out by opening the Apple menu and selecting Chooser. If your printer shows up in the left half of the Chooser, your driver is correctly installed. If not, you'll have to go look for it.

How do I install my printer's driver?

Printer drivers are kept in the Extensions folder inside the System Folder on your main hard drive. If your printer came with a disk that doesn't include an Installer, look for your printer driver on that disk. When you find it, drag and drop it on the System Folder or in the Extensions Folder. Now you'll have to Restart your Mac to get it to recognize the new printer driver.

Printer drivers are usually named something like the printer they're for, like "DW Series 500" for my DeskWriter 540. Also, in a list view, the file type is Chooser Extension.

If your driver is properly installed, it should now appear in the Chooser window. If you think of your Macintosh as a multi-line office telephone, the Chooser is where you pick what line you're going to use for this conversation. To select your printer for printing, just click its icon (see fig. 18.2). Next, tell Mac what port the printer is connected to by clicking on the printer port icon or the modem port icon. Then, it's time to set up your printer driver.

If you have a PostScript printer (or a printer that's other connected to your Mac via a network), you won't get a port choice. That's okay—it just means your Mac already knows that the printer's connected.

*Click here to select your
printer driver.*

*Then click the window to tell Mac
which port you're using.*

Fig. 18.2
Using the Chooser, tell
Mac what printer driver
to use and where the
printer is connected.

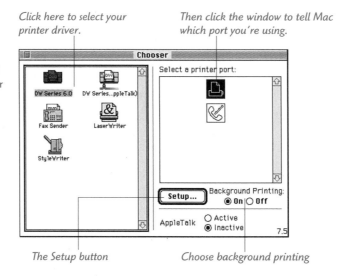

The Setup button

Choose background printing

Clicking on the Setup button gives you a dialog box that is very specific to
your printer (see mine in fig. 18.3). Here's where you may have to choose
some specific things about the way you want your printer set up. It's not fair,
I know, but my setup happens to be pretty easy. I just choose the name of the
printer I own.

Usually there's not a whole lot to set up, unless you're using a "generic"
printer driver that can be used with many different printers. If your setup box
lets you choose specific information about your printer, then do so. If it
doesn't, no problem.

Fig. 18.3
Here's my printer setup
dialog box. I hope
yours is this easy!

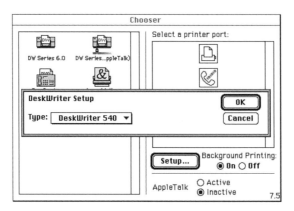

Now we can decide whether or not we want to print in the background. The idea here is this: Background printing allows us to continue working on other documents while the printer churns away. If that sounds like a good idea, click the On button under Background Printing in the Chooser. Now, when you tell your application to print, it will use the Print Manager to print in the background.

 Plain English, please!

> Printing in the **background** just means the Print Manager will worry about printing things while you continue working. If you print in the foreground, you can't do anything else with your Mac until it's done printing.

How do I print a document?

After you set up your printer correctly you'll be able to print. If this is the first time you're printing to your printer, or if you have multiple printers, remember to check the Mac's Chooser, just to make sure you have things set up correctly.

Q&A

I chose my printer in the Chooser and it told me to choose Page Setup in all open applications. Why?

This warning means that your open applications need to know that you've changed printers. You let them know by opening the Page Setup dialog box, making sure the settings are correct, and clicking OK. Every printer prints a little differently and your application needs to know this so that it can send the document correctly. You'll find Page Setup in the File menu of your applications.

Some last minute choices

With a document open and the printer chosen, you're ready to print. Pull down the File menu and select the **Print...** command. Up pops the Print dialog box (see fig. 18.4). Here's where you make some last minute decisions.

Depending on the printer you use, you may be able to decide how many copies to print, what level of print quality you want, and where the paper should come from.

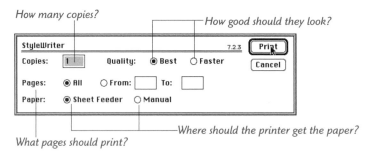

Fig. 18.4
The standard StyleWriter print dialog box. Here's where you make your last minute printing decisions.

Once you've made all the decisions you're going to make, the time has come to print. Click on Print in the Print dialog box and your document's off to the printer.

Do you want to monitor your progress? Depending on your printer, printing your document may activate your Mac's Print Monitor. Check the Application menu for any new entries. If you see the Print Monitor, select it in the Application menu to switch to it. Now you can watch the play-by-play on your printing!

Can I share my printer?

Built into every Macintosh is the capability for it to **network** to other Macintoshes. Just like picking up and dialing a telephone, your Macintosh can call out to other Macs it's connected to and share information. What does this mean to the user? If all the computers and printers are connected correctly, you can have access to any printer linked to the network.

The first thing you need to do is connect your Macintosh computers together. We'll talk about connecting a LocalTalk printer to your network. If you have a serial printer, consult your manual for help on networking serial printers.

Connecting your printer

A LocalTalk printer can't plug directly into your printer port. You need two LocalTalk (sometimes called PhoneNet) adapters, one that plugs into the Mac and one for the printer's LocalTalk port, and you'll need some cabling (usually telephone wire style, or "RJ11") to stretch between the two.

Here's how to connect your LocalTalk network, in a nutshell:

1 Connect a LocalTalk adapter to the Mac's printer port and the printer's LocalTalk port.

2 Connect the phone cable to the "in" port of each LocalTalk adapter.

3 Connect a terminator (included with your LocalTalk adapter) to the "out" port of each LocalTalk adapter.

The **terminator**, by the way, is just a device that tells your Mac that there are no more connections to look for. When AppleTalk counts things up, it will figure out that there are only two computers connected.

Macintoshes talk AppleTalk on LocalTalk

If you've heard these terms bandied about at all, you may be confused as to what exactly they refer to. **LocalTalk** is the wiring that you use to connect Macintoshes together. If someone says, "Do you have a LocalTalk network?" they mean, "Are the cables, ports, and connectors that you use following the LocalTalk standard?"

AppleTalk, on the other hand, is the software program your Mac uses to talk to other computers. It doesn't matter if you're using LocalTalk connectors or any other kind of networking hardware (like, for instance, Ethernet or Token Ring). So if someone says, "Do you have an AppleTalk network?" they really mean, "Are you using AppleTalk software to share your files and printers?"

For quite some time, LocalTalk was the most popular way to network Macs in the office. However, EtherTalk is becoming more popular for two reasons: It allows Macs to deal with Ethernet, probably the most popular network protocol for IBM-compatibles, and it works very fast. Many new Macintosh and Power Macintosh models come with Ethernet hardware built in.

 **{Note}** If you don't plan on sharing your printer with another Mac, move down to Setting Up AppleTalk.

Connecting the other Mac

In order to share the printer, we need to connect another Mac to the mix. You'll need another LocalTalk adapter.

1 Connect the LocalTalk adapter to the second Mac's printer port.

2 Pull the phone cable from one of the other connectors' "in" ports and plug it into the new adapter's "in" port.

3 Connect another phone cable between the new connector's "out" port and the original connector's "in" port.

Why this crazy scheme? You must connect LocalTalk devices in a **daisy-chain** fashion, which means each connection has to continue a chain from one device to the next. In the above example, what we've done is a lot like adding a freight car to the middle of a train. The only difference is, our train, or daisy-chain, has to have two cabooses (terminators).

Restarting your Mac

AppleTalk has to be active for your Macintosh to recognize that there's a LocalTalk connection in place. AppleTalk is the manager, LocalTalk is the employee. Just like any good manager, you have to wake AppleTalk up to get it to recognize that the employees have arrived for work.

To do this, you restart both Macs after you have the LocalTalk connections in place. Now, if you have a standard System 7.5 installation, you should have everything in place for sharing your printer. To activate AppleTalk, open each Mac's Chooser and turn on the AppleTalk Active on Restart option. Then you restart each Mac, again.

Choosing the printer

All you do now is select the printer driver for the networked printer in each Mac's Chooser. Then, you pick the printer from the list of available network printers (there's probably only one). Now you're in! Check Setup to make sure your printer is configured properly and start printing!

I started AppleTalk and selected my network printer, but it still asks if I want to use the Printer or Modem port. What did I do?

You probably don't have an AppleTalk printer driver loaded. Check your printer's disk again. You should find one there.

What You Need to Know About Fonts

In this chapter:

- What are fonts and how do they work?
- How do I add fonts to my Mac?
- I never use these fonts. How can I delete them?

Remember the saying "It's not what you say, but how you say it?" That's why you need fonts!

If your documents don't have the impact you need, maybe you should try a new font. What are fonts? **Fonts** are collections of letters, numbers, and punctuation marks with an identifiable typeface. Some fonts look like newspaper text print, some are rounder like Century Schoolbook, others are plain like Helvetica. You can get fonts that make text look handwritten and friendly or big and bold!

Plain English, please!

Technically a **font** is a collection of letters, numbers, and punctuation marks with a particular typeface, weight (bold or not bold), and size in plain or italic. However, the word is frequently used to mean a typeface with a particular design.

In the System Folder on your Mac is a folder called Fonts. Inside this folder are your font files, which serve two different purposes. First, font files tell your printer how printed text should appear. Second, they tell your Mac how to display text on the screen (see fig. 19.1).

 **{Note}** If you have System 7.0 or 7.01, you don't have a Fonts folder. Instead, fonts are held directly in the System file, which is a file in the System Folder with an icon that looks like a Mac Classic. We'll talk more about the differences later. For now, just think System file whenever I say Font menu.

Fig. 19.1
Sure, fonts change your printout. But your Mac has to know what fonts to use on the screen, too, every time you select a new one for your document.

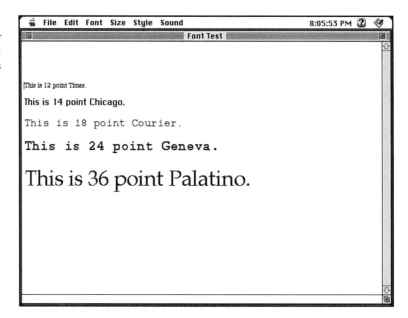

When you select a font in your application, the application lets your System software know. If you type a letter, the System software will try its best to display that font correctly. And, when you print, the System software will try to tell your printer how you want the font to look. The success of this depends, for the most part, on what kind of font technology you use.

What kind of font should I use?

There are three different "kinds" of fonts that you might be using with your Macintosh: TrueType fonts, PostScript fonts, and bitmap fonts. Each has its own little quirks, but for the average user they're all pretty easy to work with.

TrueType fonts always look good

Most modern Macintosh computers use a font technology called **TrueType**. Compared to other kinds of fonts, TrueType is like cable TV—it always looks good. TrueType fonts are very easy to resize because they're outline fonts. They're also very easy to manage and they almost never look bad on your screen or on your printer.

 Plain English, please!

An **outline font** is a font file that describes what the basic shape of a font is to the System software. From there, it's up to the System software to decide how to "fill in" the outline with dots, depending on the point size you choose for the font. An outline font is sometimes called a scalable font.

If you're using your Macintosh at home and you only print your documents to your printer (instead of taking them to work or something), you should be just fine using TrueType fonts. How do you know if you're using TrueType? If you haven't added any extra fonts to your system, you're using TrueType. All the fonts that System 7.0 and above installs are TrueType fonts.

 Just about any printer can work well with TrueType fonts, and they come with your System Software. If you're already tired of worrying about fonts, just use TrueType.

PostScript fonts look great on paper

If you own a laser printer, you may be dealing with **PostScript**. Things can get a little hairy here. PostScript creates great looking printed output, and, if you have the correct printer font files installed, there's almost no need to worry about your printouts with PostScript.

But, PostScript does some crazy things to fonts on the screen. Why? Because PostScript uses two different font files to get things done. Where TrueType is used for both the screen display and the printed text, PostScript needs separate printer font files and screen font files to work correctly. So, if one or the other is missing, you'll see jagged fonts.

Why PostScript looks jagged on the screen

If TrueType and PostScript are both outline fonts, why does PostScript look bad on your screen? The capability to show TrueType fonts on your screen is built into the System software, while the capability to show PostScript fonts is not. This means that TrueType fonts, no matter what point size you make them, always look clean and crisp. PostScript fonts, however, only look good at certain point sizes.

In order for your Mac to show you PostScript files, the System software has to use something called a bitmap font. This is the PostScript screen font, the font that will show up in your document window after you select it in the Font menu. But, by definition, a bitmap font will only show up correctly in certain point sizes. Choose the wrong point size and your font comes out jagged (see fig. 19.2).

Why doesn't everybody just use TrueType?

From the way I've described it, TrueType sounds like the best font technology out there. And for ease-of-use, it is. But there are a couple of great reasons to use PostScript, too.

Reason number one: PostScript does more than fonts. TrueType is a font technology. PostScript, on the other hand, is a **page description technology**. All that means is that PostScript is used for printing both fonts and graphics. To desktop publishers and graphic artists, PostScript is something to swear by. It's incredibly useful for high-end graphics, photos, and other professional printing tasks.

Reason number two: A lot of folks use PostScript. PostScript has been around a lot longer than TrueType, and it's still popular. In major printing houses, pre-press stores, and anywhere else that you find professional Mac users, you'll find PostScript. It's so popular, in fact, that most laser printers designed for the Mac feature PostScript technology built-in.

So, if you've got a laser printer and want to get the most out of it, you'll want to use PostScript fonts. If your printer doesn't support PostScript, or you just don't want to mess with it, stick to TrueType. It's a little easier, and things still look great.

Plain English, please!

A bitmap font file is a map of all the dots required to create the font at a given point size. Because of this, each bitmap font only looks good at its one, specific point size.

The point sizes that will look good

Fig. 19.2
Bitmap fonts representing their PostScript cousins. Select a point size that's not outlined and you'll get "jaggies."

Some good bitmap fonts

Some not-so-good bitmap fonts

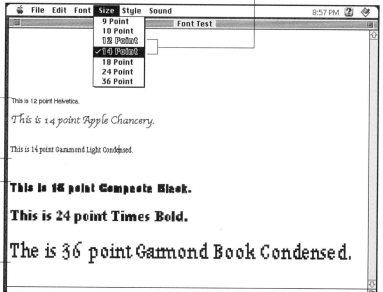

(Tip) There's an easy way to tell which bitmap screen fonts you have for a given PostScript printer font. In your Font menu, the "outlined" point sizes are real bitmap fonts. The point sizes in regular text will be jagged (refer to fig. 19.2).

So why do bitmap fonts look bad? The same reason photocopies look worse when you enlarge them. A 10 point bitmap font has a certain number of dots that make it look good at 10 points. Enlarge it to 20 points, and those same dots have to fill more space. Now things look jagged.

Remember, though, that your PostScript printer fonts *are* outline fonts. So, even if they look bad on-screen, they'll look good on paper.

Q&A

I'm using PostScript fonts and I've got jagged fonts on my printout. What's the problem?

That generally means you're missing the actual PostScript printer font file. Get the disk that came with your printer, or any disks of fonts you've bought, and reinstall the fonts to your System Folder (see "How do I add fonts?" later in this chapter).

Getting rid of the jaggies

There is a way to avoid jagged edges with PostScript screen fonts. What you need is a program called Adobe Type Manager, or ATM. What ATM does is something similar to what TrueType does. It acts as a go-between for your System software and your PostScript fonts. Whenever an application asks for a screen font, ATM looks at the PostScript font, changes the outline to your point size, and fills it in. Now all screen fonts look great (see fig. 19.3).

Fig. 19.3
Ahh, that's better. Same font and point size, but they're no longer rough around the edges.

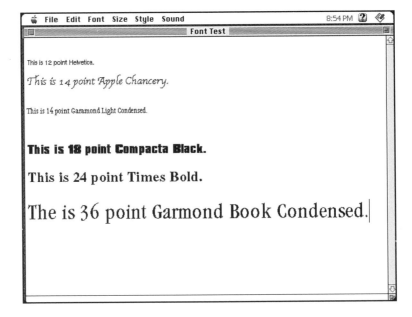

ATM isn't free—you'll have to pick up a copy from your local computer store (it's between $40–$125 depending on the fonts included). Once you've got it, pop in the disk and run the Installer program. It will set you up with all the proper files, including the ATM Control Panel (see fig. 19.4). The Control Panel is where you need to make a few decisions to get everything working correctly and efficiently.

Turn on Adobe Type Manager to end those jaggies, or if you plan to print PostScript fonts to a non-PostScript printer.

Fig. 19.4

You'll have to install a copy of the ATM Control Panel to see all your PostScript fonts cleanly on the screen.

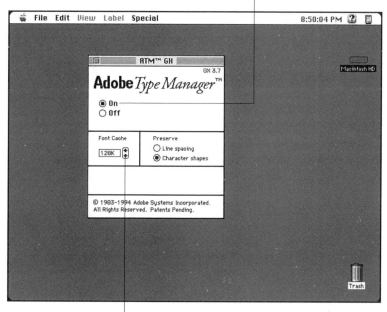

Choose your cache size; a larger cache means fonts show up on the screen faster, but it also takes away from available RAM

ATM's Control Panel is pretty straightforward. Once you turn it on and restart, it will use the printer fonts in the Font folder (in your System folder) to generate screen fonts on the fly for your viewing pleasure.

Q&A

> ### ATM *didn't fix things! I installed it, but my fonts still look bad.*
>
> Remember that ATM needs the printer font file to be in your System folder so it can create the screen fonts. If you deleted or moved the printer font file, it won't work. Also, many PostScript printers have the printer font files built into the printer themselves, which means they can print PostScript without the printer font file in your System folder. But, ATM doesn't like that. Adobe Corp. sells a package called Adobe Type Basics ($125) that includes the duplicate printer font files you need for ATM to work correctly.

There's another reason you might want to own ATM. If you have a QuickDraw printer (inkjet or other printer that doesn't include the PostScript language) you can use ATM to print PostScript fonts that look great. Why would you want to do this? In case you need a font not available in TrueType or your work uses PostScript so you need to at home, too. It's not a bad way to get good looking printouts from your inexpensive printer.

Bitmap fonts: One size fits all?

Bitmap fonts were actually the original type of font that the Mac used for both the screen and the printer. If you have bitmap fonts installed, you can still print with them.

Just remember that these fonts are not at all scalable. The outlined point size in your program's menu is the only point size at which a bitmap font will look good. Usually these are standard sizes, like 10 point, 12 point, and sometimes a few others. Stick with these and things will be okay. Stray at all from these point sizes and your printouts probably won't look much like actual words!

Moving your fonts around

Hopefully, you won't have to move your fonts around too much. If you're installing new fonts from a commercial package, more than likely they'll find the right place to go on their own. If you install fonts that don't include an Installer program of some kind, it's a fairly simple process. But be careful.

 If you're adding your own fonts, take care that you don't leave a PostScript font and a TrueType font with the *same name* in your Font folder (or System file). This can cause your Mac to crash or "freeze-up" if it has trouble deciding which to use. You can use both TrueType and PostScript fonts as long as the font files have different names.

How do I add fonts?

To add a single font, just drag and drop the font file onto the System Folder icon (not the open System Folder window). A dialog box appears, making sure it's okay to add this file as a font. Click OK to let your Mac know that it's doing the right thing (see fig. 19.5).

Fig. 19.5
After dragging the font onto the System Folder, Mac makes sure you know what you're doing.

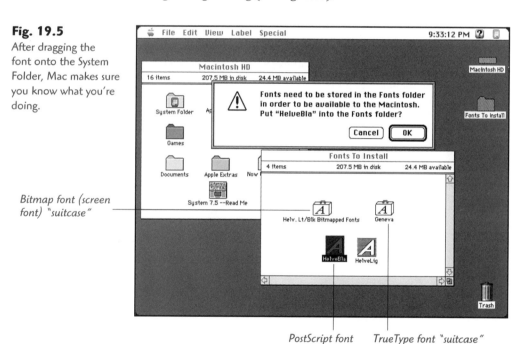

Bitmap font (screen font) "suitcase"

PostScript font   TrueType font "suitcase"

Now, Mac will put the font in the Font folder for System 7.1 and above, or in the System file for System 7.0 and 7.01. Either way, you've got the font in the right folder, and it should be ready to use the next time you start an application. (For System 7.0 and 7.01, you'll need to restart your Mac.)

Notice how the TrueType and bitmap fonts are in suitcases (refer to fig. 19.5)? A **suitcase** is a special type of folder for TrueType and bitmap fonts on your Mac. It allows you to group similar fonts to make them easier to keep track of and to make it easier to move families of fonts into and out of the font folder.

How do I delete fonts?

To delete a font, just open the Fonts folder and drag and drop the font to the Trash. Then empty the Trash. If you're deleting a PostScript font, remember to drag and drop associated bitmap files to the Trash, too.

In System 7.0 or 7.01, double-click on the System file. It should open like a folder, showing you the fonts that are installed. You can drag and drop them out to the Trash just as if they were in a folder. Of course, you don't have to move them to the Trash. You can always move them to another folder (even one you create called "Disabled Fonts," for example) so that you can use them again later.

You can't move or delete font files without closing your applications first. This is Mac's way of keeping you from deleting or losing a font while an application that needs it is still active.

Part VI

My Mac Can Do That?

20

Easy DOS It: Talking to IBM-Compatible PCs

Liz from sales comes over and hands you a PC disk with the monthly sales figures on it. Now what do you do?

In this chapter:

- Can I use a Mac at home and a PC at work?

- Can I make my Mac look like a PC and run PC software?

- Will my Mac work with Windows files?

DOS is the system software that runs most IBM-compatible personal computers (PCs). Like the Mac's operating system, it acts as a buffer between applications and the actual computer hardware, doing things like showing text on the screen and interpreting messages from the keyboard. As you may already know, applications are generally written to work only with a specific operating system. So, programs written to work with DOS can't be used directly on a Macintosh and vice versa.

Why should you care about DOS? If you're in business, there's a pretty good chance that your company uses PC computers and DOS, even if you're lucky enough to use a Macintosh. To exchange files and information with someone who uses a PC, you have to deal with DOS. Plus, there are a good deal more programs written for DOS than there are for the Macintosh. If you ever want to run one of them, you'll need some emulation software or a similar solution.

Can my Mac work with PC disks and documents?

If your Mac is running System 7.5 or higher, you're in luck. Your Mac can read and write directly to DOS formatted disks. If you have a DOS disk you'd like to get some documents from, just put it in your floppy drive. The PC floppy icon should appear on your desktop (see fig. 20.1).

You can treat this just like any other floppy disk icon. Double-click to view its contents and drag and drop files to your hard drive folders to copy them.

Fig. 20.1
The PC Floppy icon on Mac's Desktop.

②Q&A

> ***I put my MS-DOS disk in the Mac's floppy drive, but it says it can't read it. Why?***
>
> Your MS-DOS disk may not be correctly formatted (initialized) or it may be compressed with an MS-DOS utility like Stacker or DoubleSpace. (**Compressing** files increases the amount of data you can store on a disk.) If you think there is data on the disk, *do not* initialize it. Take it back to an IBM-compatible computer and check. Also, check to make sure that the PC Exchange Control Panel is properly installed in your Control Panels folder, and that On is selected in PC Exchange's window.

If you don't have System 7.5, you still have options. Some earlier System software versions include Apple File Exchange, a program designed to translate between Macintosh and DOS formats (consult your Mac's User Manual). Or, you can purchase a program called PC Exchange, which gives your Mac the same DOS-handling capabilities as System 7.5.

 *{Note}* _____ | Many Performa models using an earlier version (pre-System 7.5) of the System software come with the PC Exchange utility program.

Picture this. Liz down in sales comes over and hands you a floppy disk with the monthly sales figures on it. You put the disk in your Mac's floppy drive and up pops the PC Floppy icon. You can move the files around, but how do you open the document? That depends on the application Liz used.

These days, many Macintosh applications can open files created in DOS applications. All you need to do is use the File, Open command in the application (see fig. 20.2). Check to see if the DOS document is listed (you may have to tell your application what type of files to look for). If it's listed, go ahead and open it. Your application will automatically translate between the two formats.

MS-DOS files should appear here

Fig. 20.2

Here's an example Open dialog box from WordPerfect. Once I find my MS-DOS documents, WordPerfect will translate anything it recognizes.

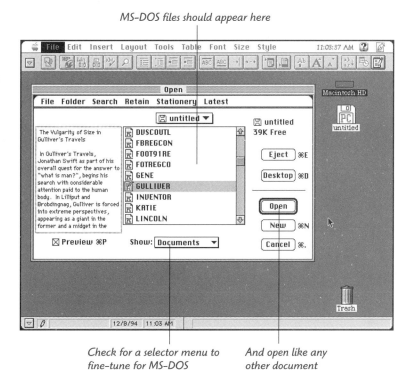

Check for a selector menu to fine-tune for MS-DOS

And open like any other document

If your application won't directly open a DOS file, you still have a couple of options. First, see if you can get the DOS application to save in a file format your Mac application will recognize (like Microsoft Word for Mac or something similar). Second, if this doesn't work, save your MS-DOS document in a common text format, like Text or Rich Text Format (RTF) for word processing and Comma-Delimited text for spreadsheets and databases. You may lose some formatting information, but most Mac applications can deal with these files.

Can a PC work with Mac disks and documents?

PCs can't read Mac disks, but as long as you use a DOS disk, the PC may be able to work with your documents. Just do things in reverse. Say you're working in your Macintosh word processor on a report you want to give back to Liz in sales. Make sure you have a DOS floppy disk in the floppy drive, and use the Save As... command to save your document to the DOS disk. Or, if you're in the Finder, just drag and drop your file on the PC Floppy icon. Now, eject the disk and give it to Liz. She may be able to open the file with her DOS word processor.

The same tips above apply in this situation. If the DOS application can't open your Mac document, try using the Save As... command to save the document in an RTF, Comma-Delimited, or some other PC application's format.

When is a Mac not a Mac? When it's a SoftPC

Just as a flight simulator lets you think you're flying a plane, DOS emulation software lets your Mac think it's a PC. The best known of these software programs is SoftPC from Insignia Solutions, which enables you to run DOS applications in a Macintosh window (see fig. 20.3).

Fig. 20.3

You can use MS-DOS applications on your Mac, thanks to SoftPC from Insignia Solutions.

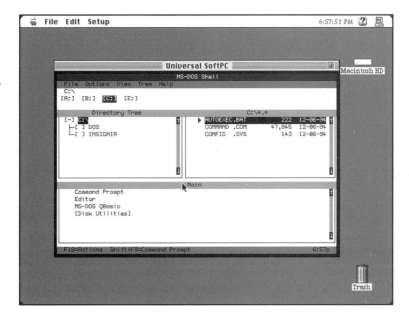

SoftPC works just like any other Macintosh application. Install it from the floppy disks and double-click its icon to start it. Then you'll have a Macintosh window that looks like DOS. SoftPC makes DOS applications think your floppy drive is just like a PC's floppy drive, so you can load DOS applications from within SoftPC. That's the good news. The bad news is now you'll have to learn how to use DOS.

✹ {Note}

SoftPC also emulates an IBM-compatible hard drive so that you can store DOS applications and files. This "virtual hard drive" converts space on your Mac's hard drive for DOS use. Just remember that any space you dedicate to the DOS hard drive takes away from your available hard drive space for Macintosh files.

What about Windows?

Microsoft Windows is the closest thing to a Mac on a PC. It's basically a graphical user interface (GUI) add-on to DOS that gives PCs some of the features of the Mac, including things like icons, menu bars, and, of course, windows. Windows runs "on top" of DOS, starting just like any other DOS application.

Programs have to be written specifically for Windows to take advantage of these graphical elements, which is why you'll hear people refer to both DOS versions and Windows versions of programs.

 The Microsoft Windows I'm talking about is Microsoft Windows 3.1, not Microsoft Windows 95. The new version of MS Windows will likely offer differences that make its programs and documents less compatible with the emulation programs currently available for the Macintosh, but that remains to be seen.

Can I use Windows documents on my Mac?

Windows 3.1 uses the same file format as DOS, so you don't have to do anything different to use Windows documents on your Mac. Just pop the disk in the drive and drag Windows documents to your Mac's hard drive. Many Macintosh applications can open documents created in Windows applications just like they can open DOS documents. (See "Can my Mac work with PC disks and documents?" earlier in this chapter.)

Apple's Houdini: The DOS-compatible Mac

 In the fall of 1994, Apple introduced a new line of upgrade cards (code-named Houdini) that Macintosh owners can use to add an actual Intel processor to their Macs. Apple offers cards for the Power Macintosh computer, while a company named Reply Corporation manufactures them for various Quadra and Centris models.

If you really need to run DOS and Windows applications at full-speed, look into one of these cards. They offer processing speeds well beyond what SoftPC or SoftWindows is capable of. In fact, these cards are as powerful as full-blown IBM-compatible computers!

Plus, some of them even support IBM-compatible sound and networking. And, the cards are priced much lower than a new IBM-compatible computer. That's a heck of a magic trick for those of us who want the best of both worlds!

Can I use Windows applications on my Mac?

As with DOS, Insignia Solutions offers Windows emulation software called SoftWindows (see fig. 20.4). SoftWindows can run most MS Windows programs in a window on your Macintosh. Just load it up and you're ready to go.

 **{Note}** In spite of the name, SoftWindows is just a slightly different version of Insignia's SoftPC that includes MS Windows. Since Windows is an application for DOS, SoftWindows is actually an emulator for DOS, just like SoftPC. If you have SoftWindows, you don't need SoftPC!

Fig. 20.4
SoftWindows lets you run Windows applications on your Macintosh.

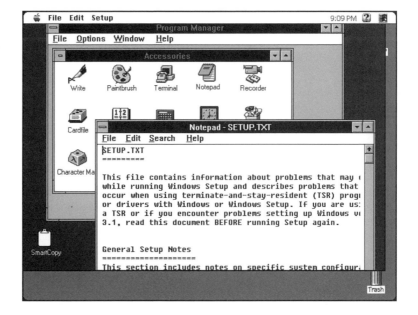

SoftWindows works just like SoftPC—just run the install program, pick the size for your virtual hard drive, and go. You can still use the Mac's floppy drive and the Mac's CD-ROM drive from inside SoftWindows just as if they were IBM-compatible!

What if I have a Power Macintosh?

If you have a Power Macintosh, make sure you buy SoftWindows for Power Macintosh. Basically, it gives you the same capabilities as SoftWindows for older technology Macintoshes. The difference is that the Power PC processor's power allows SoftWindows to run at a much faster speed (currently somewhere around that of an Intel 486SX processor in the IBM-compatible world).

It so happens that the PowerPC processor is very good at emulating other operating systems. This capability and its implementation by Insignia's SoftWindows is part of the reason the Power Macintosh is such a serious contender in the world of business computing.

21

The Multimedia Mac

In this chapter:

- What the heck is multimedia, anyway?
- Do I have to buy more equipment?
- What applications do I need?
- Best buys in games and edutainment

Multimedia isn't just cool games...it's a new way to communicate your ideas using your computer.

Multimedia may be the most overused word in all of computer marketing. Everything you buy these days is multimedia. Multimedia computers, multimedia kits, multimedia applications. So what is multimedia? **Multimedia** is the integration of sound, text, and video for the purpose of communicating an idea or entertaining. Put more simply, it means your computer can communicate about as effectively as your television. Television is a multimedia presentation, with sound, text, and video input in the communication of an idea.

What's so exciting about multimedia?

The key to multimedia on a computer is that it's interactive. It goes farther than television as a medium because the action can be directed by the user. Not just stopped and started, like a VCR tape, but outcomes can be changed, storylines altered, and topics probed further. Interactive multimedia, then, is what we're after for business presentations, education/reference, and entertainment. If you want to be on the "cutting edge" of any of these topics, multimedia is definitely for you. You'll just need to make sure you have the right equipment.

Do I have everything I need?

Your Macintosh already has the capability to display video and play advanced audio. Depending on your model, you may even already have two stereo speakers, a high-resolution color monitor, and a CD-ROM drive. If you do, you're set.

Television on your Macintosh

Yes, you can watch TV on your Mac, but not all Macintosh computers have the capability built in. Most Macs require a special expansion board. There are some models that include this ability, like some Performa 630-series computers, the AV Macintosh (Quadra/Centris 660AV, 840AV), and Power Macintosh AV computers.

With an AV or Power Mac AV, you can hook up a VCR and run an included program called Video Monitor to watch television on your screen. Change channels on the VCR and you'll see the change on your screen. With the 630-series computers, you can connect your cable TV cable directly to the back of your computer and even change TV channels on your Mac (that's what the 630's remote is for)!

I'm watching television on my Mac!

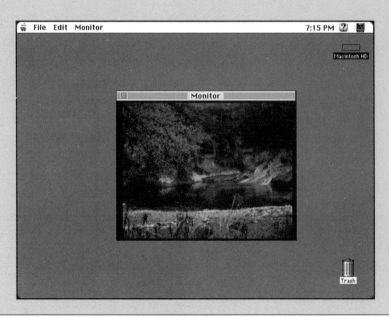

Plain English, please!

A CD-ROM drive is sort of like a floppy drive that uses CD-ROM discs instead of floppy disks. A CD-ROM disc looks and acts almost exactly like an audio CD, except it has the capability to store an incredible amount of computer data (around 600–700 megabytes). ROM, incidentally, stands for Read Only Memory. You can't save to a CD-ROM disc, you can only read data from it.

A CD-ROM drive is essential

If you don't have a CD-ROM drive, you'll need one. Multimedia applications generally require a CD-ROM drive because it is the most convenient way to store a great deal of data. And all that video and audio takes up a quite a bit of space.

The current minimum is a **double-speed** CD-ROM drive, which just means a drive that spins at twice the speed of a normal audio CD player. This allows files to move more quickly from the CD-ROM to your Mac's memory so that all those neat digital movies and sounds play smoothly.

CD-ROM drives work a little like a combination between an audio CD player and your floppy drive. Depending on your CD-ROM drive, you'll either load a CD-ROM caddy or the actual CD-ROM into the drive.

Plain English, please!

A CD-ROM **caddy** is a hard plastic shell that you put your CD-ROM disc into. You then load the caddy into your CD-ROM drive much as you do a floppy disk.

Loading and unloading discs

If you have a caddy-style CD-ROM drive, make sure your CD-ROM disc is properly placed in the caddy and then slide the caddy gently into your CD-ROM drive opening. It should catch and pull the caddy in, just like a floppy disk.

If you have a drawer-style CD-ROM drive, press the release button. The drawer should open automatically, like most audio CD players. Place the disc in the drive (label up) and press the button again. (As with many audio CD players, you can also nudge the drawer a little to get it to close.)

When the disc is properly loaded, a CD-ROM icon will appear on the Desktop (see fig. 21.1). This works just like a hard drive or floppy disk icon. Just double-click to open its window.

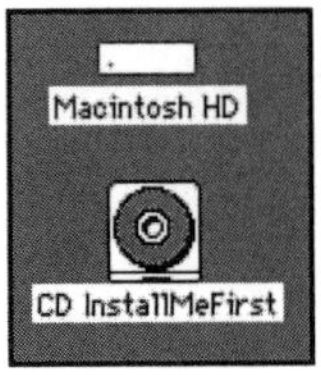

Fig. 21.1
A CD-ROM disc's icon
on the Desktop.

Unloading a CD-ROM disc works the same way as unloading a floppy disk. Just pick up the CD-ROM disc's icon and drag it to the Trash. Out pops your CD-ROM caddy or drawer.

Running CD-ROM applications

Often, CD-ROM applications don't start directly from the CD-ROM disc—they load some portion of the application onto the hard drive and you start it from there. Why? CD-ROM discs transfer data much more slowly than your hard drive does. (In fact, many CD-ROM drives are slower than a floppy drive.) So, in order to optimize speed, some of the application runs from your hard drive.

Your best bet is to look for an Installer program (see fig. 21.2). As with floppy disks, you double-click the Installer icon and your application will be installed on the hard drive.

 **{Note}**

There's a good chance that, even if you launch the application from your hard drive, you'll still need the CD-ROM disc in its drive. That's because the application may require data files from the CD-ROM.

Fig. 21.2
Double-click the
Installer icon to
put the CD-ROM
application on your
hard drive.

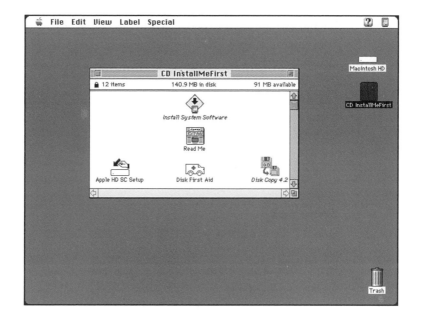

Copying and using CD-ROM files

If your CD-ROM doesn't have an Installer program, or you simply want to
move some of the files from the disc to your hard drive, it's easily done.
Again, it works much like a floppy disk. Just drag and drop the files from the
disc's window to a folder on your hard drive. You'll get the Copy dialog box
with a bar graph to show its progress.

 Remember that CD-ROM discs can store over 600 megabytes of data. There's a
good chance that your hard drive can't hold all those files, so think before you
copy a large number of files. Also, copying files from a CD-ROM disc can take
a long time. Be prepared to wait a few minutes if you copy a large number of
files from the CD-ROM disc to your hard drive.

Once the file arrives on your hard drive, you can treat it like any other
document or application. Just double-click to open it.

By definition, CD-ROM discs are *read only*. That means you can't drag and drop files *to* a CD-ROM disc. You can only drag and drop them *from* the CD-ROM disc.

QuickTime must be installed

There's something else you'll need for your multimedia Mac—the QuickTime extension. QuickTime is software technology written by Apple that allows your computer to play digital movies on the screen.

Realize, however, that installing QuickTime just gives your Mac the movie-playing *capability*. You still can't do anything until you have an application that supports QuickTime. You'll need at least a QuickTime movie player application to do this.

You don't necessarily need a dedicated movie player application to use QuickTime movies. The latest versions of Microsoft Word, for example, enable you to add QuickTime movies to your documents and view them by double-clicking! And many other applications offer similar capabilities.

How do you know if QuickTime is installed? You can open the System Folder, double-click on Extensions, and check (see fig. 21.3). If you've got it, you're ready to get a movie player and some movies to watch. If you don't have it installed, you may find it on your System disks, or you may have to search for it on an online service like eWorld or America Online.

Q&A

Nothing happens when I double-click a QuickTime movie. What's wrong?

Even with QuickTime properly installed in the Extensions folder, you still need a "movie player" application to view QuickTime files. Apple's Movie Player is included on the System 7.5 CD-ROM. Others are available for downloading via online services. You can also play QuickTime movies through QuickTime-enabled applications like Microsoft Word.

Fig. 21.3
If the QuickTime extension is in your Extensions folder, you're in business.

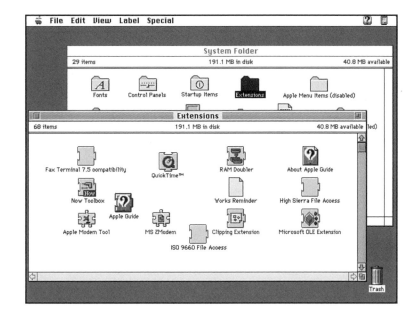

Once you've found the extension, just drag and drop it to the System Folder icon. Your Mac will automatically install the extension in the Extensions folder. Restart your Mac and you're QuickTime-ready! See chapter 23, "Taking Pictures and Making Movies," for more info on creating QuickTime movies.

The best games and edutainment CDs for Mac

It seems to be pretty much a rule in the world of computers—games are almost always farther along on the cutting edge of technology than are other programs. And multimedia is no exception. Most people hadn't really thought of the valuable implications of multimedia when games like *Myst* and *Seventh Guest* began to arrive.

Remember that you'll need pretty powerful equipment to enjoy the best games. On high-end Quadras and Performas, QuickTime movies can play at somewhere between 25% and 50% of the screen and still look decent. On Power Macs these percentages are a little higher, but not much. What are the best multimedia games? To start, try *Myst* ($50), *Seventh Guest* ($40), and *Star Wars Rebel Assault* ($50).

🄸 (Tip)

> The smaller a QuickTime movie's window is, the easier it is for your Macintosh to display all the frames crisply. If you play a QuickTime movie and it looks awful, make its window smaller.

And there's more to multimedia software than games. In homes with CD-ROM equipped Macs, the paper-based encyclopedia is a thing of the past. It's been replaced by CD-ROM titles like Microsoft's *Encarta '95* ($90) and Compton's *Interactive Encyclopedia* ($80). Hundreds of educational, reference, and "edutainment" titles are available. These range from home titles like *3D Home Architect* ($60) and the *Mayo Family Health CD* ($35) to entertaining and educational titles like the *Microsoft Art Gallery* ($60) or Time's *20th Century Almanac* ($40).

And once you've had your fill of that, move on to chapters 22 and 23. There we'll talk about creating your own music, sound effects, digital graphics, and QuickTime movies. Are you ready for Hollywood, New York, or Nashville? Your Mac is!

The latest and greatest: QuickTime VR

QuickTime keeps getting better and better at displaying small movie clips on your Macintosh. Today's QuickTime shows more frames of the movie in a larger window on your screen, thanks to faster computers and advances in programming.

The latest QuickTime, **QuickTime VR**, takes the whole idea one step further. QuickTime VR allows multimedia programmers to create virtual reality worlds in QuickTime movies. These movies let the viewer pan around an entire 3D room, for instance.

QuickTime VR also lets programmers embed "hot spots" in the video. Now, while you're watching a QuickTime VR movie, you can click a certain part of the window and, if it's a hot spot, something else happens. You can move forward or backward, open or close doors, anything.

What does this mean? It means some great simulations for architects, direction-finding kiosks, and designers. It also means some incredible games and reference tools are on the way!

The Mac as a Sound Machine

In this chapter:

- What is digital sound?

- How do I record sounds and play them back?

- How can I send a verbal message or a jingle with my e-mail?

- I'd rather make music than listen to it

Your Macintosh is a great communications tool, even if you prefer to communicate through sound and music!

These days it seems that most cars come with some kind of car stereo as standard equipment. Likewise, every Macintosh model comes with the basic capability to deal with sound. Some have more powerful sound capabilities than others, but, in general, any Mac can play sounds, and most can record sounds, too. Many even include the ability to record sounds from an external microphone, a CD-ROM drive, or some other source.

The Macintosh has two major ways of dealing with sound. Any Macintosh can record and play back **digital** sounds, which are simply computer-coded recordings of actual sounds, music, or speech. The second type of sound is called **MIDI** (**Musical Instrument Digital Interface**), and while many Macs can play these sounds, you may need additional equipment.

What is digital sound and how does it work?

Most of the sounds you deal with on your Mac are digital sounds, or **samples**. Digital sounds are recorded much in the same way that sound is recorded to an audio CD. Ultimately, each sound is broken down into numbers that the computer can understand. This data tells the computer what electronic signals to send to a speaker in order to make it play the sounds correctly.

 ### Plain English, please!

Recording music on a computer is called **sampling** because the computer takes thousands of quick samples of a sound and turns them into numbers. The sampling rate, therefore, is important to the quality of a sound. 22KHz (or 22,000 samples per second) generates higher quality than 11 KHz (11,000 samples per second).

Depending on your Macintosh model, you probably have the capability to record sounds up to a rate of 22 KHz (see fig. 22.1). Power Macintosh and AV Macintosh computers can sample sounds up to 48 KHz, which is widely regarded as CD-quality.

Bypass your Mac's speaker for decent sound

The single speaker that comes with most Macintosh models isn't exactly something you'd be proud to mount in mahogany and display next to your 100-disc CD-changer in the living room. It's cheap and it doesn't do justice to your Mac's capability to generate sound.

Your best bet is to get yourself a set of computer speakers, which you can easily plug into the back of your Mac. Remember that the Macintosh requires powered speakers, so you'll need to get some that either run on batteries or plug into your power strip.

Another word of caution: Always buy shielded speakers. Some standard home or portable stereo speakers aren't magnetically shielded...and they can make big trouble for your monitor's picture or any floppy disks you store near them.

Fig. 22.1

In my Sound Control Panel, I can choose the sample rate for recordings. (My Mac is an AV model, allowing sample rates up to 48 KHz.)

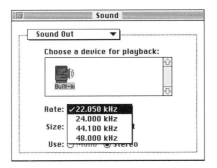

Digitized sounds take up a lot of hard drive space; and size is directly dependent on the sample rate you choose for a sound. Recording one second of a sound at 11 KHz, for example, creates an 11 KB file. At 22 KHz, it's a 22 KB file. So, one minute of sound at 22 KHz creates a file about 1.3 MB in size!

How to record sounds

For most folks, the quickest and easiest way to record digital sounds is through the Sound Control Panel we discussed in chapter 10. After choosing Alert Sounds in the selector menu, simply click Add... to record your sound. You can use a microphone or other external device to record 10 seconds worth of sound to use as your new alert sound.

Want to record more than 10 seconds? You'll need another application. The application HyperCard was included with many Macs in the early 1990s (not the HyperCard player that's standard now) and it could do great things with sound. You can also record with MS Word's Voice Annotations feature described later in "Using sound in applications."

How to play sounds back

As we've already seen, you can play back digital sounds by using your Sound Control Panel. Just click on one of the alert sounds and it will play that sound for you (remember, you've now selected it for your alert sound).

But there is another way to play back sounds. Like fonts in earlier System software (see chapter 19), your alert sounds are stored in the System file in your System Folder. To get to them, just find the System file and double-click to open it (see fig. 22.2). See the alert sounds? If you want to, you can drag sounds out of the system file and put them on your Desktop or in folders.

Fig. 22.2
System 7 sound files are stored in the System file when you record them with the Sound Control Panel. If you don't want them there, drag them out.

Drag it onto the Desktop

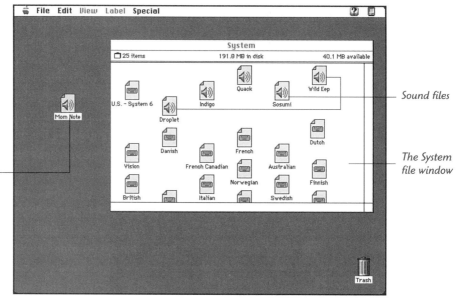

Sound files

The System file window

The question is, why would you want to do this? Well, a System 7 sound can be played through the speaker just by double-clicking. So, how about if I record a sound—say something like "Todd, don't forget a card for Mother's Day," in the Sound Control Panel. I can jump to the System file, drag that sound to the Desktop, and name it "Click Me Before Sunday" (see fig. 22.3). Now, I've got a little voice reminder to help me out with one of those ultra-important things in life!

?Q&A

Why can't I drag sound files out of my System file?

The Mac assumes that any open application is using the System file and that the application requires access to all those sounds and fonts. So, you need to close all applications to drag a sound out. Or try this trick: Hold down the Option key while you drag the sound file out onto the Desktop. This will create a duplicate copy of the sound file, which you can double-click. Remember that the original is still in the System file, taking up disk space.

Fig. 22.3

Here's my little voice memo sitting on the Desktop.

 (Tip)

Here's another neat trick. If you'd like to hear a reminder the next time you turn on your Mac, just drop the sound file in the folder called Startup Items in your System Folder. The sound will play every time the Mac starts until you take it out of that folder. This works great for "Billy, stop playing games...", too.

How to send music or speech in your documents

More and more applications are becoming multimedia inclined. Microsoft Word, for instance, has a feature called Voice Annotation, which allows you to save a sound file *inside* your word processing document. You just end up with a little sound icon right there in the text (see fig. 22.4). Now, if you're sending electronic memos back and forth to people you work with, it's easy enough to send a little sound file along with it—whether it's you talking, a sample of the new jingle, or baby's first words.

Fig. 22.4

Part of a Microsoft Word document including a Voice Annotation icon. Just double-click the icon to play the sound.

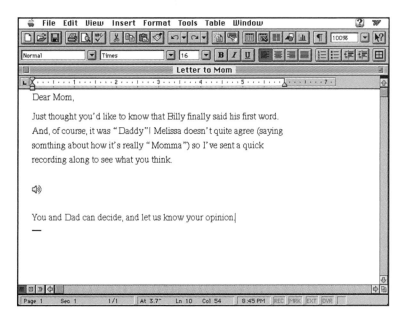

 **<Caution>** | Don't forget what I said about the amount of hard drive space a sound sample takes up. If you record long voice annotations at a high sample rate, your word processing file will end up being many megabytes in size, which could make it difficult to edit and take a long time to transfer over your office network or via modem.

Having more fun with sound

Frankly, recording all your digital sounds in the Sound Control Panel and then dragging them out of the System file can be a pain. Luckily, there are some digital sound applications that can take some of the pain out of this, making sound creation a breeze.

SoundMaster applications

We've talked before about SoundMaster, a shareware application available on most online services. SoundMaster is great for assigning digital sounds to system events, but you can also record sounds using SoundMaster (see fig. 22.5). The advantage is that you can save these files anywhere you want to without having to bother with the System file.

Fig. 22.5
SoundMaster's Control Panel gives you a little more flexibility when saving sounds.

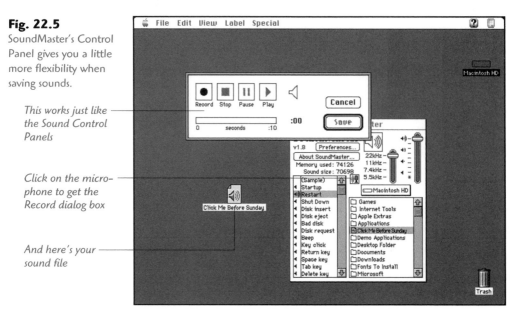

This works just like the Sound Control Panels

Click on the microphone to get the Record dialog box

And here's your sound file

Also, a number of commercial applications have these capabilities, and more, like Kaboom ($35) from Nova Development.

Sound editing applications

A number of applications will also let you edit digital sounds to your heart's content. You can play with pitch and bend, rearrange words and sounds, and generally have a great time. Look for some great versions online, or, once again, Nova's Kaboom Factory is a great digital sound editor.

Making music with your Macintosh

Unlike digital sound, MIDI technology is almost exclusively for music. MIDI is a standard language for electronically communicating musical notes between a synthesizer and a computer. Once a MIDI song is in a "computerized" format, it becomes a document file—like a word processing or spreadsheet document. With the right program, you can edit this song, change the key, add more notes, or whatever. Then you send the revised music file back to the synthesizer and have it played automatically.

To record MIDI music, you generally need a music synthesizer (most often a keyboard, although other digital instruments can also be used), a MIDI interface (a box and cable that plugs your synthesizer into your Mac's modem port), and some sequencing software. What **sequencing software** does is allow you to record what you play on the synthesizer and then edit the song (see fig. 22.6). You can rearrange notes, change mistakes, and change the pitch, tempo, or even the instrument sound. Then, depending on your keyboard, you can record another track of sound and put the two together.

Plain English, please!

Each **track** of music is something like each instrument in a band. You might play the piano on one track, a guitar on the next, a sax on the next, and so on. Then with sequencing software you can overlay the tracks and make your synthesizer sound like an entire band.

Fig. 22.6
MusicShop is an example of MIDI sequencing software. With my keyboard hooked up, it can play enough sounds to imitate an entire rock band.

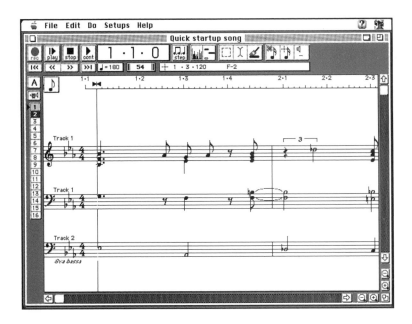

Listening to MIDI without a synthesizer

Most of the time you play back MIDI sounds, you'll do so with a keyboard. There is another way—but it's tricky.

Remember QuickTime—Mac's movie playing technology? Well, QuickTime version 2.0 (and above) also has the built-in capability to play MIDI songs. There are two problems. First, you've got to get QuickTime 2.0 and the QuickTime Musical Instruments Extension. Second, you've got to convert MIDI files into QuickTime movies.

The only place I've ever seen QuickTime 2.0 and the QuickTime Musical Instruments is on the System 7.5 CD-ROM disc. Apparently Apple is not releasing these to the general public,

although more new applications—as they support QuickTime's MIDI capabilities—will probably include these files.

If you've got QuickTime 2.0 and the music extension already in your Extensions folder, you just need to convert your MIDI files to QuickTime. A freeware program called All MIDI (by Paul C.H. Ho and Pink Elephant Technologies) enables you to convert MIDI files to QuickTime—look for it, and others, online.

Once everything's in place, just load the QuickTime MIDI file with a QuickTime movie player and start it running. You should hear music through your Mac's speakers. If your Movie Player knows anything about MIDI, you'll probably be able to change instrument sounds, too.

There is some software available that lets you create MIDI songs using just the Mac's keyboard or your mouse to write the songs in music annotation on a standard looking music staff. If these programs are to create actual MIDI output, though, they still require you to have some sort of synthesizer for playing the music.

 (Tip)

Not every MIDI synthesizer is a $1,000 keyboard. Some less expensive models, like the Miracle Piano, can play basic MIDI sounds. If you're just getting your feet wet, look around for an inexpensive MIDI-compatible keyboard.

23

Taking Pictures and Making Movies

Mac the movie star? Get pictures and movies into your Mac for presentations, public relations, or posterity.

H ere's the other side of multimedia: photos and video. Any Macintosh model has the capability to deal with **digitized photos**—that is, photos that have been translated by the computer into numbers that represent the color and location of each little dot in the picture. This is done in a variety of ways, from special cameras to photocopier-like scanners for the Macintosh. The Macintosh is also very adept at playing video movies, thanks to QuickTime movie technology.

What are digital images and what can I do with them?

Ultimately, digital images give you a distinct advantage over photocopying things and pasting them onto your printed output. Using digital images in your publications allows you to avoid the "generational" loss that you see when you photocopy a photocopy of a photocopy, etc. It gives your documents a more professional look. That's the bottom line. Whether you're creating company newsletters, presentation slides, or Christmas cards, you can drop in your digital image and print away (see fig. 23.1).

Fig. 23.1
What about digital photos for salespeople? Here's a quick real estate flyer that's the perfect excuse for buying a digital camera or scanner.

But there's another reason to use digital images—you can edit them. With the right software, you can take nearly any photo and work with it to your heart's content—recoloring, reshaping, cropping, or superimposing. Whether this is for jazzing up the family album, editing for publication, or sending in freakish photos to the grocery-store tabloids, digital images just sit there waiting to be messed with.

How do I create digital images?

There are a good number of ways you can get digital images on your Mac. Nearly all of them cost money, depending on your Mac's built-in capabilities. But if using photos in your newsletters, family cards, and other publications sounds like a great time to you, read on.

Get your photos developed on a PhotoCD

If you have a fairly recent CD-ROM drive, a PhotoCD may be the perfect way to get digital images into your Mac. Developed by Kodak, the PhotoCD allows you to take standard pictures with standard 35mm film and have the photos developed onto a CD-ROM-compatible disc. All you have to do is bundle up your film and send it away to Kodak or an authorized developer.

What you get back is all your photos on a CD-style disc (see fig. 23.2). If your CD-ROM drive is designed to read PhotoCDs (most are), it's relatively easy to take those photos and place them in a graphic, desktop publishing, or even a word processing document. From there you can add the photos to whatever document you're creating.

Another great thing about PhotoCDs is that they can hold about 100 images. And you don't even have to send in 100 images at once. You can send the CD and new film back to your developer to have more photos added.

 **<Caution>** Get a multi-session, PhotoCD-compatible CD-ROM drive. If you don't, you can't send your PhotoCD back to the developer to have more photos added to it.

Fig. 23.2
Using the viewer program, I can look at PhotoCDs and zoom in and view them in a slideshow.

?Q&A   *My CD-ROM drive is compatible, but I can't seem to use PhotoCDs.*

You may need a special extension in your System Folder. Some versions of the System software include the PhotoCD access extension. Consult your manual if this doesn't work, or check the disks that came with your drive.

Use a scanner

Another great way to get photos into your Mac is by using a scanner. A **scanner** uses the same basic technology as an office photocopier, allowing you to copy printed material into a graphics file. Scanners can copy actual photo prints, printed documents, magazine pictures, hand sketches, or just about anything else that can be photocopied.

There are three different types of scanners, and, depending on how serious you are about scanning things, each has its ups and downs.

?Q&A   *My software says I don't have a scanner connected. What should I do?*

You've got SCSI problems. If your scanner is connected correctly on the back of your Mac, you probably need to configure it to work with your other SCSI hardware. Consult your scanner's manual for instructions on changing the scanner's SCSI ID number.

Flatbed scanners

These things look like the top of a photocopier that has been lopped off and connected to your Mac by a cable. They work almost exactly like photocopiers, too. Just lift the cover, put your document face down on the screen, and tell your software to scan away. What you end up with is a graphics file that you can load into your favorite paint program and edit—or, just drop it in your word processor, add it to your newsletter, and print (see fig. 23.3).

Plain English, please!

I'm talking about **graphics files** as if they're different from other files because they are. Most graphics files are saved in a standard format so that many different programs can load them. These formats include PICT, TIFF, and EPS, among others (see details later in this chapter).

Fig. 23.3

Here I'm cleverly editing a scanned image using my favorite paint program.

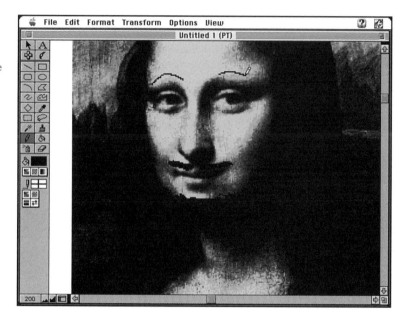

Be aware that flatbed scanners are your more expensive option—somewhere around $500 for a grayscale scanner or $750 and up for a color model. You also need to worry a little bit about the resolution of your scanner. Make sure your scanner offers a resolution that's at least as good as your printer (probably either 300 or 600 dpi). That'll help things come out crisp and clean.

Flatbed scanners will often give you the option of adding a feeder, just like a nice office copier. This will let you scan more than one photo or document without sitting next to the scanner for hours.

Hand scanners

If flatbed scanners sound a bit expensive, consider a hand scanner. Hand scanners use the same technology as flatbed scanners—but instead of laying your page face-down on a scanner's glass, you leave it face up and roll the hand scanner slowly down the page. This presents two problems.

First, it's tough for the average human to pull a scanner in a perfectly straight line; so sometimes hand scans come out looking a bit distorted. Second, the typical hand scanner is only about 4.5 inches wide. So, if you want to scan an entire page, you'll have to do it with two tries and get your software to "stitch" the graphic together.

(Tip) Use a nice solid straight-edge (like an artist's T-square) to help you guide the scanner. Or, better yet, buy a specially designed hand scanner guide for perfect scans every time.

Sheet-fed scanners

These recent arrivals are something of a hybrid between the two other scanner types. Usually about 9 inches wide and only a few inches high and deep, these scanners work a lot like the friction-feeder on a typewriter. Just stick the document into the scanner's opening and it automatically pulls it past the scanning gizmos, spitting the page out on the other side.

Generally these scanners produce decent quality and high-speed. They're perfect for faxes and laser-printer copies, and not bad for quick black-and-white scans of the kids for your newsletters or homemade greeting cards.

How to use a scanner

With any type of scanner, you'll probably get software that helps you create the scan. Once you have your page properly situated, the scanning software will look at the image and convert it into a digital file (see fig. 23.4). Then, your software will probably give you the choice of various file formats to saving it in (TIFF is a very popular choice—see the discussion later in this chapter).

(Tip)

Scanned images, especially color, can be huge hard drive hogs (megabytes in size)! If your software lets you, use fewer colors in your scan or crop the image *before* it's scanned in. Some scanners have a special preview mode that lets you see and crop the scan before creating a final copy (see fig. 23.4).

Fig. 23.4
Popular scanning software at work. Here I can crop the image and change color levels to make a smaller file.

Lower color levels

Cropping for a smaller scan

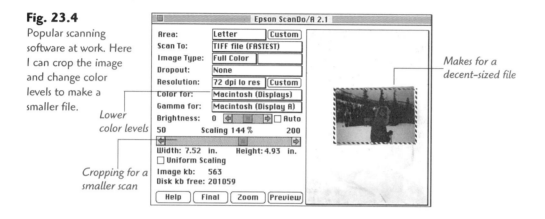

Makes for a decent-sized file

What do you get when you cross a scanner and a fax modem?

If you've read along so far thinking you don't need a scanner, think again. A scanner is not only great for scanning images, it's good for scanning text, too. Especially for things like faxing.

Scan the document you want to fax and then use your fax software to send it off. It's just about that easy. Of course, for best results, you'll need to exercise that credit card and buy at least a sheet-fed scanner, if not a full-blown flatbed scanner.

Another advantage? With a high-quality printer, you can use this setup for basic photocopies, too.

If you're building your home office are or just frugal at work, a scanner is a great alternative to thousands of dollars in major office appliances.

Incidentally, there are some new printers out there that will solve all these problems for you. "Printer/Scanner/Fax" machines are becoming very popular with home and small offices. Most are about the size of a laser printer, but, by adding a scanner and fax circuitry, they allow you to scan, fax, and even make photocopies. They're generally a couple of hundred dollars more than comparable printers, but they may be worth it for your office.

Once the scan is saved in a standard graphic file format, you can easily open it in most popular paint, desktop publishing, and word processing formats. Then you can add all the fake mustaches you want!

Grab frames from your home video

Some Macs have this way-too-cool capability built-in and others can add it with plug-in expansion boards. With your VCR hooked up to the back of your Mac, you can grab a single frame of a video, create a digital file, and use it the same way you'd use a scan or a PhotoCD image (see fig. 23.5). All you need is the right program and hardware.

Fig. 23.5

My Centris 660AV can digitize with no extra hardware, and even includes a program. All I do is run Video Monitor and choose Copy from the Edit menu.

If you've got an AV Macintosh/Power Macintosh or the Performa/Quadra 630 with the Apple Video System, you've got this capability built in. Just use video-grade RCA cables (often spotted roaming around Radio Shack) to connect your VCR's video out connector to your Mac's video in. Then run the program included with your Mac for video capture.

If you don't have one of the above computers, a simple digitizing expansion board, like the Video Spigot, is a great answer. These boards plug into an expansion slot inside your Mac and add ports to the back for plugging in your

VCR. Then, with included software, you can do the same thing the AV Macs can do.

Buy a digital camera

Our final way to get photos into our Macs is to use a digital camera. Until fairly recently, digital cameras were incredibly expensive and very complicated. But now Apple has come to the rescue with the QuickTake100 camera ($700). This thing is cool. With a fully charged battery you just point and shoot like any other camera. You can take up to 32 low-resolution or eight high-resolution photos. Then, when you get back to Mac, just plug in a cable and transfer the photos. Instant digital pictures. There's no film, no scanning, and no messy residue.

What's the best way to save my images?

Here's the quickest ever primer on digital file formats. There are three basic formats you'll have to deal with: PICT, TIFF, and EPS. What you use depends on what you're doing and how much you care.

- **PICT**—PICT files are the most standard Mac-based graphics. This is the format the Mac's Clipboard uses when you cut and paste. They work fine with nearly every Mac application. Realize, though, that PICT files are not as accurate as other formats. If you're a picky graphics-type, you might need to use another format.

- **TIFF**—This is usually the default choice for scanners and many graphics programs. Unfortunately, the TIFF standard is very broad, and not all programs can open all TIFFs. They are very accurate, however, and are good for high-quality printing.

- **EPS**—These are Encapsulated PostScript graphics files, basically PostScript printer instructions for creating graphics. They're highly accurate and the choice of many graphics professionals. They can be a real pain, though, and not particularly useful if you don't have a PostScript printer.

What's the verdict? Use PICT if you don't mind it, TIFF if you need more quality, and EPS once you know what you're doing.

 **{Note}** Most other graphics formats, like GIF, JPEG, or IBM-style TIFF files, require a program to convert them (or just view them) to Mac-style formats.

How can I create a digital movie?

If you're ready to add more than just still-frame photos to your Mac, you're talking about digitizing movies. If a digital photo is something like a photocopy, a digital movie is something like a VCR recording. And the same advantages apply. Digital video makes your presentations and documents more exciting. And unlike a typical VCR recording, digital video is easy to edit.

Creating QuickTime movies

When you digitize video on your Mac, what you're actually doing is creating QuickTime movie files—the same QuickTime we talked about in chapter 21. To do this, you'll need the same Macintosh models you use for capturing video—an AV Mac, certain Performa/Quadra 630s, or a digitizing board like the Video Spigot. Hook up your VCR and fire up the digitizing software that was included with your Mac or with your digitizing card (see fig. 23.6).

Fig. 23.6
With my AV Mac, I can use the included software to digitize video—with controls that are a little like my VCR.

Choose the right window size

Your video monitor window

Hit Record

When you digitize video, you need to consider two things. One is file size. Digital videos take up incredible amounts of hard drive space; you'll need to make sure you have plenty of room on your hard drive for your QuickTime movie.

(!) (Tip) — A smaller capture window makes for a smaller QuickTime file. Setting your digitizing software to recognize fewer colors will make the file smaller, too.

Second, video quality degrades as your window gets bigger. The smaller your window, the crisper and cleaner your QuickTime movie will be. Video quality is measured in frames per second (fps), or how often the screen is redrawn (frames) as the video plays (seconds). TV-quality is 30 fps, a decent QuickTime movie can get away with 15 fps. You'll have to experiment with your software as you try to get the most frames per second while maintaining a decent-sized image and picture quality.

Compression is the key to video capture

Capturing video can be frustrating even on an AV Macintosh because a decent looking movie just ends up being tiny on your screen. If you're interested in tweaking things for quality and size, here are a few tips that seem to work for me...uh, sometimes.

Go ahead and capture long (over 10 seconds!) QuickTime videos to your hard drive, but pick the right compression scheme. Apple's built-in QuickTime schemes are good. If you're capturing from a VCR, choose the Video, Composite Video, or the YUV Codec scheme. Second, choose to have your videos post-compressed. You'll need many megabytes of free space on your hard drive, but you'll get more frames per second this way.

If you're digitizing a very short movie, close all your other applications and give your digitizing software as much memory as possible (with the Get Info... command). Then capture to RAM with compression on (don't post-compress). That will enable you to capture a few seconds of video at higher quality.

My final advice? Add a compression board. Hardware compression can potentially boost your capturing ability to TV-looking full-screen QuickTime movies. And compression boards only cost between a few hundred and a few thousand dollars. (Yea!)

Q&A

Why did my digitizing program quit? I wasn't finished recording!

You probably ran out of memory for the application, or you might have run out of disk space. Close the digitizing program and use the Get Info... command in the Finder's File menu to increase the program's memory requirements. Also, check your hard drive to make sure you still have space left.

Editing QuickTime for the small screen

With the right software, you can turn QuickTime movies into mini Hollywood productions, complete with some of the special effects and titles that the big kids use. Even without special software, you can play some music behind your movie, chop out all the silly bits, and edit it to make your vacation actually look interesting.

Simple copy and paste editing

Here's a neat trick. If you'd like to piece together a couple pieces of QuickTime movies (like vacation video you just want to edit), you can just cut and paste using your QuickTime movie player program. Just load the different QuickTime movies you want to edit together, create a new movie, and copy and paste everything you want to keep (see fig. 23.7). You can cut and paste each individual frame or hold down the Shift key and drag the slider bar to select entire clips at once.

(Tip)

Your best bet for a crisply edited movie is to digitize each different segment in the same sized-window (160 x 120, for instance). That way, every frame in the final movie will appear to be the same size.

Fig. 23.7

QuickTime is just electronic data, so you can copy and paste just like text. Select your clip and copy. Then, select the final video's window and paste.

Use the Copy and Paste commands

My raw video

My finished video window

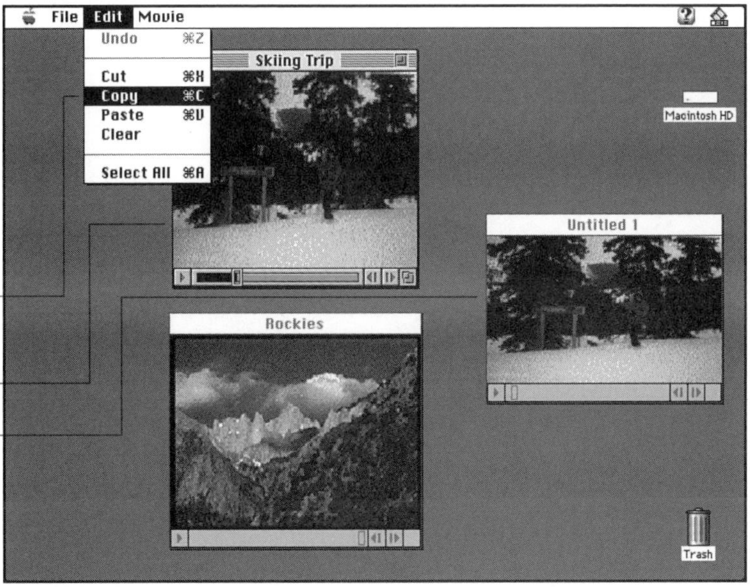

Digital editing software

If you want to do something more with your videos, you'll need extra software. (Actually, some of this software may have come with your digitizing board.) For the most part, you should be able to do some of the editing basics with nearly any application: like titling, fades and wipes, and other special effects. QuickFLIX! ($150), by VideoFusion, is an example of a home-oriented editing program that includes some nice bells and whistles. At the higher end, Adobe Photoshop ($700) lets you add special effects like fancy text and backgrounds, but it can be tedious and time-consuming to work frame by frame.

24

Presenting Information on the Mac

Create a presentation on your Mac with special effects, color, 3D graphics, music—even animation and video.

In this chapter:

- How can I create a simple business presentation?

- How do I add all the bells and whistles: music, sound, and video?

- Great presentation programs for kids

I t's true...not every business presentation requires animation, video, and sound. In fact, many presentations can be crisp, clean, and effective with just slides and graphics that the presenter can easily control. Other presentations can be jazzed up with multimedia—maybe with a little music thrown in or even some digital video.

Once you decide what level of presentation you need, you'll want to get the right tools. There are a lot of applications out there that are designed to make creating presentations quick and easy—so that you can concentrate on the content.

What presentation programs do I need?

The tools for presentations range from business graphics programs to multimedia authoring tools. Some programs are designed to help you create attractive slides, transparencies, or printouts for your stand-up presentations (see fig. 24.1). Others allow you to add more automated features—like sound, narration, or even digital video.

Fig. 24.1

Here's Microsoft
PowerPoint, a
slideshow-style
presentation
application.

*This slide is based on a
template, which gives
it clean, consistent
graphics and text.*

*Like a drawing
application, I can
use tools to add to
the artwork.*

*I can click here to add
different objects, like
charts, graphs, and
pictures.*

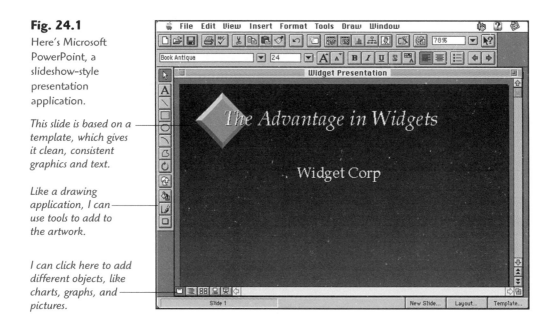

The most extensive professional applications allow you to create actual
multimedia *programs*. These applications can be expensive and often require
programming experience. But, they're also great for creating truly interactive
presentations—the kind of thing that can sell your product in a kiosk or
teach your employees in on-screen training sessions—even if you're not there
to supervise.

Build a slideshow for a business presentation

The simplest type of presentation you can create is a slideshow presentation.
Displayed on a computer screen, these presentations can be an effective and
entertaining replacement for conventional slides and transparencies. Plus,
the more popular applications have a "click-and-type" interface that enables
you to create a slick presentation without serious drawing or programming.

I'll start my presentation by choosing a format for my slides. In Microsoft
PowerPoint, there is a Wizard gizmo that helps me do this—some other
programs do it other ways. I choose one of the pre-defined styles and apply
it to the slide background. Most of my slides will follow this format (see
fig. 24.2).

Fig. 24.2
I've picked my
background so now
most of my slides will
look this way.

*Click and type to
change points*

*Choose a consistent
background*

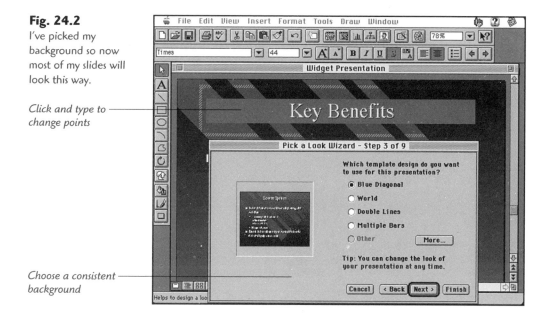

Hints for an effective presentation

I'm probably not the foremost expert on presentations, but there are a couple of things that I like to see people do when they create one. These are those:

Use fonts consistently and sparingly. You don't need a thousand different fonts to prove the capabilities of your program. Use the same font in each title (it can be a little wacky if you like) and then use clean, communicative fonts in your discussion points.

When possible, use stylesheets. Unless you really, truly are an artist, you probably have an eye that's about as bad as mine is for color. Use the professional stylesheets that come with your

software. People who know a lot about "color warmth and texture" designed those things.

Use special effects, but not over and over. Again, people fall into the "isn't this cool" trap. Yes, it is cool the first time and maybe the second. But the fifteenth time something jumps around the screen for no discernible reason will take away from what you're trying to communicate.

Have a cool intro and an effective summary. If you want to use neat effects and crazy fonts, use them at the beginning of your presentation to grab people's attention. Then, at the end, give the key points one more time. Be up front about what you have tried to communicate and try to anticipate questions.

Next, I can use either the Outline view or view each slide and type in my information. In Outline view I can get a good idea of how I'm presenting the information. In Slide view I can see how things are going to look.

⓵(Tip)

> Unless you've got a really good reason, don't change your backgrounds. That one color scheme will really help people focus on what you're trying to say instead of distracting them from your message.

Now, deeper into my presentation, I've decided that the default slide isn't going to present information the way I'd like it. I need a chart. Luckily, I created a perfectly nice one in my spreadsheet and saved it as a graphics file. I can place it in a specially designed slide format that accepts graphics (see fig. 24.3).

Fig. 24.3
Graphics are an important element of many presentations. In fact, you might even want to add QuickTime movies or digital images if your program allows them!

Here I've imported my chart and dropped it in.

I've changed the slide to one that accepts graphics.

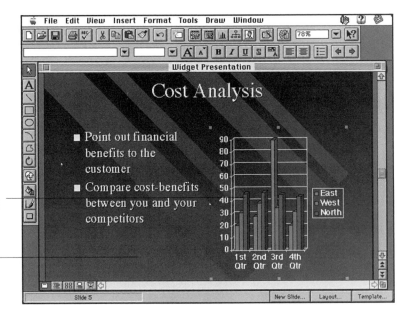

With all my information typed in and my special slides created, it's time for the fun stuff. In thumbnail view, I can look at a small picture of each slide and decide how it will interact with the slides before and after it. This is that effect that people have spent thousands of dollars for in slide projectors.

Just by selecting each slide and telling it what effect to use, I can change the "wipe" or "fade" from one slide to the next (see fig. 24.4). This is a great way to jazz up a presentation without detracting from the content. A nice clean entrance and exit to a slide makes things seem more polished.

Fig. 24.4

Transitions are a big part of the slideshow presentation. PowerPoint, for instance, offers quite a selection.

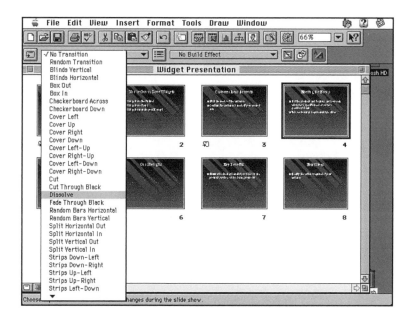

Finally, I add some other elements to spice it up. PowerPoint, for example, is QuickTime compatible, so any QuickTime movie file I create will be played automatically when the slide appears. That's a great way to add some excitement to the beginning of my presentation, or even drop in narration or music for a self-running slideshow.

①(Tip)

> Remember QuickTime MIDI? QuickTime movies don't have to have a picture; and in your presentation program, they don't even have to show up on the screen. Even a "video-less" (sound only) QuickTime file will play automatically in your show.

My final presentation actually only took a few hours at the most to build, and with a powerful enough slideshow program, it's also easy to create speaker's notes, printed handouts, or slides/transparencies for a more conventional show. And once the presentation is built, it's easy enough to modify it for any audience. I can move slides around, change wording, update figures, or even personalize the slides for the audience I'm dealing with!

What presentation software should I buy?

At the high-end of traditional slideshow creators are Microsoft PowerPoint ($400) and Aldus Persuasion ($500). Some other packages, like ClarisImpact ($400), offer presentation features in a more comprehensive "business graphics" package. Others, like Gold Disk's Astound ($399), offer fancy tools for adding animation and sound.

 (Tip)

> Microsoft Excel has the capability to create fairly rudimentary slideshows, complete with charts and your spreadsheet information. They might not be the best looking, but it's a great money saver (if you already own Excel) that still communicates effectively.

Create a family album with music, sound, and video

Here's a pretty well-kept secret: Many drawing programs and works applications, like ClarisWorks, have the capability to create presentations from within their drawing modules! In ClarisWorks, you can set your Mac to show each page of your drawing as a slideshow, including QuickTime videos (see fig. 24.5). With QuickTime's capabilities you can add music, sound, and movies.

For my multimedia family vacation show, I start by drawing a background and some common elements for each page. To do this, use the **Edit Master Page** command in the Options menu. This allows me to define a standard background for every page of the presentation. For ClarisWorks' slide viewer, I need to completely cover my page with the background for a full-screen effect (see fig. 24.6).

To create text, I just click on the Text tool, click on the page, and start typing. I use the Rectangle tool to create some little photo boxes and some boxes for holding my captions about the vacation.

Fig. 24.5
Here's the intro page to a ClarisWorks multimedia family album.

Fig. 24.6
I set up my presentation pages by editing the master page. Now all my pages will have this background.

Use a gradient fill to give it that "pro" look

Background color covers the entire master page

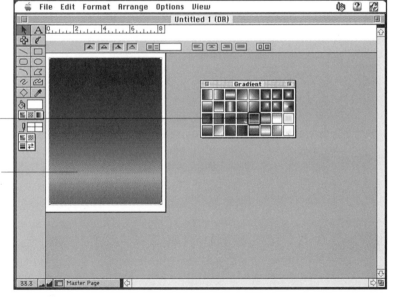

 (Tip)

To add pages to your presentation, pull down the Format menu and choose Document... . Then, in the size box, change the number of pages *down*.

With my master page set, I can start drawing elements on each page. What I like to do is create some standard elements—like title text, picture boxes, and caption boxes—and copy and paste them onto the other pages. Using the Page View command from the View menu, I can see more than one page at a time. Now I can paste multiple elements into each page (see fig. 24.7).

Fig. 24.7
Copy and paste let me quickly add most of the elements I want for my presentation.

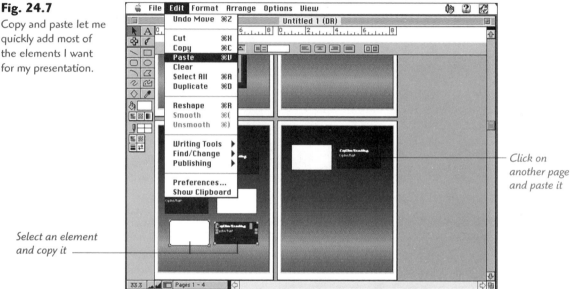

Click on another page and paste it

Select an element and copy it

Next, I'll add some photos. These can be PhotoCD photos, scanned photos, or even artwork and clip art. From the File menu I select the Insert... command. Now I can browse for the graphics files I have of my vacation. Select a file and it pops up on-screen. Now, I just position it in a graphics box and edit the caption text (see fig. 24.8).

I can also insert QuickTime movies in this presentation. ClarisWorks will automatically play QuickTime movies when it gets to a page with one on it. The easiest way to place a QuickTime movie is to pull down the File menu and use the Insert command. You can also copy the movie from the Movie Player (as illustrated in chapter 23) and paste it onto the page.

 **<Caution>** Don't forget that adding a QuickTime movie makes your presentation file pretty big. It may be difficult to put it all on a floppy disk and send it away to Grandma!

Fig. 24.8

Here I've added some multimedia excitement. With photos and QuickTime, I can add narration, music, or video!

Insert the graphic file ———

Position it in ———
the photo box

Even paste ———
QuickTime movies

It's Melissa - Heads Up!

Melissa is decked out in all of her Winter splendor. Including, I must say, a very fine cap.

Click Here to see Melissa in action!

Edit the caption text

With all the pages of my presentation in place, I can now use the slideshow viewer to show it on the screen. In the View menu is the Slide Show... command. Selecting this brings up a dialog box with a number of options. Here I can decide to have fades between each slide, how long each slide will stay on the screen, and how the slideshow will show QuickTime movies (see fig. 24.9).

Notice that I can decide whether my presentation will be driven by the user or if it will be automatic. For instance, if I select the Advance every _ Seconds check box, the show will move itself along. If I don't check it, each slide will move when the mouse is clicked.

The same goes for QuickTime. Without Auto Play selected, I'll have to manually double-click each QuickTime movie to play it. This could be fun for the family, however—especially small kids. It adds a powerful level of interaction for your homemade presentation.

Fig. 24.9
Add the fancy stuff
from the Slide
Show dialog box.

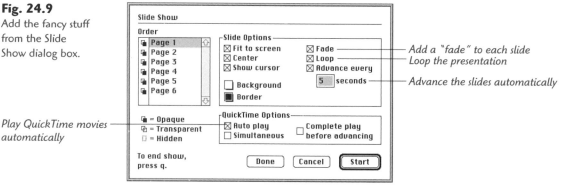

Add a "fade" to each slide
Loop the presentation

Advance the slides automatically

Play QuickTime movies
automatically

So there we have it. Even without fancy editing equipment, ClarisWorks and the Mac let us create pretty snazzy presentations for home, work, or just playing around with family pictures. Does this beat the family album? It just might, especially if you took your camcorder on vacation with you!

Create a class project or school report

Some really great presentation tools are designed just for kids, complete with animation, sound, and slideshow capabilities. Many of these are designed to help kids tell stories, creating interactive "books" on the computer. They feature easy tools for adding pictures, sound, or even video. Kid Pix Studio

Showing your Mac's screen on TV

Your Mac monitor is probably pretty small. Wouldn't it be cool to display your Mac's screen on a TV! Unless you have an AV Macintosh model, your Mac's picture was not designed for showing on a standard TV. Frankly, a TV can't live up to the Macintosh's display quality.

But, with the right amount of money, nearly anything can be fixed. What you need is called an

NTSC Encoder ($150–300 and up). This is usually a little box you hook up between your Mac's video output port and your TV. The encoder translates Mac monitor output to TV-type signals, making the picture of your Mac's screen as crisp and flicker-free as possible.

With your box hooked up, you can display away. You'll still probably notice that your Mac display is cleaner and crisper—but, for presentations, a 32-inch TV picture might have some advantages, too!

($50), shown in figure 24.10, and Microsoft Fine Artist ($40) are popular examples.

Fig. 24.10

With photos, freehand drawings, and the program's special effects, kids can create entertaining presentations for the family or schoolmates.

These programs are great for playing around, but kids can also find them useful for class projects or school reports. Using a program with sound and animation capabilities, kids can use a computer to explain their science projects, present their research papers, or even create a multimedia book report. And chances are they'll wow their teacher as well as their buddies!

Part VII

Getting on the Information Superhighway

The Online Essentials

25

You can do a little shopping, stop off and chat with some distant friends, or head down to the Library of Congress.

In this chapter:

- Which modem should I buy?
- How do I use communications software?
- I want to send and receive files. How do I do that?

Owning a Mac without a modem is like owning a car that never leaves your driveway. You can turn on the radio, use the heater, even toot the horn—but you never go anywhere or see anything! If you're not online yet, try it. Chances are there's something out there that will expand the usefulness and pleasure you get out of your Macintosh. And getting online is (usually) incredibly easy.

What kind of modem do I need?

As we discussed in chapter 2, a modem is just a little box that connects a computer to a phone line, enabling your Mac to call up and talk to other computers around the world. There are really only two decisions you need to make concerning modems.

Actually, a modem can also be a little circuit board inside your Mac that lets you do the same thing (especially with PowerBooks). If you think you may have an internal modem, check the back of your computer for phone connectors. If you have some, plug 'em in!

Does speed matter?

As with most computer-related things, modems keep getting faster. The speed of a modem is measured in how many bits per second (bps) of computer data it can transfer. Common bps numbers are 1200, 2400, 9600, 14,400, and 28,800. So what speed should you get? Right now, most of the big name online services are switching over to 14,400 bps as their fastest connection. These modems are actually down in the $150–200 price range and are probably your best choice.

Don't buy a 2400 bps (or lower) modem. If you got one with your Mac, play with it a little and you'll see why I say that. It's only marginally useful these days, and, within months, it'll just be annoyingly slow.

You might go ahead and get a 28,800 bps modem, especially if you plan on using an Internet provider for a modem connection to the Internet (see chapter 27, "In the Fast Lane—Using the Internet," for more info). The latest graphical tools for the Internet demand a lot from your modem, and it's in your best interest to be able to move up to 28,800 bps service when it's available.

 Plain English, please!

You may also hear the word **baud** used to refer to a modem's speed. Baud rate is the number of changes in a signal in a communications channel that can occur per second, and 300 baud equals 300 bps. However, with higher bps rates, its relationship to baud is basically irrelevant to using your modem. Realize that, in most cases, if some tells you the "baud" of a modem, they really mean the bps rate, which is the true measure of a modem's speed.

Do I need a fax modem?

Well, a more useful question might be, "Do you have any choice?" Most modems available today also include fax capabilities, which, with the right software, enable your Mac to send and receive faxes over phone lines (see fig. 25.1). This is a really cool trick, except for one caveat: You can only fax things that are already in your computer. Of course, if you want full fax capabilities, you can use a scanner like we discussed in chapter 23.

(Tip)

Fax modems also use bps ratings to indicate speed, but don't go nuts trying to find the fastest fax modem around. If your modem can handle fax connections of 9600 bps, you'll be as fast as 90% of the fax machines out there today.

What some of the numbers mean

You'll find plenty of strange numbers and letters on the side of the modem box to tell you how fast it is. These numbers are just version numbers of the communications standard set up by an industry standards board.

This number	Means
V.22bis	2400 bps
V.32	9600 bps modem
V.32bis	14,400 bps modem

This number	Means
V.34	28,800 bps
V.42	Error-correction built-in
V.42bis	Data compression technology built-in

Notice, incidentally, that these last two are not bps-related. Nearly any speed modem can feature error correction and data compression.

Fig. 25.1
Here's a "preview" of
my Mac getting ready
to send off a fax.

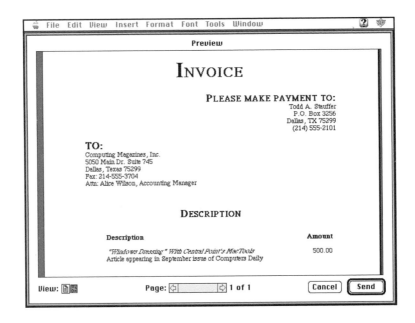

For the most part, a fax/modem is fairly easy to use. Using the Fax Sender software from Apple, for instance, all you have to do to send a fax is hold down the Shift and Control keys while you pull down the File menu in nearly any application. This replaces the Print... command with a Fax... command, which you use to "print" the document to the fax modem. Instead of the Print dialog box, you get one for faxing, including a little phone book of people you often call and a way to create the cover page (see fig. 25.2).

*Click here to select
a cover page.*

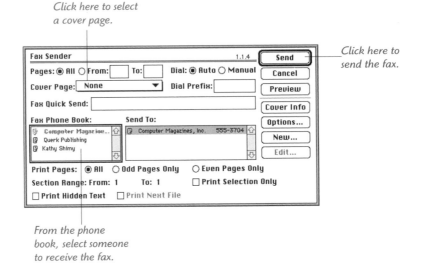

Fig. 25.2
The Fax Sender
dialog box replaces
the Print dialog box
in most applications
to make sending a
fax easy.

*Click here to
send the fax.*

*From the phone
book, select someone
to receive the fax.*

Generally, faxes are received automatically as long as you have configured your fax software to receive and you leave your Macintosh powered-on to take the call. Check your fax software's manual to see how it will let you know there's a fax. Some software (like Apple's Fax Terminal) just shows up in the Application menu. Other software may pop-up a dialog box or even make your Apple menu icon blink.

**\<Caution\>** | If you use the same phone line for data transmission and phone calls at your home, realize that your Fax Terminal and your telephone answering machine might be racing to answer the phone. Both will usually try to pick up after 4 rings. If you know you're receiving a fax, you can set your modem to pick up earlier. Check your modem software's manual.

Do I have a built-in modem?

As we discussed in chapter 2, the GeoPort Adapter allows you to connect your AV Macintosh or Power Macintosh computer directly to your phone line. Because these computers have modem capabilities built in, they only require extra software to get going.

When you buy your GeoPort Adapter, it comes with all the software you need to get it up and running. Just run the Installer program on the disk that came with your adapter.

? Q&A | *I've got a Macintosh AV computer and all my software is installed, but the GeoPort won't dial out.*

First, make sure your software is properly configured. Then, make sure you've selected the "GeoPort" in your communications application. Finally, make sure that Speech Recognition is turned off (on AV Macs), and your Sound Out (in the Sound Control Panel) is set to 24.000 KHz.

Why do I need communications software?

Your Macintosh needs special communications software in order to work with the modem and display text and graphics on your screen. This software is also used to transfer files between your Mac and the computer you're connecting to. Some software is specifically designed to connect to the computers operated by a service like America Online or CompuServe. Other software, sometimes called terminal emulation programs, allow you to connect to most computers around the world.

 Plain English, please!

Communications software is called terminal emulation software because most of these programs can act like those dedicated screen/keyboard combos you would use to do work on a big mainframe computer. For instance, you're likely to see bank tellers and airline reservationists using terminals. **"**

There are a fair number of communications programs available for the Macintosh, and how much you spend for your program should be based on how much you think you'll use it. Most of the retail programs, like Microphone Pro, Crosstalk, or Smartcom, offer a full set of features for communicating with other computers and transferring files.

You may also be able to find useful communications software as shareware on an online service. If you already have the America Online or eWorld software, your best bet might be to use it to connect to the service and then look around for shareware communications software. One of my favorites, ZTerm by Alverson Software, is available this way (see fig. 25.3).

You may also take a look around your hard drive and floppy disks to make sure you don't already have some communications software. Many Macs come with modems and include some kind of online software. Most works applications, like ClarisWorks, Microsoft Works, and WordPerfect Works, also include a communications module.

Fig. 25.3

Here's an example of a session with ZTerm. I've called a local bulletin board system and I'm looking at a listing of Apple Newton software they have available for downloading. ZTerm is simple, but it gets the job done.

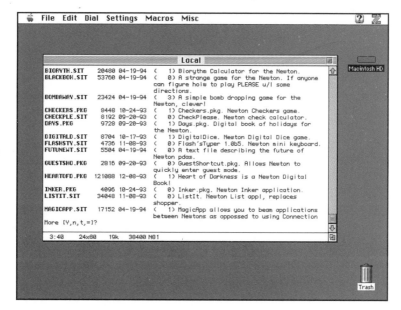

Setting up the software

The first time you load your communications software, you'll need to make sure you have it set up correctly. First, find the command in your software that allows you to tell the software which modem you're using. This is often a command called something like Connection... or Modem... in a menu called Settings.

If your exact modem is listed, select it. Some software will include descriptions for many different modem types. If yours isn't one of the choices, you may need to use a standard connection like Express Modem or Hayes Compatible and set your bps rates by hand. Most other choices will be set automatically (see fig. 25.4).

(Tip)

You may need to check your modem's manual to figure out what standard connections it's compatible with.

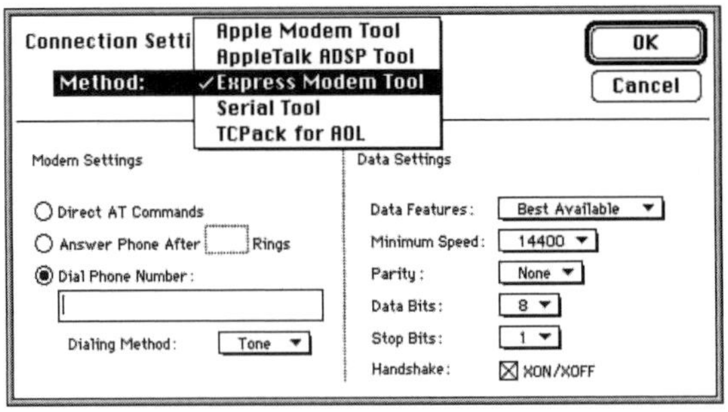

Fig. 25.4
ClarisWorks' communi-
cations tool lets me
select the modem tool
I want to use and other
settings for a proper
connection.

Connection Setti	Apple Modem Tool	OK
Method:	AppleTalk ADSP Tool	Cancel
	✓Express Modem Tool	
	Serial Tool	
	TCPack for AOL	

Modem Settings

○ Direct AT Commands
○ Answer Phone After [   ] Rings
● Dial Phone Number :
[   ]

Dialing Method : [Tone ▼]

Data Settings

Data Features : [Best Available ▼]
Minimum Speed : [14400 ▼]
Parity : [None ▼]
Data Bits : [8 ▼]
Stop Bits : [1 ▼]
Handshake : ☒ XON/XOFF

The next thing you need to do is set up your terminal emulation. Usually you'll find a Terminal command under Settings in the communications program's menu bar. You need to know what type of terminal the host computer is going to expect you to use. A couple of common terminal emulations are:

- **TTY**—teletype style terminal where each line follows the last; almost no graphical elements.

- **VT100/102**—standard terminal setting for full-screen control; allows you to use cursor keys to move around and choose menu items with some computers.

- **ANSI**—something of a PC standard, ANSI lets the host computer send some color and graphical elements.

 Plain English, please!

By host computer I mean any computer that you use your Mac's modem to call. Your Mac can be a host computer, too, if you set your communications software to answer the phone.

In general, most host computers can communicate with your Mac if you set your terminal to TTY, but you should find out what else it supports as soon as you can. If the host computer sends ANSI signals to your TTY or VT100 terminal emulator, you *can* read things, but only just barely (see fig. 25.5)

Q&A

> ## When I connect to the host computer, I get a lot of junk, but some things are readable. Why?
>
> For VT100 and ANSI terminals, the computer sends extra information (to tell it things like text color and graphics elements). Experiment by setting your terminal to different emulators *while you're connected.* Chances are you'll eventually find an emulator that makes things easier to read.

Fig. 25.5
See the difference? Since the host was sending ANSI signals, TTY showed me a lot of junk on the screen, which ANSI turns into graphics.

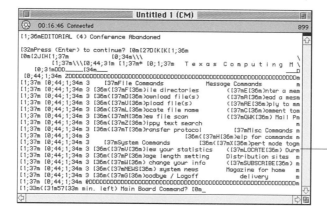

This session is set to TTY.

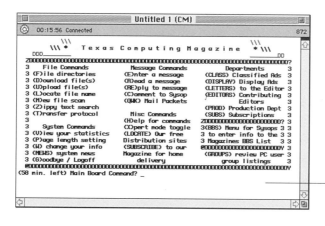

This session is set to ANSI.

Dialing another computer

Now, with the communications software set up for the appropriate modem and terminal, you can dial out. Different software handles this in different ways, but you should be able to find a Dial or Open Connection command somewhere (see fig. 25.6). Choose that command, give your program a phone number, and it should start dialing!

If you need to dial non-standard numbers to get an outside line, use a comma for a pause. For instance entering 9,555-2345 will dial the 9, pause two seconds, and finish dialing the number.

Fig. 25.6
ClarisWorks has its Open Connection command in the Session menu.

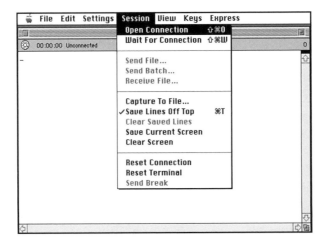

You should hear your modem dial and then the host computer connect. (If you dial a wrong number, you might hear somebody say "hello.") When the host computer picks up, you'll hear some electronic screaming as the two modems try to communicate. When they finally decide the best way to get things done, you'll see something on your screen like:

```
CONNECT 9600
```

When you see this, hit Return. You're online. If you called a friend's computer, start typing and you should be able to chat back and forth. If you called some other kind of service, you'll probably need to enter a user ID and password.

Q&A   *I'm connected! Why do I see double (or nothing) when-ever I type?*

If you see something like, "HHeeyy MMiikkee, wwhhaatt''ss uupp!!" then your Echo setting is wrong. Look in your Terminal setup for an option called Local Echo. Make sure it's *not* selected. On the other hand, if you're seeing nothing when you type, you should turn Local Echo *on*.

Transferring files

Once you've been online for a while, especially with an online service or a local bulletin board (see chapter 26, "Finding Your Superhighway Ramp"), you'll realize that one really great reason to be online is all the programs and other files you can get. To get these files from the host computer to your Mac, you'll need to download them. To do that, you need to select a transfer protocol.

 Plain English, please!

Downloading is the term for transferring a file from a host computer to your computer. Its opposite is uploading, which means sending a file. The **transfer protocol** is a standard that your computer and the host computer use for transferring the file. It's a little like deciding whether you're going to send something by Federal Express or by U.S. Mail—the protocol determines how quickly and safely the file is transferred.

There are some standard transfer protocols that you should be aware of. Although there are some computer-nerd differences among them, I'll just point out why you'd pick one.

- *XModem.* One of the older (and more widely used) protocols. You can transfer one file at a time with limited error correction.

- *YModem.* Slightly faster and enables you to transfer more than one file with a single command (called a "batch" transfer).

- *Zmodem.* Currently one of the most popular and fastest protocols, works well with high-speed modems and allows batch transfers.

- *Kermit.* Named for the frog. Slow, but sometimes your best bet for transferring files to older, mainframe style computers.

 **<Caution>** Downloading software is one of the two most likely ways you can get a computer virus. (The other is using a floppy disk or magnetic tape that's been used by other computers.) See chapter 29 for more info on avoiding viruses.

When you're ready to download a file, tell the host computer what protocol you'll be using. Then, head to your File menu and look for a command like Receive File... and choose the protocol you'd like to use (see fig. 25.7). (Depending on your program, you may also need to decide where to save the file.) In most cases, your best choice is ZModem if the host computer supports it. ZModem is generally faster, easier, and more reliable than other protocols.

{Note} Some online services, like America Online and eWorld, use their own transfer protocols and systems. Using their special software, you don't need to worry about the protocol—it's chosen automatically.

Fig. 25.7
ZTerm's receive commands. Here I select the protocol that I've told the host computer I want to use.

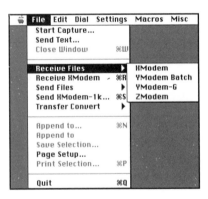

If your software *doesn't* have a Receive File... command or something similar, it may be designed to receive files automatically. Look for a command like Transfer Settings or something like it and choose your default protocol there. Then, when the host computer begins to send a file, your program will automatically try to download it.

Using compressed files after downloading

A remarkable number of the files you download from online services or BBSs will be **compressed** or **archived**. Compressing a file makes it smaller so it's cheaper (and faster) to transfer by phone. These files won't run as they are on your Mac; they need a special program to rebuild them.

The most popular format for compressing Macintosh programs is the StuffIt format. StuffIt is a shareware program that's available on most BBSs and online services. You'll need StuffIt or StuffIt Expander (a decompressing-only program) to use these programs.

There are some other standards out there, too, like Disk Doubler and Compact Pro. Often, however, these files are saved as **self-extracting archives**, which means you can double-click them and they'll decompress themselves. In fact, StuffIt-compressed files may be self-extracting, too. If you don't have StuffIt, try double-clicking the file first.

26

Finding Your Superhighway Ramp

There's an incredible world of information, ideas, and really cool near-free programs out there waiting for you.

In this chapter:

- What services do I get from an online service?
- What's a BBS (Bulletin Board System)?
- How do I find and use a local BBS?

The hype and publicity that have surrounded the Information Super-highway have fueled an incredible growth in all aspects of the online world. Once on it, you can enjoy years of information, education, and fun. But first you need to decide how you want to get on.

Which online service should I use?

Online services are information services and social clubs. That's about the extent of it. But as you'll see in the next few pages, the emphasis placed on information versus social stuff varies, as does the cost of each service.

eWorld

eWorld is Apple Computer's own personal information service. You use eWorld graphical software to get online—you'll find the software on your System 7.5 CD-ROM disc, or you can buy a subscription kit for around $20 in your local computer store (see fig. 26.1).

Fig. 26.1

eWorld's interface is friendly, easy to navigate, and... well...cute.

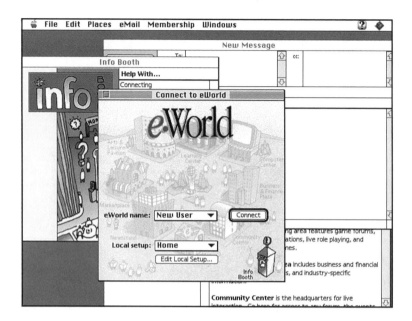

eWorld was designed from the ground up to be easy to use and fun. It's a great looking service—arguably the most "Mac-like" in look and feel. It's definitely a chatter's network; while it has decent business tools and some online reference capabilities, it seems destined to be a fun place to hang out.

eWorld is still relatively new, and for all that, needs a little time to grow. Its current user base isn't quite enough to sustain a healthy level of conversation in all the different interest areas, but that may change. eWorld currently charges about $9.00 a month for membership and $3.00 per hour that you're connected.

 **{Note}**

eWorld may be your most direct link to Apple Computer, Inc., and it's definitely a good place to go when you need some help. It may not be the *best* place, but don't be surprised if Apple offers some "exclusive" Macintosh tidbits that aren't available on other online services.

America Online

The second most Mac-friendly online service is America Online (AOL). AOL offers an attractive Macintosh interface that does everything "behind-the-scenes" for you (see fig. 26.2). Just enter your name and password at the start-up screen and follow the on-screen instructions. AOL's software is often shrink-wrapped with popular Macintosh magazines, and it's available free from their customer service number (1-800-827-6364).

Fig. 26.2

America Online's interface is Mac-friendly, attractive, well organized, and very marble-y.

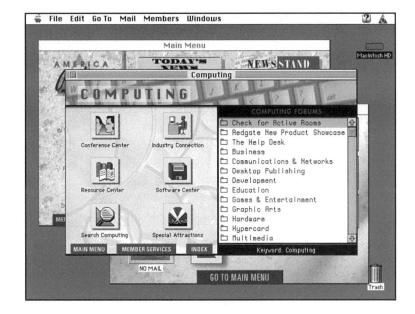

AOL is perfect for the chat-a-holic and great for some folks with strong hobbiest-type interests. If you're looking for a replacement for your *Wall Street Journal*, forget it. AOL offers basic news and financial services, but you'll want to move on to the heavy-hitters for the serious scoop on money.

 (Tip)

One of AOL's strong points is that they don't charge extra for 9600 or 14,400 bps service. Depending on where you live, AOL may be one of the cheapest "national" services for downloading files.

AOL is growing strong, with more than 1.5 million users—and more each day. That means the chat-rooms and bulletin boards get a lot of play—people send lots of messages on tons of subjects. In addition, AOL offers some nice Internet features, which, it is promised, are soon to be full access—including a graphical interface. If you'd like a quick and easy primer to the Internet, AOL is a great place to start. AOL is priced at about $10.00 a month and $2.50 an hour (after 5 free hours a month).

CompuServe

CompuServe offers two different interfaces—plain text through your communications program or the CompuServe Information Manager, which is a slightly graphical program for accessing some of CompuServe's services. CompuServe gets about a D+ on Mac-friendliness, but, then again, maybe it doesn't care.

This is definitely the service for you newspaper readers. The financial and news sections of CompuServe are unparalleled—and their exclusive guest hosts and celebrity appearances are difficult to match, too. (Although services like America Online are catching up.) CompuServe has built up vast stores of financial database information, and if you're seriously corporate about your money, it's where you should be.

 CompuServe and a few other online services offer access to some databases and information that can be overwhelmingly expensive. This can be a good thing for the independently wealthy, but a bad thing when Young Timmy gets ahold of the computer and downloads the individual prospectus of each of the S&P 500 companies.

Frankly, many people have their company or organization pay for access to CompuServe. It's not cheap. Access to the "basic services" is less than $10 a month, but those services don't go far (CompuServe plans to expand these "free" services). And CompuServe charges many different rates for many different services. By the time you read this, CompuServe will probably have lowered their rates to somewhere around $5 an hour for most bps rates. But you still need to watch out for surcharges on many of the "higher-end" features like corporate research.

But, if you need the best and the brightest for finance, news, business, and computing, CompuServe is the answer—if you can afford it.

Prodigy

Most people are a little surprised with Prodigy's interface at first—it's a bit abrasive, highly graphical, and, of all things, Prodigy has commercial messages online. Get past this, however, and it's not a bad place to hang around.

A couple million users make Prodigy interesting. There is a whole lot to chat about on Prodigy, with interest groups for nearly everything. It's a good service for "the family" with a lot of kid orientation and not a lot of ways for kids to bump up the monthly bill.

There's a decent amount of Mac-specific content online, even if the interface isn't quite as Mac-savvy as I'd like it. If any two services compete directly, it's probably America Online and Prodigy. Both offer similar features, similar users, and just about the same rates (about $10 a month and $3 an hour).

The other guys

Who's the best of the rest? Both **GEnie** ($9/month, 4 hours free then $3/hour 6pm-8 am or $6/hour 8 am-6 pm) and **Delphi** ($20/month for 20 hours, then $2/hour) are text-based services with some outstanding features, if not exactly a strong Macintosh-bias. GEnie is the "sleeper" of newspaper-style services with great financial and business resources. Delphi has nearly complete access to the Internet, although it's all text-based. Look for some graphical interfaces soon, though.

How do I connect to an online service?

Depending on the service, connecting to it may be just like installing a new application. Text-based services will require that you determine what phone numbers, account numbers, and passwords you need beforehand. Most graphical services will walk you right through it.

First, get your hands on the software. Some services may come bundled with your Mac—just find them on your hard drive and double-click. Others will require that you run an Installer program and load the software on your hard drive. Once it's up, you'll get a startup screen (see fig. 26.3).

Next, the software will probably call a main computer to find a local access number for the service. Once you have that (if one is available), your software will call the local number and get you up and running on the service. After you answer a few questions, give them a form of payment and settle on your password for the service—you're in!

Fig. 26.3
The first time you load eWorld, it starts up and automatically calls the 800 number to help you find local access.

 **<Caution>** Here's some standard online advice. Keep your user name and password written in different places (if you need to write them down). And remember that your password is the key to your monthly bill. Never give it out to anyone while you're online, no matter how official they seem.

Getting to know the locals online

Before there were PCs and Macs in offices, there were hobbyists in their garages building computers. And before there were national online services, there were hobbyists in their basements creating their own online services. And they're still there. Local bulletin board systems (BBS) have grown up around the country covering nearly any interest and every area code.

> ## Plain English, please!
>
> A **bulletin board system** can be nothing more than a computer hooked to a phone line with special software. They are often called BBSs or just boards.

These BBSs can offer you something that the national services probably never will—a feeling of community. Just like you have local news and sports programs, a local BBS can let you know what's going on in the world of computers right in your home town. Get to know people online who you could actually meet in that pub down the street or get in on the latest gathering of professionals and investors in your neck of the woods.

What is a bulletin board system?

More often than not, a BBS is run by a computer sitting in someone's house, with one or more modems that sit and wait to take calls. Using special software, this computer can automatically handle incoming calls, allowing callers with a membership password onto the service. The software then tracks the user's progress, lets them post messages and read electronic mail, and sends them any files they request to download.

BBSs can come in different sizes and shapes; and they can be completely free, require a certain amount of participation, or make you pay a regular fee. What is there to do? Depending on the BBS, there are probably message areas similar to the forums on online services, where a topic is declared and people discuss matters by exchanging electronic messages (see fig. 26.4).

Many BBSs also have online games (usually text games) where you might be able to "gamble" for extra time or just post your high score against others. Finally, many boards offer access to shareware and freeware files for downloading. Many local BBSs even offer access to Internet e-mail and discussion groups. If your interest in the Internet stops at the ability to send messages worldwide, you might find that a local BBS is the most effective (and least expensive) route you can take.

 **{Note}**

Some BBSs have upload/download ratios that work differently than national services. In order to download from this BBS, you must first upload (send to the host computer) some shareware or freeware software they don't currently have. Then you can download files given a certain ratio—like, 5 files for every 1 file you upload.

Fig. 26.4

A local BBS's different message areas. Pick your interest and dive into the conversation.

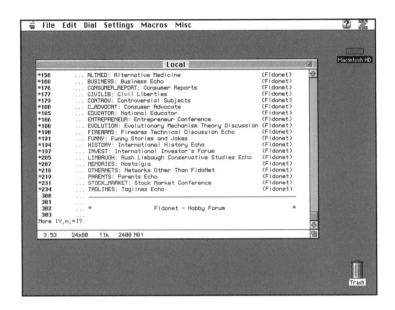

```
 File  Edit  Dial  Settings  Macros  Misc                    
                                                              Macintosh HD

                            Local
*156    ... ALTMED: Alternative Medicine              (Fidonet)
*168    ... BUSINESS: Business Echo                   (Fidonet)
*176    ... CONSUMER_REPORT: Consumer Reports         (Fidonet)
*177    ... CIVILIB: Civil Liberties                  (Fidonet)
*179    ... CONTROV: Controversial Subjects           (Fidonet)
*188    ... C_ADVOCAT: Consumer Advocate              (Fidonet)
*185    ... EDUCATOR: National Educator               (Fidonet)
*186    ... ENTREPRENEUR: Entrepreneur Conference     (Fidonet)
*188    ... EVOLUTION: Evolutionary Mechanism Theory Discussion (Fidonet)
*198    ... FIREARMS: Firearms Technical Discussion Echo (Fidonet)
*191    ... FUNNY: Funny Stories and Jokes            (Fidonet)
*194    ... HISTORY: International History Echo        (Fidonet)
*197    ... INVEST: International Investor's Forum     (Fidonet)
*205    ... LIMBAUGH: Rush Limbaugh Conservative Studies Echo (Fidonet)
*207    ... MEMORIES: Nostalgia                       (Fidonet)
*218    ... OTHERNETS: Networks Other Than FidoNet    (Fidonet)
*219    ... PARENTS: Parents Echo                     (Fidonet)
*231    ... STOCK_MARKET: Stock Market Conference     (Fidonet)
*234    ... TAGLINES: Taglines Echo                   (Fidonet)
 300    ...
 301    ...
 302    ... *                Fidonet - Hobby Forum             *
 303    ...
More [Y,n,=]?

  3:53    24x80    11k    2400 N81                                     Trash
```

How do I find BBSs?

BBSs really are everywhere, but the trick will be to find the one that has people with interests similar to yours. If you're lucky enough to have a local computer magazine, check there first. Also stop by some local computer stores and look for postings or ask the salepeople if they know of any good services.

Check your local newspaper, especially the classified ads. Ask around at church, the civic organization you belong to, or anywhere else where people share your interests—chances are these people know where to find the BBS that you'd enjoy. You might also check national publications like *BoardWatch Magazine* for BBS listings.

(Tip)

If you're really stuck, you might try asking for local phone numbers in the communications forums on America Online, eWorld, or another service.

After you've looked around, call up some of the numbers you get and request access as a guest. Most BBS hosts, or sysops, are interested computer-community souls who will be happy to help you find a BBS that meets your needs—or they may even post a listing of popular local BBSs.

Plain English, please!

Sysop is an acronym for system operator, or simply, someone who manages the user lists and files for a BBS. Generally, this person also owns the equipment and phone lines that the BBS uses.

What to look for in a BBS

As a general rule, a BBS will not be the slick, graphical whiz-bang of America Online or eWorld. It will also usually be much more tightly focused on some area of interest—from backpacking to writing. For the most part, you should look for good conversation and like-minded people—with services and forums set up to promote these ideas (see fig. 26.5).

You can also just as easily find BBSs dedicated to nothing more than swapping shareware games or hints for retail games. Some BBSs are even dedicated to networkable games, which allow two people to play against each other over phone lines.

There are a good number of BBSs dedicated to trading "adult" (X-rated) graphics files and electronic movies via modems. Most of these services make some attempt to make sure their clientele is over legal age. If you have children, or if such material offends you, be warned.

Fig. 26.5

The Manuscript, a Dallas, Texas-area BBS, is dedicated to fiction and non-fiction writers, as suggested by its discussion areas.

```
                             Local
+---The--M-A-N-U-S-C-R-I-P-T------------------------------------------+
+--------------------------------------------------------------------+
|              Message Menu                                          |
+--------------------------------------------------------------------+
| [R] General Roundabout  [F] Fiction            [N] Non-Fiction     |
| [T] Fantasy             [M] Modern Dark Fantasy [S] Science Fiction|
| [P] Poetry              [E] Editorials         [W] Writing Life    |
| [O] News on the Street  [B] Reviews                               |
+--------------------------------------------------------------------+

[-] Previous Menu
[Q] QWK Message Area
[*] Message to Sysop
[L] Length of Call
[G] Goodbye ... Logoff the System

Command: _




31:58    24x80    108k  9600 N81
```

Is it always true that you get what you pay for? Many BBSs are pay services, so approach these with care. Usually you'll get a trial period to look around the BBS and decide if you see things you like. Don't forget, too, that BBSs are generally run out of the pockets of their owners, and that donations to free BBSs generally go to improving their services. If you find a BBS you really enjoy, help to support it!

Using BBS services

The majority of local BBSs do not have their own special software; you just use the standard communications software we talked about in chapter 25. Set your software to dial the service and listen for an answer. When the host modem picks up, you should get a response on your screen telling you that you're connected. The majority of BBSs will give a short announcement as to who they are and then ask you for your name.

 **{Note}** Remember that not all BBS services are 24 hours. The polite thing to do is call the number with a handset first and make sure you hear modem tones (high-pitched squeals). Then call back with your modem.

After entering your name, the BBS will recognize you as a new user. Enter whatever information they require for access, which may include your real name, address, and home phone number. Realize that many BBSs will either automatically call your home to verify your phone number or you may get a call from the sysop to verify your number and welcome you to the BBS (see fig. 26.6).

Fig. 26.6
A typical call-back verifier program. When the BBS hangs up, type **ATA**. Then, when the phone rings, hit Return to finish the answer command. The two modems will connect and the BBS will ask you for your name and password.

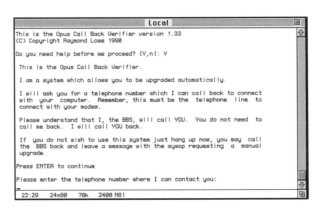

Save time and money with offline readers

We've already talked about how many BBSs and online services use compression software to make files smaller for transfer. But there is other software that makes reading messages easier and less expensive, too.

Many BBSs offer offline reading services, where, given the right command, the BBS will package all new messages on a particular subject (or written directly to you) and allow you to download them like a shareware file. Then, using special software, you can read the files while you're not connected to the service—saving any toll charges and leaving it open for others.

Since most BBSs offer saved messages (as opposed to real time "chatting"), there's no immediate reason for you to read all those messages while you're online. Just browse them for a while, make whatever responses you like, and have your software prepare a reply file for uploading.

Connect back to the BBS and use its special upload command for offline replies. Your replies are automatically inserted in the correct message areas, ready for your online buddies to read!

To and From information (it's a public message, but the discussion is between two specific people)

Here's a typical offline reader for BBS messages.

A listing of the messages I haven't yet read

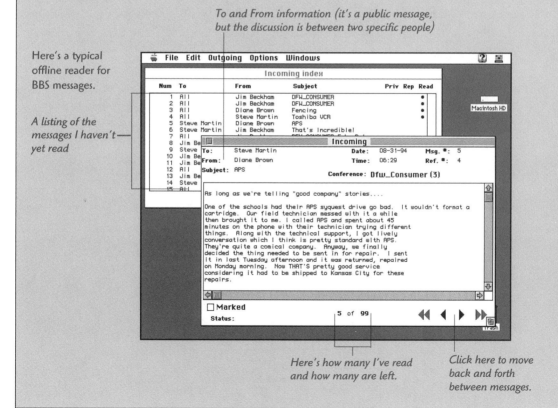

Here's how many I've read and how many are left.

Click here to move back and forth between messages.

Once you have access, you use the BBS's commands (usually by choosing a letter from a menu, like "M" to move to the message areas or "G" for Goodbye) to get around on the BBS. Take a little time to explore. Get used to the interface and see what this BBS has to offer. Pretty soon you'll be an expert. If you have trouble, most BBSs offer a quick tutorial or help with their specific commands.

27

In the Fast Lane— Using the Internet

The Internet is a lawless, uncontrolled frontier, rather like the old Wild West. If you're ready for serious online adventure, warm up your modem!

I f national online services make up the Information Superhighway, the Internet is the *fast lane*. If you've been spending most of the last year on this planet, you've probably heard something about the Internet. It's easily the fastest growing and most publicized aspect of computing in the United States.

What is the Internet?

Saying, "I'm going to use the Internet" is something like saying, "I'm going to use the international telephone system." It just doesn't mean that much. If you're making an international call, you're using the telephone system—but that doesn't really matter. What matters is who you're calling.

The same goes for the Internet. Technically, the Internet refers to the networking hardware that connects somewhere around 30 million computers around the world. The Internet is not a particular place or a particular host computer; it's information that's available from literally millions of sources. What's important, then, is not that you're going to use the Internet for the connection, but who you're going to "call."

What can the Internet do for me?

Giving your Mac access to the Internet will enable it to send and receive electronic mail messages worldwide. You can also access file transfer centers (like downloading on an online service), databases of information, and discussion groups on nearly any topic. You can play games against live opponents 24-hours a day or "chat" with other folks by sending messages back and forth. And you can browse millions of pages of information on nearly every topic known to humankind.

✱ *{Note}* — The things you do on the Internet are actually a lot like the things you can do on national online services. The difference is that there are many more people involved on the Internet, so there are a lot more people talking. Also, many services on the Internet are university, scientific, government, or otherwise nonprofit, so there's a lot of great information, but things tend to be less polished.

The quickest Internet history in history

The Internet was created in 1969 as the ARPAnet, a government experiment in secure networks that would allow military communications to continue in case of catastrophic war. In reality, the ARPAnet was used more often by scientists and researchers working for the government and universities.

In 1986, the National Science Foundation created the high-speed NFSNET to connect scientific supercomputer centers around the country. By 1991, NFSNET and other associated networks lifted their ban on commercial traffic and more and more regional networks began to connect to these government networks. Ultimately, all these interconnected computers became known as simply the Internet.

You can also use the Internet for your own personal business. Send electronic messages to clients, the folks in the office, or to your grandkids. Transfer files from your office computer to your laptop while on a business trip. With the right connection, you can even use the Internet for desktop video conferencing by using two Macs, some small video cameras, and the right software. Impressed yet?

How do I connect to the Internet?

The first thing you have to do to use your telephone is get the phone company to connect it for you. The first thing you need to do to access the Internet is decide what service you'll use. There are some trade-offs for each, but you'll probably find the right service for your circumstances.

Use an online service to connect

Are you ready for the easiest way to get Internet access? Use an online service. Nearly all the big names are offering access to the Internet or they soon will. Delphi has led the pack in text-based access with inexpensive rates and a quick and easy way to get going. America Online has taken the most graphical approach and should have a full lineup of Internet services by the time you read this. Most other online services are right behind.

 **<Caution>** Read any material your online service (like AOL) provides you concerning the Internet and its conventions and etiquette (sometimes called netiquette). The Internet, like any other community, has its own way of doing things. And people aren't afraid to barrage you with nasty electronic notes if you do things wrong.

Fig. 27.1

AOL's Internet services. They've put a graphical interface on nearly everything, making navigation a little easier for the "newbie" user.

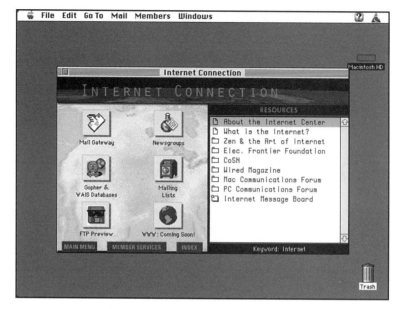

The one thing to remember with a national service is that you're being charged for every minute you spend reading messages, browsing information, and chatting on the Internet. Considering that this costs between $3 and $10 an hour (depending on the time of day and the online service), you could be talking some serious bucks. Plus, many online services do not offer full access to the Internet. You may be able to browse a few databases and work with electronic mail, but the full benefit of the Internet can only be experienced through a direct connection or a personal account.

So online services are, if nothing else, a great place to get your feet wet.

Use a direct connection

Another way to connect to the Internet is to work or go to school somewhere that already has access. In that case, you'll want to talk to your IS department or system administrator about exactly how you can start getting e-mail and access to other Internet applications on your Mac. If you're connected through your local area network, consider yourself lucky—you've got a very high-speed connection that's perfect for the latest graphical interfaces to the Net.

Get a personal Internet account

The best way to get access to the Internet from home is through a dial-up SLIP or PPP connection. Essentially, these connections allow your Mac to use its modem as a network device—almost as if you had a networking cable stretched between your computer and the Internet. A SLIP or PPP connection is limited by the speed of your modem, but otherwise, it's just like being there.

 Plain English, please!

SLIP and **PPP** are both just networking protocols specifically for connecting to the Internet over phone lines. Since you don't have Internet wiring coming into your house, you use phone lines to connect to a computer network that *does* have wiring connected to the Internet.

Think about this. The Internet is a huge, global network of computers. What's a network again? It's computers connected by wires that allow them to transfer information. Just like telephones are all connected by wires. (I'm ignoring cellular phones.) Unfortunately, you don't have Internet wiring strung along the poles outside your house (you will, soon). So, you can't just call the Internet company and have them hook you up.

The next best thing is your phone. Using a modem, you can *simulate* a network connection by using the right software (PPP or SLIP) and calling an **Internet provider**. When you call your provider, the software pretends that you're a computer connected to the provider's network, and you are free to use your own computer to roam the Internet—just as if you had a direct connection (see fig. 27.2).

My e-mail program, connected to the
Internet by modem over a PPP connection

Fig. 27.2
Using a SLIP or PPP
connection, I can run
Macintosh Internet
applications (like
Eudora) to manage
my e-mail from my
Desktop.

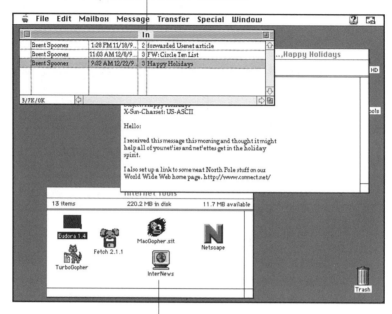

These other programs can be used to
access information on the Internet, too

Are SLIP/PPP connections too slow?

If you were directly connected to the Internet,
say, through your office's network, you'd be able
to transfer data at some absurdly fast rate—*ideally*
around 10 megabits (10,000,000 bits) per second
(although the distance and limitations of the
Internet would slow that down considerably).
Connected over a phone line, you transfer data
at somewhere around 14.4 kilobits (14,400 bits)
or 28.8 kilobits (28,800 bits) per second. Much
slower. (By the way, 8 bits make a byte—so, 1
megabyte takes about 280 seconds to transfer at
28.8 kilobits per second, or roughly 5 minutes.)

It's kind of like those "town meetings" the Pres-
ident is always having. He's on a big TV screen

and it's a little like he's there—but he can't see
and hear everything that goes on. A SLIP/PPP
connection gives you full access to the Internet,
but at the cost of speed.

At 2400 or 9600 bps, things are way too slow. But
at 14.4 Kbps or 28.8 Kbps (most new modems),
the Internet becomes tolerable. In fact, the only
thing that remains slow is transferring files and
graphics, and you don't always do that on the
Internet. With a SLIP/PPP connection, you can
do everything someone with a regular connection
can—it just takes a little time.

How to find an Internet provider

An Internet provider is usually a company that has high-speed data lines and a bank of computers and modems in their building. You subscribe to their service and they allow you to call up and use your SLIP/PPP connection to become part of their network. (Almost like you plugged your computer in at their building.) With this access you can use your own Internet programs to get e-mail, download files, and browse information.

Ask around for the best Internet provider. Stop by your local computer stores and user groups or ask the computer guru in your office. You want a quality provider who isn't overburdened with users. Generally you pay a flat amount per month for unlimited access—but if you get a busy signal every time you call, this won't seem worth it.

 **⊗<Caution>**

For the most part, you want to avoid "dial-up" or "terminal" accounts to the Internet. This sounds a lot like a SLIP/PPP account, but it's not. Usually when you dial up, you use a communications program to connect to a host computer. Then you use the host computer to access the Internet. The problem is that you can't use your own Internet software—and you usually get stuck using cryptic UNIX or DOS commands to get around!

How to set up the software and test your connection

When you find the right Internet provider, chances are they'll be able to help you get your Mac ready to connect to their specific service. In general, there are a couple things you'll need to do.

First you need MacTCP. **MacTCP** is a Control Panel that tells your Mac that you want to connect to another computer using TCP protocols (see fig. 27.3). Just drag and drop the icon on your System Folder icon to install it. Like any other Control Panel, you can just drop MacTCP on the System Folder to install it.

Plain English, please!

MacTCP lets your Mac speak the "language" of the Internet. It makes it compatible with the computer language that Internet computers use to talk to one another. MacTCP comes with System 7.5 and is available from a number of sources for free if you have earlier system software (check online services and Mac user groups). PPP and SLIP are special Control Panels that allow a MacTCP connection to be made over phone lines. **"**

Fig. 27.3
MacTCP looks a little like the Chooser. I could use MacTCP to network two Macs together, just like LocalTalk. Here I've selected a PPP (modem) connection.

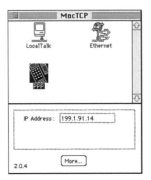

To use a PPP or SLIP connection, you need either the PPP Control Panel or the SLIP Control Panel loaded in your Control Panels folder. Since PPP/SLIP is the control panel that actually starts up your modem and calls your Internet provider, you'll need to enter all the correct codes and phone numbers (you'll need to ask your Internet provider for this information).

⊛ {Note} You only need one or the other—either PPP or SLIP. Each is a slightly different way to connect. You may want to discuss which is better for you with your Internet provider.

Fig. 27.4
My Config PPP Control Panel. Some of this can get pretty cryptic, so make sure your Internet provider gives you good instructions.

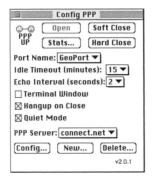

When you've got everything configured, you can use your PPP/SLIP Control Panel to test the connection. In figure 27.4, I've clicked on the Open button to connect to my Internet provider. If everything works, I'll get the PPP UP message.

Generally, you don't have to go through this step to connect to your provider. Whenever you start an Internet application, it will look for a MacTCP network connection. MacTCP, in turn, will tell PPP or SLIP to call the provider and try to connect.

What can I do with my Internet connection?

Here's the real advantage in a direct or SLIP/PPP connection to the Internet. You can use Macintosh applications to do stuff on the Internet! It used to be that you would use a communications program to call an Internet computer and use cryptic UNIX commands to fumble around the Internet. But now it's as easy as double-clicking!

 {Note}

I'm about to introduce you to a bunch of applications you can use to access different parts of the Internet. Most of these are available online or through user groups. There are also tons of books available on the Internet and many include free versions of this software.

Send and receive mail

Usually your Internet provider (or your company if you have a direct connection) will have a computer called a **mail server** that knows your e-mail address on the Internet. To get your Internet e-mail, you need a program like Eudora (see fig. 27.5). When you start Eudora, it checks the provider's mail server to see if anyone's sent you any mail. If they have, you can read it and answer it or send mail to others.

Plain English, please!

E-mail stands for electronic mail. To send e-mail over the Internet, you must know the recipient's correct e-mail address.

The first thing you should know about your e-mail account is your Internet mail address. Usually it will be something like your name, followed by the @ symbol, the name of your Internet provider, a . (period), and the type of organization your provider is.

For instance, I have two Internet e-mail addresses. One is *TStauffer@aol.com* (America Online is a commercial entity, so it gets a "com" at the end of the address); and the other is *stauffer@connect.net* (Connect is my Internet provider's name, and "net" is the type of organization it is—a network provider). You'll also see addresses with "gov" for government, "edu" for educational facility, and "mil" for a military facility. If there is an additional period and more letters, that is an international address (".FR" for France, for instance).

Fig. 27.5
Eudora is a popular Internet e-mail program for the Macintosh. It allows you to view and answer mail sent to your Internet address. If you have an Internet connection at work you may receive your Internet mail through MS Mail or cc:Mail.

Mail I've received   *Reading a mail message*

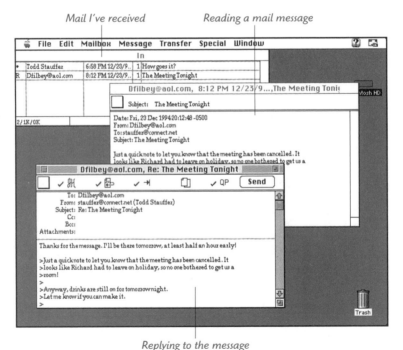

Replying to the message

When you read an Internet address aloud, it goes like this. *TStauffer@aol.com* would be read:

TStauffer *at* a-o-l *dot* com

Just say "at" when you see "@," and "dot" when you see ".", and everybody'll think you're a hip Netter.

Participate in discussion groups

I've never really been completely sure why UseNet groups are called "newsgroups," since these are actually the forums or bulletin boards of the Internet. This is where all the discussions are on just about every topic imaginable. In fact, UseNet newsgroups are a lot like local BBSs or forums on AOL or CompuServe, except for one thing. They're HUGE! Millions of people read and respond to UseNet messages everyday.

Before you head for the newsgroups, it's important to know a little "netiquette." Never type messages in all capital letters. IT'S CONSIDERED SCREAMING! Also, post messages in the appropriate groups. Random "Help me..." messages will get you a lot of not-so-nice e-mail messages sometimes called "flames."

Using UseNet newsgroups is easy—you just need a newsreader application, such as InterNews (see fig. 27.6).

UseNet newsgroups are message areas that cover a wide variety of topics. Messages are entered to begin a new subject and then others chime in with their replies. This creates a message **thread**, which means the same idea or topic is discussed from response to response. Most newsreader programs are designed to notice these threads so that you can follow a particular conversation.

Fig. 27.6

The InterNews application lets me read the UseNet messages from start to finish in whatever topic areas I choose.

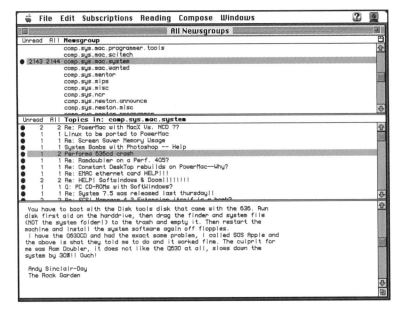

The different topic areas are broken out by main interest and then more specific interests. For instance, **comp.os.mac** is a newsgroup that falls in the main category "Computers," the subcategory "Operating Systems," and a further subcategory "Macintosh." Here you should find discussion concerning the System software for the Macintosh.

Transfer files over the Internet

The **File Transfer Protocol** (**FTP**) is the standard protocol for transferring files over the Internet. How can you do this? With a program like Fetch (see fig. 27.7), an FTP application for the Macintosh.

The real joy in FTP are all the anonymous FTP sites that you can find on the Internet. These are computers dedicated to allowing just about anyone to download shareware, freeware, and other files to their own computers. Fetch even comes with a few anonymous sites built-in. You can add more as you find them.

 *{Note}*

Although your user name for an anonymous FTP login is "anonymous," proper netiquette dictates that you send your e-mail address as your password. (Anonymous FTP doesn't actually require any password.)

Click here to send a file

Fig. 27.7
Using Fetch to down-
load files over the
Internet.

*This pop-up menu lets
you change directory
levels*

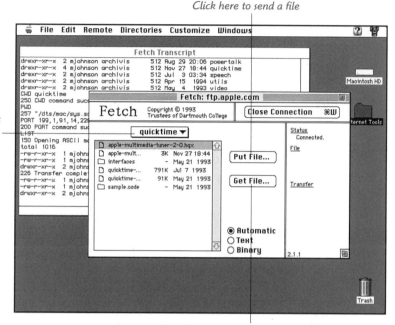

Click here to receive the highlighted file

Fetch is pretty simple. After you open a connection to the Internet, browse
through their file directories until you find what you want. (File directories
are like looking at list views in the Finder. Just double-click on a folder to see
its contents.) When you find a file you'd like to download, highlight it and
click on Get. If you'd like to send a file, click on Put and tell Fetch what file
you're sending.

> Many popular FTP sites are actually working university or business computers.
> During office hours, outside connections may be limited. You'll always have
> better luck downloading files later in the evening and at night.

Use Telnet for specific connections

Remember when we discussed terminal emulation in chapter 26? Well, on
the Internet, you may occasionally want to connect to public Internet BBS
computers, just like you connect to a BBS computer with a modem. Or, you
might want to connect to a computer at your work or school to get some
stuff done. You do this with a **Telnet session**.

You'll probably only Telnet to computers that you have a user account on unless they allow anonymous connections. If you're connecting to a work-related computer, make sure you have the appropriate user name and password for the system.

Burrow for information with Gopher

Another reason many people want access to the Internet is all the information you have access to. **Gopher servers** let you "burrow" under the Internet, looking for neat and interesting things. If you'd like to get lost for a few days traveling around to the world's Gopher servers, get a program like TurboGopher (see fig. 27.8).

Universities, businesses, and government offices around the country offer Gopher server computers that place information out on the network for you to browse. Everything is very menu-driven. To choose an option, just double-click on it in your TurboGopher menu. This will move you from topic to topic and occasionally from computer to computer. That's the magic of the Internet, it doesn't matter where the computer is. If one computer is linked to the other, you just move along.

If you don't want to worry about a Gopher application, just stick to Mosaic or Netscape (the World Wide Web browser programs). These applications can read Gopher server info, too.

Gopher is a great way to get down and dirty with Internet information. It's been around for a while, and a lot of organizations have Gopher servers just waiting for you to use. So explore!

Fig. 27.8

Here's TurboGopher in action. Right now I'm checking out the job listings at Texas A&M University!

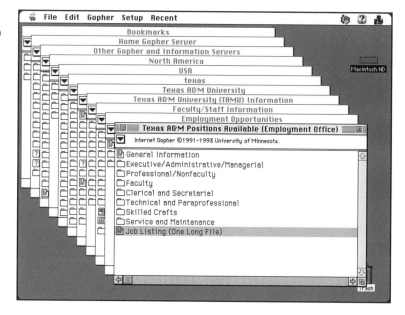

Navigate the Internet the easy way

One of the most exciting developments on the Internet recently has been the exploding popularity of the **World Wide Web** (WWW). This makes a lot of sense. The WWW is the most graphical of Internet services; and it's an exciting way to be introduced to the Internet. WWW applications are also often capable of a number of other functions—like dealing with Telnet, FTP, and Gopher info. What does this mean to you? If you get any single Internet application, get a WWW browser.

The two most popular browsers are Mosaic and Netscape. Mosaic is freeware, Netscape is shareware (around $35 to register for individuals, $100 for business users, and free to educational/government users) and both allow you to see the Internet in all its glory (see fig. 27.9).

Fig. 27.9

Netscape is a great way to browse (or "surf") the World Wide Web. Just click on a link to move to a new page.

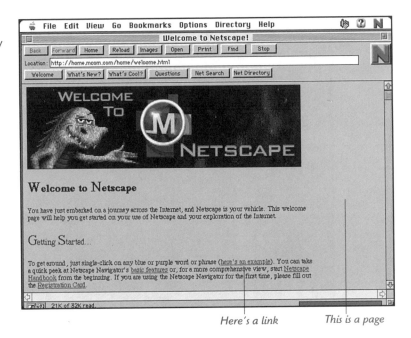

Here's a link   *This is a page*

Here's how the World Wide Web works. Each screen you see in Netscape or Mosaic is called a **page**. On this page are a number of **links** to other pages. In fact, it's the hypertext concept we talked about in chapter 9. You read along the page until you find something that interests you. Then you simply click on the word to move to another page.

Pages can be anywhere—on another hard drive on another computer or even in another country. That's why it's a *web*. The hypertext pages allow WWW writers to weave their pages in and out of other people's information all around the world.

What's made the WWW so popular, though, are its multimedia aspects. Unlike most other Internet services, the WWW has the capability to transfer graphics and formatted text as well as just plain textual information (see fig. 27.10). You have to have a special program to view things, but this graphical approach makes things much more enjoyable.

Fig. 27.10

The WWW and its browser programs allow it to display graphics and formatted text. It can even send QuickTime movies and sound files to your Mac!

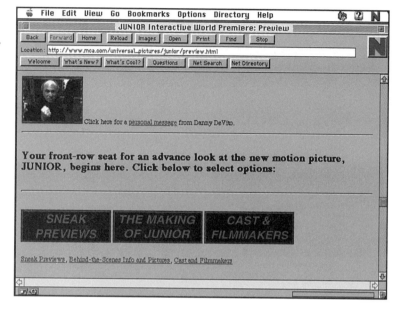

Each individual page can be set up to give you whatever information you like. Some people equate this to setting up your billboard on the Information Superhighway. With the right software, companies can advertise their wares, show you pictures, movies, and play sounds of their products, and even take credit card orders! Suddenly it's clear why people think the WWW may be the future of the Internet. It makes money for people!

(Tip)

Try this out. Think of a company you'd like information from. Then, type its WWW address into the Mosaic or Netscape's address window (usually at the top of the browser window). How do you get the WWW address? Just guess. Try "www.(company name).com". Here's your first one: www.apple.com.

Part VIII

Keep Your Mac Smiling

28
Inside the System Folder

Understand what all that
stuff in the System Folder
does, and you're well on
your way to becoming a
Mac guru!

In this chapter:

- What's an extension and how do I use it?
- Using the Extensions Manager
- Managing Control Panels
- What's all this other stuff in the System Folder?

A t the heart of every Macintosh's System software is a little folder called the System Folder. This is where a lot of decisions are made. Throughout this book we've used Control Panels, the Font folder, and the System File to make changes in the appearance and functionality of our Macintosh.

Those changes may have been enough for you to get started. There's a lot you can do to enhance your Mac's appearance and performance—and most of that is done in the System Folder. Learn a little more about how things work on your Mac and you'll be better able to troubleshoot problems, too.

? Q&A

I can't seem to move, copy, or delete anything in the System Folder. Why?

You probably have the System Folder protected in the General Controls (System 7.5 and System 7.1p for Performa models). When the System Folder is protected, everything is automatically locked to keep you (or children, more likely) from accidentally deleting things.

What is an extension?

An extension is a small program that is loaded when the System software starts up. After you see the Happy Mac and the Welcome to Macintosh boxes, you'll see some little icons flashing across the bottom of the screen. These are extensions being loaded.

 Plain English, please!

> **Extensions**, sometimes called **inits**, are just small computer code files designed to increase your Mac's capabilities to deal with the things you plug into the back of it or the software you're running.

An extension literally *extends* the capabilities of your Macintosh. At its most basic, the System software knows how to do certain things—like draw text on a standard screen, display fonts, and move windows around. Other functions though, like connecting to your specific brand of modem or printer, require extensions to the System software (see fig. 28.1). These little snippets of computer language code tell the System software what it needs to know to deal with your particular computer.

Fig. 28.1
Here are a couple of the extensions I have in my Extensions folder. Notice the names of these files; they have very specific purposes that customize the System software for my Macintosh.

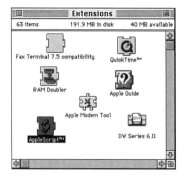

Managing your extensions

Extensions can be added to your Extensions folder in a number of ways. To add an extension yourself, drag and drop an extension file to the System Folder icon, and the System software will automatically recognize it as an extension and place it in the Extensions folder.

 **<Caution>** If you drag and drop an extension to install it, make sure you drop it on the System Folder's *icon*...not its open window. Dropping it in the window will not automatically place it in the correct folder.

But extensions get added by other programs, too. Many application Installer programs will add extensions to your Mac. The Installer program for my printer, for example, added extensions that allow the System software to send data to the printer, allow the printer to appear in the Chooser, and so on. Many applications (even word processing and spreadsheet programs) add their own extensions, too.

The problem is, these extensions take up RAM. The more extensions you have with your System software, the less RAM you'll have available for your programs. So, you'll want to manage your extensions to get the most out of each of your applications.

That's why the Extensions Manager was included with System 7.5. The **Extensions Manager** is a Control Panel that allows you to see every extension (and Control Panel) that's currently being loaded to determine if they're all necessary (see fig. 28.2). It also allows you to create custom "startup scenarios" with different extensions marked for loading, depending on what you want to do.

Fig. 28.2
The System 7.5 Extensions Manager makes dealing with your system files easier. If there's a check mark next to an extension, it'll load.

Click to "check" an extension for loading

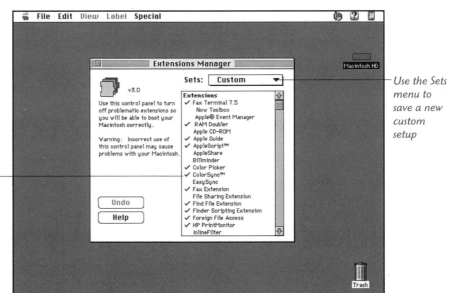

Use the Sets menu to save a new custom setup

 **{Note}** If you're using pre-version 7.5 System software, you can usually find shareware Extensions Manager software on online services. Also, Now Utilities (discussed in chapter 12) includes a very nice Extensions Manager Control Panel.

To determine whether an extension will load the next time you turn on or restart your Mac, click once just to the left of its name. This will place a little checkmark next to the extension name. When you restart, that extension will load automatically.

You can also save sets of extensions by pulling down the **Sets** selector menu and choosing the **Save Set...** commands. Name it something meaningful like "Standard Plus Modem" or "No Network Files" and you'll be able to load the minimum extensions you need to get a particular task done. This is especially useful when you have a limited amount of RAM.

Fixing extension conflicts

Occasionally your Mac will choke on an extension. Sometimes this happens because you don't have the equipment the extension is designed for, and sometimes it happens because it just isn't happy being loaded with another extension. These are **extension conflicts**. To deal with them, you need to spend a little time sitting in front of your Macintosh and restarting.

How to tell if an extension isn't working

The first sign of an ill-behaved extension is a big X through its icon on the `Welcome to Macintosh` screen. This won't tell you why an extension isn't working—only that it isn't. To figure out why, you'll need to experiment with your Extensions Manager.

> ### My Mac can't get all the way to the Finder—it freezes while loading an extension. What should I do?
>
> You can do two things. First, try restarting your Mac manually (some Macs have a Restart button; others use the key combination Ctrl+Command+Power Key on the keyboard). Now, hold down the space bar through the Happy Mac and `Welcome to Macintosh` screens. The Extensions Manager should appear. Choose the **System 7.5 Only** set from the Set menu and restart. Then troubleshoot as described below. If you can't get the Extensions Manager to appear, hold down the Shift key when you restart. Your Mac will load with *no extensions* and you can edit your setup manually (see sidebar below).

Isolating the conflict

With the Extensions Manager open, choose the **System 7.5 Only** set from the Sets menu and go and put a check next to the extension that was Xed out. Now, restart your Mac. Does the extension still not work? Then it's either incompatible with System 7.5 extensions (get rid of it) or you're having a problem with your hardware. Check your port connections and try again.

If it did load correctly, you have a problem with another extension. This could take some time. What you need to do is go through your list of extensions, adding one at a time and restarting. When that extension icon is Xed on the `Welcome to Macintosh` screen, you'll know that the last extension you loaded is probably the conflict.

> Some extension management software, like Now Utilities, helps you isolate bad extensions with a little less pain. You may want to look into one of these if you're having a lot of trouble.

What do I do with a bad extension?

My best advice is: Make sure you need the extension. Look at the extension it's conflicting with—do they have similar purposes? Are you loading two CD-ROM extensions or two different Network Extensions? If so, figure out which one you need and deselect the other one.

Managing without an Extensions Manager

You don't have to have an Extensions Manager to work with your extensions. In fact, System 7.5 is the first System software to include it.

Here's the key. Your System software loads an extension if it is *in the Extensions folder or the System Folder.* So, if you don't want an extension to load, create a new folder and put your unwanted extensions in it.

I like to create another folder in the System Folder called "Extensions (disabled)". This allows

me to drag and drop an extension from the Extensions folder to this new folder, thus keeping it from loading (see accompanying figure). You can call your new folder anything you want ("Bad Extensions," "Extensions I Hate").

Incidentally, the "Extensions (disabled)" folder is automatically created if you are using the Extensions Manager. All the Manager actually does is move files in and out of the Extensions folder according to what you've checked. It just has a pretty way of doing it!

Just drag and drop offending extensions on your "disabled" folder.

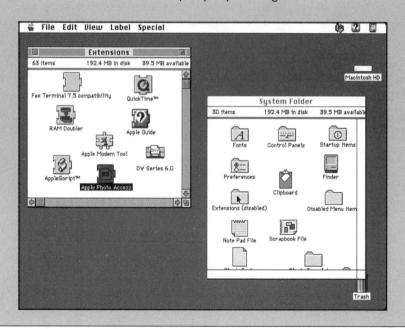

If things are more complicated than that, I suggest either calling the company that wrote the offending extension or looking around for people who've had the same problem online, your local Mac User Group, or computer store.

> Need to figure out what company wrote an extension? Use the Finder to get to the extension in your Extensions folder. Select the extension's icon and use the Finder's Get Info... command in the File menu. Look for the company's name and copyright on the "Version" line.

How do Control Panels work?

The major difference between a Control Panel and an extension is this: a Control Panel gives you options. An extension is something like QuickTime, which just gives your Mac new capabilities. A Control Panel may give your Mac new capabilities, too, but it also gives you the ability to change settings on your Macintosh. We've talked a lot about Control Panels throughout this book—they're what we used to change the Desktop pattern and the Finder's Label menu, for instance.

How do I add Control Panels?

Again, the easiest way to add a Control Panel is by dragging and dropping it onto the System Folder icon. It will automatically be put in the Control Panels folder. Also, be aware that Installer programs can add Control Panels, too—especially customizing applications like Now Utilities or disk fixing software like Norton Utilities.

How do I manage Control Panels?

You can manage your Control Panels just like you manage your extensions—with the Extensions Manager. Scroll down the list of extensions in the Manager's window, and you'll eventually get to a new heading—Control Panels (see fig. 28.3). Just use the same checkmarks to enable or disable Control Panels.

Fig. 28.3
You can also use the
Extensions Manager
to turn your Control
Panels on and off.

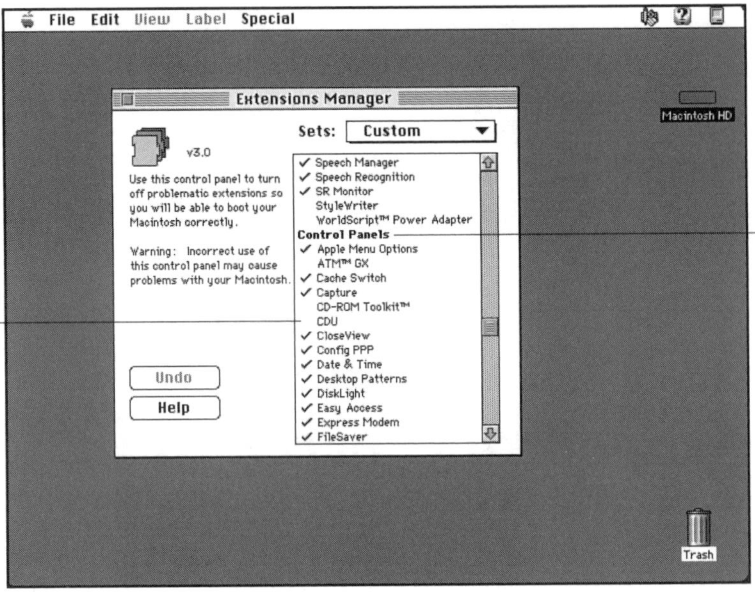

Click to enable or
disable Control
Panels

The Control
Panels listing

Why would you want to disable a Control Panel? Generally you'd do this
because Control Panels take up RAM, and you can get more for your applications by disabling the Control Panels you don't use. Also, you can have
Control Panel conflict just like you can have extension conflict. You troubleshoot them the same way, too.

(Tip)

You can manually manage your Control Panels the same way you do extensions, by creating a "Control Panels (disabled)" folder and dragging and
dropping unwanted Control Panels into this new folder.

What is all this other stuff?

The System Folder is basically a repository for all the files that aren't applications or documents designed for you to use. The other stuff in the typical
System Folder includes the Preferences folder, Startup Items folder, Fonts
folder, the Apple Menu Items folder, the Scrapbook file, the System File, the
Finder, the Note Pad file, and the Clipboard file.

Your application preferences

This folder should contain most of the files that your applications use to save the way you like to do things. Some of these files hold the actual settings you select (in Microsoft Word, for instance, you can choose whether or not to use the toolbar and what your default font will be) or just information the application needs to know about your system.

For the most part, you don't need to worry about these Preference files. Except...you don't need Preference files for programs you've thrown away. Some programs come with an Uninstall program that will delete Preference files automatically. But, most don't (see fig. 28.4).

Fig. 28.4

Most applications keep settings and other information in the Preferences folder, but you can toss out preferences for applications you've deleted.

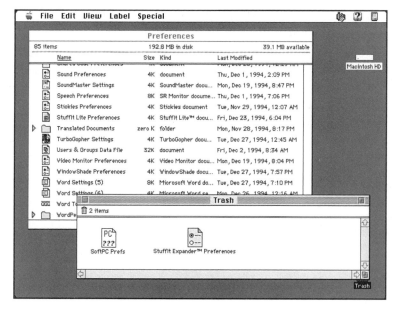

It's a good idea to check your Preferences folder every once in a while to see if you're wasting disk space by holding onto files that belong to applications you've long since thrown out. If you find any, you can toss them in the Trash.

Q&A

What if I throw out a Preferences file for an application I'm still using?

Try starting the application. More than likely that application can create another one, but you will lose any custom changes you've made to that application's appearance. If the application won't load, you may have to reinstall it from its floppy disks.

The Startup (and Shutdown) folder

Put something in the Startup folder and it starts—as if it were double-clicked—when your Mac is turned on or restarted. You can put nearly anything in here—a document, System 7 sound file, QuickTime movie, an application, or an alias—and it will start up with your Mac (see fig. 28.5).

 **{Note}**

If you can't normally double-click a file, it won't work in the Startup folder, either. Extensions, for instance, should always go in the Extensions folder.

Fig. 28.5
A typical Startup folder. Anything in here will start up automatically when you turn on your Mac.

Is this useful? If you use the same programs every time you use your Mac, then, yes. System 7.5 Stickies, for instance, is a great program to put in the Startup folder. So is Microsoft Word, if you always use it. If you have a PIM program or calendar you always like to have open, put it in here as well.

 (Tip)

You can stop your Mac from loading Startup items by holding down the Shift key *after* your Mac loads all its extensions and Control Panels. (Begin holding it down right as the Welcome to Macintosh screen and all your extension icons disappear.)

System 7.5 also adds a new Shutdown folder that lets you do the same thing as the Startup file whenever you shut down your Mac. What is this good for? If you have an anti-virus program, disk-fix utility, or something similar that you'd like to run every time you end a session, you can put it in this folder and it will run automatically. It's also a good place to put a System 7.5 sound that says something like "See ya later!"

The Fonts folder

We discussed this one in-depth in chapter 19, but there are a few essential things to remember. In System 7.1 and above, all your fonts go in the Fonts folder. (Before System 7.1, you install fonts by dragging and dropping them on the System file.) But, you can only have 128 items in the Font folder, so use suitcase folders to hold fonts that are similar. Also, you want to avoid having TrueType and PostScript fonts with the same name in your Fonts folder.

The Apple Menu Items folder

You can put just about any icon in the Apple Menu Items folder and it will appear as a selection on your Apple menu. Plus, with the hierarchical menus of System 7.5, you can use folders to represent another level of hierarchy in the Apple menu. (See chapter 9 for more on using and organizing your Apple menu.)

The Scrapbook file

Remember the Scrapbook program in your Apple menu? It's a neat little program that lets you store pictures, text, QuickTime movies, and anything else you can copy and paste to and from your applications. It's a great place to put stuff that you'd like to share between applications or that you just want to store away for safekeeping.

Well, the file where all that is stored is the Scrapbook file in the System Folder. You can't really do much with it—double-click it and it automatically starts the Scrapbook program. You can, however, see how much disk space the Scrapbook file is using with the Get Info... command or by selecting one of the Finder's list views (see fig. 28.6).

Fig. 28.6
Using the Get Info...
command tells me how
much space I'm using
for the Scrapbook file—
just in case I'm running
a little low on hard
drive space and need
to get rid of some-
thing.

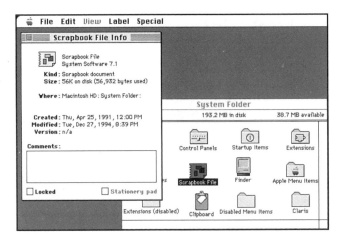

The Clipboard file

Here's another neat one. Every time you cut or copy something in your application, you're actually sending it to the Mac's Clipboard. That's interesting, but where is the Clipboard? It's a file in your System Folder.

You can view the Clipboard's contents by double-clicking the Clipboard file in your System folder. Up pops the last thing you cut or copied. If you want, you can make an alias of the Clipboard file and drop it in your Apple Menu Items folder. Whenever you want to view the Clipboard's contents, just pull down the Apple menu and select Clipboard alias (or whatever you rename it to).

You can also view the Clipboard by selecting the Show Clipboard command from the Finder's (and some other applications') Edit menu.

Keeping Your Mac Happy

Bombs, freezes, strange sounds, and Sad Macs: this is not fun stuff but you need to know what to do next.

In this chapter:

- My Mac's getting slower. What's the problem?
- Prevention is always better than a cure
- It won't work. What's the cure?

Hopefully you won't ever need to worry about Sad Macs, bombs, and freezes. But, even if your Mac doesn't meet with catastrophic problems, there are some things you should know about prevention that can keep your Mac clicking along nicely. And if you ever do encounter some out-of-the-ordinary problem, there are some steps you can take on your own to cure your Mac before taking it back to the service center.

Why is my Mac slowing down?

We've talked before about your Macintosh-based filing system—how you arrange your folders and icons to get work done. Your Mac also has an internal filing system—how it keeps track of your folders and icons. This is the nitty-gritty, technical, behind-the-scenes way that your Mac deals with data. What Mac does is keep a database of information about all the files you save and where it put them on the hard drive. Sometimes, if this filing system gets confused, it can slow down your Mac.

This database, called the **Desktop file**, is a little like a city map for your Mac's hard drive. Whenever you double-click an icon, Mac looks up that file's location in the Desktop file and tells the hard drive where to find it. The hard drive finds the data on its disks and sends it back to Mac's RAM so that you can use it.

In System 7 and above, the Desktop file is actually two hidden files on your Mac's hard drive. You can't normally see these without a special utility program—but they're there.

Your desktop file may be getting too big

The most common cause of a Macintosh slow-down is a bloated Desktop file. Over time, the Desktop file gets used a lot. Files get added and deleted, icons and other information get shuffled around, and the Desktop file keeps getting bigger. Eventually, every time you double-click an icon it has to search a large file (that map of your hard drive) to find the information—thus slowing down your Mac. The Desktop file can also slow down startups and shutdowns.

The Desktop file is where icons and other information about your programs are stored. If you suddenly start to see different or generic icons for your applications or documents, you know your Desktop file is messed up.

To fix this problem, you have to tell your Mac to rebuild its Desktop file. You do this by restarting your Mac and holding down Option+⌘ all the way through the `Welcome to Macintosh` screen until Mac asks you if you want to rebuild the Desktop file. Click on OK and it will re-create the Desktop file by taking a quick look at the hard drive to see where everything is, storing the correct information and doing away with old or bad Desktop data.

Rebuilding the Desktop is generally safe, although it does have one unfortunate drawback. It deletes any notes you've entered in a file's Get Info box.

Q&A _____

My Mac gets to the end of rebuilding the Desktop file and starts over. What should I do?

You've probably got worse problems than just a bad Desktop file. You need to use a disk fixing program, like Norton Utilities' Disk Doctor, to fix your disk. Then rebuild again.

Your files may be fragmenting

When your Mac saves a file to the hard drive, it does its best to save that file *contiguously*, or, all in one spot. If it can, it will find a large enough space on the hard drive to simply drop the whole file in so that, when you double-click on that file's icon, it just has to look in one place and it can quickly send the file to RAM. It's a little like laying ceramic tile on a floor. You lay one row of tiles all in a neat, straight line. Then you lay another row right next to it, and so on, until you cover the floor. That's what Mac tries to do with files on your hard drive.

Unfortunately, every time you delete a file, you're picking up one of those tiles—leaving a small hole in your neat little system. Over time, a Mac's hard drive looks less like a tile bathroom floor and more like an old tile mosaic—with little holes where files used to be.

Now when your Mac goes to save a file, it tries to fill in these gaps. If the gap is too small for your file, the file has to be split up and put in two or more of these gaps. Suddenly, you're saving files that are **fragmented**, or spread out all over the hard drive.

You'll need a special utility program to defragment your Mac's hard drive (see fig. 29.1). What this program does is determine the best way to pick up your file fragments and lay them back down in a contiguous pattern. Not only does this keep your Mac moving quickly, but it also makes your files less likely to be corrupted.

Plain English, please!

A **corrupted** file is generally a file that has had part of its data mixed or confused with data from another file, making it either garbled or impossible to use.

Fig. 29.1
Norton Utilities is a great program for defragmenting your Mac's hard drive.

A "mosaic" representation of my files

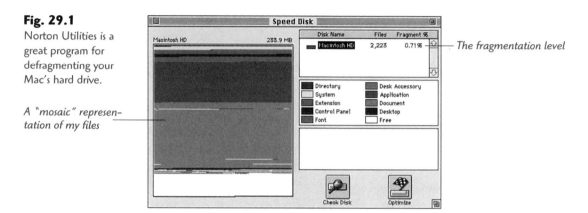

The fragmentation level

Preventive health care for your Mac

In order to defragment files and do a number of other things to keep your Macintosh healthy, it's a good idea to buy a copy of Norton Utilities or a similar program to take care of these little ailments. Generally these software products are actually packages of smaller programs, each with a particular task.

If you'd like to avoid spending the big money on Norton Utilities or a similar software title, look for shareware programs on your favorite online service. Just remember that a poorly written utility can do more harm than good—check around and see what other folks online or in your user group recommend.

Optimize your hard drive

Optimizing your hard drive goes hand in hand with defragmenting. When a utility like Norton's Speed Disk optimizes your drive, it's actually putting your files in order on the hard drive so that they are (1) more readily available to your Mac, and (2) less likely to become fragmented. For instance, by putting all your applications in one place (because you're less likely to delete applications) a program can make fragmentation less likely.

Recover files you've Trashed

Ever feel like picking up everything in your office or living room and just tossing it all in the dumpster? This happens to a lot of Mac users with their files. One day they wake up, look at their Macintosh HD window, and realize they've used up hundreds of megabytes on their hard drive. Then they go completely nuts deleting things.

And then they realize they've thrown away their presentation to the Board. Uh, oh.

With just you and Mac, there's no way to get that file back. But some clever utility programs, including one that comes with Norton Utilities, enables you to recover files you've thrown away (see fig. 29.2).

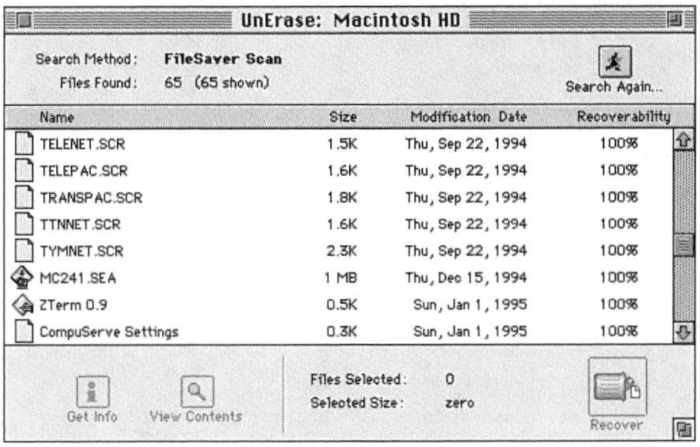

Fig. 29.2
Here's Norton's Undelete, which lets you get back files you've accidentally Trashed.

The trick is that when you Trash a file, it's not actually deleted from your hard drive. Instead, Mac just makes a mental note to itself that it's now okay to overwrite that file with the next one that comes along. So, for a while anyway, the file is still there on the hard drive. With the right utility, you can get it back.

(Tip) _____ | Some undelete programs can run all the time and keep their own database of your files. That way, even if a file is fragmented or otherwise difficult to find, you've got another way to search for it, and you're more likely to be able to undelete it.

When you need to delete a file forever

The flip-side of undelete is often called wiping files. Because your Mac doesn't actually delete files when they're Trashed, it's possible for you to recover them. Right?

Well, it's also possible for other people to recover them. Maybe this is a little cloak-and-dagger, but it's perfectly possible for your IS department to rummage through your Mac, undeleting all those embarrassing resumes and cover letters you've been generating in your "after 5" job search.

If you want to make sure they can't get at them (or, if you need to securely delete any other sensitive documents), you need a file wiping utility. Again, there's one with Norton utilities and with some other software packages.

Most file wiping utilities simply overwrite the sensitive file with random data. This effectively keeps anyone from being able to recover the file and read its contents.

Norton's Wipe Info program lets me wipe files, folders, or entire sections of my hard drive.

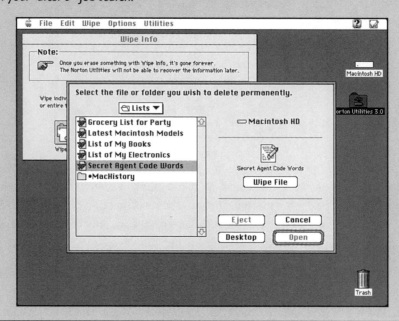

Why can't my undelete utility recover my file?

You won't like this. It's been too long since you Trashed the file and it's been overwritten with a new one. As far as I know, you're stuck. You'll have to re-create that document, if you can.

 Just to be completely clear, realize that using a file wiping utility makes it *absolutely impossible* for you to recover a deleted file.

Disk doctors and the sick Mac

The Mac is generally a fairly maintenance-free machine—some of this stems from the fact that much of the software and all the hardware for a Mac is designed by one company, Apple. But, occasionally you will have problems. Most of these are easy enough to resolve—and, hopefully, not nearly as scary as they may seem.

(Tip) The best defense against an ailing Mac is to back up your important documents to a floppy disk or some other media. You'll especially appreciate this tip if your Mac ever gets sick.

How to diagnose a sick Mac

The most important part of diagnosing a sick Macintosh is isolating the problem. You need to start by deciding if the problem seems to be disk-related, software-related, or a problem with your Mac's actual hardware. How do you do this? Here are some tips:

- *Is RAM my problem?* The actual RAM chips inside your computer may not be properly installed if you get a Sad Mac icon when you start up your Mac. The Sad Mac may also mean you've got a problem with other internal computer chips. (This should only happen if you've recently installed some chips, though.)

- *Is it a bad extension?* If your `Welcome to Macintosh` screen shows X-ed out icons or if it freezes while loading an extension program, software may be your problem. Extensions and Control Panels are usually the first culprit when you can't get a printer or CD-ROM drive to work, too.

- *Is my disk bad?* If you get the "Disk ?" icon when you start up your Mac, you may be having problems with your hard drive or the System Folder files. You may also be having disk problems if your System seems to move slowly or if you have trouble opening documents or applications.

- *Is it my applications?* Always check to make sure that your software is compatible with System 7 and above. Some software will have conflicts with other programs, so if you load a new application and start having problems, you may need to check its documentation for known incompatibilities.

 **<Caution>** If a *floppy* disk is bad, your Mac will often report that it is unreadable and ask you if you want to initialize it. Remember that initializing a disk erases everything—that's not what you want to do if you have important files on that disk.

First aid for your Macintosh

If you're having any problems with your Macintosh that you attribute to the hard drive or your System software, there's a quick solution that might either solve your problem or help you isolate it. Restart your Mac, and then, right after the Start chord, insert your System software disk called Disk Tools. This will load a very basic version of the System software and allow you to run Apple's disk doctor utility, Disk First Aid (see fig. 29.3).

Fig. 29.3

My Mac started from the Disk Tools disk, so it's the "active" drive (it's on top). Now I can run Disk First Aid on my hard drive to see what the problem *is*.

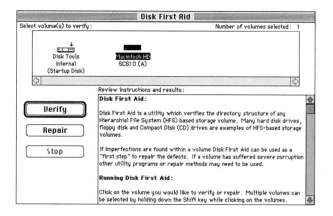

Using the Disk Tools disk does two things. First, we can run Disk First Aid, which will examine the hard drive or any floppy drives that aren't working properly for problems with the Desktop file and directory catalogs. It can fix some of these problems or at least let you know that you need to use Norton Utilities' Disk Doctor or a similar program.

If Disk First Aid reports no problems, you can be pretty well assured that your problem lies elsewhere. If your Mac works correctly when it starts from the Disk Tools disk, more than likely you're actually having trouble with your extensions (see chapter 28 for extension troubleshooting tips).

 (Tip)

Every once in a while, just *running* Disk Tools will fix your Mac, even if it reports no problems. Try restarting your Mac and see if your problem "magically" disappears (this is actually due to a bug in some Macs' ROM chips). You may still want to run a disk doctor to make sure—but Disk Tools may be all you need.

Fixing sick files and programs

If Disk Tools reports problems that it can't fix, it's time to turn to Norton Utilities' Disk Doctor or a similar program. These programs go deep into your hard drive's catalog and Desktop files to determine where fragmentation and other issues have corrupted files. Luckily for us, all we really have to do is run the program and let it do the dirty work (see fig. 29.4).

Fig. 29.4
Here's Disk Doctor rummaging through my disk, looking for problems.

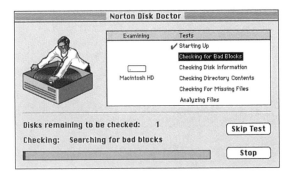

Realize that, for the most part, Disk Doctor and similar utilities will not be able to fix problems that are on your Startup disk (the disk that appears in the top right corner of your Desktop after you turn on your Mac). That usually means you'll need to start up from a disk. Norton Utilities will allow

Using Disk Tools as your utility startup disk

If your utility can't do it for you, you can use the Disk Tools disk as a Startup disk. Just remember that you can't put any other files (like the utility program) on the Disk Tools disk, since it's basically full. Here's a nice trick, though.

1   Unlock the Disk Tools disk by sliding the plastic "Read Only" tab down so that it covers the hole in the disk's top right corner.

2   Start up your Mac using the Disk Tools disk.

3   Drag and drop the Memory Control Panel from your hard drive to the Disk Tools' System Folder.

4   Open the Disk Tools' Control Panels folder and double-click the Memory Control

Panel. Turn on the RAM Disk and choose a size large enough for your utility program (like Disk Doctor).

5   Restart your Mac and then copy your utility program to the RAM disk. Start the utility program by double-clicking its icon in the RAM disk window.

6   When you're done with the Disk Tools disk and you're ready to start up with your hard drive, don't forget slide the "read only" tab to its original position.

Now you can perform whatever disk fixing you need without worrying about affecting your Startup disk!

you to create a Startup disk for this purpose. Other utilities may have different ways to get around this problem.

The fix-all for sick Macs

Here's your ace in the hole for a sick Mac. Many, many problems can be solved with this one little step: Reinstall your System software. Sound like trouble? It is, but it can also save a lot of headaches.

But, you can't just drop in Disk One and start re-installing. Your System Installer program won't replace any files already on your hard drive—it will only update them. This won't do you much good if one of those files is a problem child. The solution? You'll have to hide your current System Folder from your Mac.

Start by opening the System Folder and moving the System file to another folder (maybe your Fonts folder or the Preferences folder). Next, close the System Folder window and rename your System folder to something else— like "Old System" or something similar (see fig. 29.5). Now, restart your Mac and insert the System Install Disk 1 after the Startup Chord.

Fig. 29.5
Before I reinstall the System software, I need to hide my old System file and Folder.

2. Rename the System Folder

1. I hide the System file

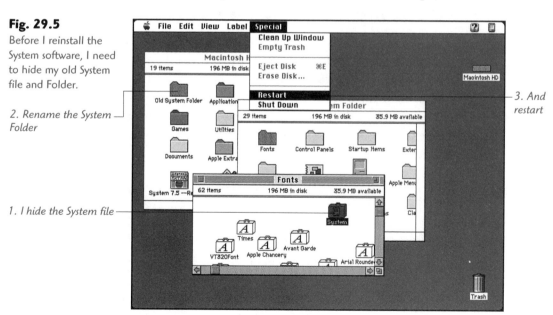

3. And restart

So, why not just throw the System Folder away? Well, your Mac won't let you, for one thing. And, you'll probably want all those extensions, Control Panels, and fonts that are already installed.

Once the new System software is in place, you need to gradually transfer extensions, Control Panels, and fonts from the old folder to the new one. Restart after moving every few extensions. If your Mac crashes again, you've isolated the problem (it's one of the last extensions or Control Panels you moved). If it doesn't crash, you're back in business!

 Q&A

Nothing seems to fix my Mac's problem. Is there anything else I can try?

There's one more fix-all, although it's weird. It's called "zapping the PRAM." PRAM is a small bit of memory reserved by your Mac for system information. If all else fails, it might (maybe, there's a small chance...) fix your Mac. As your Mac starts up, hold down ⌘+Option+P+R until you hear a second startup chord.

Does my Mac have a virus?

There's a lot of talk about computer viruses out there. Could that be what's affecting your Mac? In two words: probably not. *Unless* you download from BBSs or national online services or often use disks that have been used with other computers. Those are the only two ways you're likely to get a virus. Essentially, you'll need to transfer an infected file from someone else's computer to your computer—and then double-click that file. Then, a virus can attack.

 **{Note}**

Actually, a virus can be transmitted over any computer media (disks, backup tapes, CD-ROM), but the theory's the same.

A computer virus is simply a program designed to cause applications on your hard drive to act strangely, or, in worst cases, they may attack your Mac's filing system and mess things up. It's *possible* to lose data to a virus—but, unless you're in a high-risk group, it's unlikely that you'll ever get one.

 **{Note}** Most application vendors and major online services use anti-virus software and other measures to ensure that their files are virus-free. While you can't be too careful, if they don't catch the virus, chances are you won't either.

If you find yourself at risk, you can buy anti-virus software that periodically scans your hard drive and any floppy disks you insert for viruses. There are a number of these programs available online or in retail stores. The best of these programs run all the time, checking new floppy disks when you insert them and alerting you to abnormalities, but they may also give you some false alarms. Personally, I find they slow down my work. It's a trade-off for security, I know. Taster's choice. In any case, if you do detect a virus, one of these programs is essential for erasing it.

I wouldn't call it a pressing concern, but it's not bad to have virus detection software on hand—if it doesn't bother you to run it all the time, fine. If it does, just run it when your Mac starts acting funny.

Part IX

Indexes

Action Index

Get Started

When you need to...	You'll find help here...	
Turn on your Mac	p. 24	How do I turn it on?
Shut down your Mac	p. 65	How do I turn off my Mac?

Work With Icons

When you need to...	You'll find help here...	
Select icons	p. 40	Click once to select something
Drag-and-drop icons	p. 41	Click once and drag to move an icon
Open icons	p. 30	What are icons for?
Throw stuff away	p. 63	How do I clean up and throw stuff away?
Create an alias	p. 91	Creating an alias
Customize your icons	p. 139	Change the look of your icons

Use Files, Folders, and Windows

When you need to...	You'll find help here...	
Create a folder	p. 71	Creating folders
Name a folder	p. 71	Giving your folders names
Copy files to a disk	p. 88	How do I copy a file from one disk to another?
Put away files and folders	p. 92	Putting stuff away
Move or resize windows	p. 76	Can I change the window's size?
Close windows	p. 77	How do I close the window?

Work With Disks

When you need to...	You'll find help here...
Insert a floppy disk	p. 83 Inserting a floppy disk
Prepare a new floppy disk	p. 84 Preparing a new disk
Eject a floppy disk	p. 86 Getting a disk back from your Mac
Load or unload a CD-ROM	p. 273 Loading and unloading disks
Copy CD-ROM files to a disk	p. 275 Copying and using CD-ROM files
Use a PhotoCD	p. 291 Get your photos developed on a PhotoCD

Get Help

When you need to...	You'll find help here...
Turn on or off Balloon Help	p. 100 Showing balloons
Use Apple Guide	p. 101 The Apple Guide holds your hand

Customize Your Macintosh

When you need to...	You'll find help here...
Set up the Launcher	p. 113 Put stuff you use everyday on the desktop
Change your desktop pattern	p. 127 I hate this gray desktop
Add items to the Apple menu	p. 116 What's special about the Apple menu?
Change your alert sounds	p. 132 Changing your alert sound

Use Applications

Get Your Work Done

Print

Run DOS and Windows Stuff

Use Photos, Video, and Sound

Use a Modem

Take Care of Your Mac

When you need to...	You'll find help here...
Use the Extension Manager	p. 364 Managing your extensions
Add control panels	p. 369 How do I add Control Panels?
Rebuild the desktop file	p. 376 Your desktop file may be getting too big
Optimize your hard drive	p. 378 Optimize your hard drive
Diagnose a sick Mac	p. 381 How to diagnose a sick Mac

Q&A Index

Help with the basics

Disk problems

Problems with control panels

If this happens	Look here for an answer
I've got folders in my Apple Menu Items folder, but no hierarchical menus show up on the Apple menu. Why?	118
My Mac didn't make a sound. Why?	132

Insufficient memory

If this happens	Look here for an answer
I don't have as much memory as my program says it requires. Will virtual memory help?	145
My Mac is frozen! How can I save the data on my RAM disk?	147

Printing problems

If this happens	Look here for an answer
I started AppleTalk and selected my network printer, but it still asks if I want to use the Printer or Modem port. What did I do?	249
I'm using PostScript fonts, and I've got jagged fonts on my printout. What gives?	256
ATM didn't fix things! I installed it, but my fonts still look bad.	258

Multimedia concerns

If this happens	Look here for an answer
Why can't I drag sound files out of my System file?	282
My CD-ROM drive is compatible, but I can't seem to use PhotoCDs.	292
My software says I don't have a scanner connected. What should I do?	292

Getting connected

If this happens	Look here for an answer
I've got a Macintosh AV computer and all my software is installed, but the GeoPort won't dial out. Why?	321
When I connect to the host computer, I get a lot of junk, but some things are readable. Why?	325
I'm connected! Why do I see double (or nothing) whenever I type?	327

System problems

If this happens	Look here for an answer
I can't seem to move, copy, or delete anything in the System Folder. Why?	363
My Mac can't get all the way to the Finder—it freezes while loading an extension. What should I do?	367
What if I throw out a Preferences file for an application I'm still using?	372
My Mac gets to the end of rebuilding the desktop file and starts over. What should I do?	377
Why can't my undelete utility recover my file?	381

{ Index }

PLUG YOURSELF INTO...

MACMILLAN INFORMATION SUPERLIBRARY™

que

SAMS PUBLISHING

Hayden Books

que COLLEGE

NRP

alpha books

Brady

ADOBE PRESS

THE MACMILLAN INFORMATION SUPERLIBRARY™

Free information and vast computer resources from the world's leading computer book publisher—online!

FIND THE BOOKS THAT ARE RIGHT FOR YOU!

A complete online catalog, plus sample chapters and tables of contents give you an in-depth look at *all* of our books, including hard-to-find titles. It's the best way to find the books you need!

● STAY INFORMED with the latest computer industry news through our online newsletter, press releases, and customized Information SuperLibrary Reports.

● GET FAST ANSWERS to your questions about MCP books and software.

● VISIT our online bookstore for the latest information and editions!

● COMMUNICATE with our expert authors through e-mail and conferences.

● DOWNLOAD SOFTWARE from the immense MCP library:
- Source code and files from MCP books
- The best shareware, freeware, and demos

● DISCOVER HOT SPOTS on other parts of the Internet.

● WIN BOOKS in ongoing contests and giveaways!

TO PLUG INTO MCP: ➔

GOPHER: gopher.mcp.com

FTP: ftp.mcp.com

WORLD WIDE WEB: **http://www.mcp.com**

Home Page | What's New | Bookstore | Reference Desk | Software Library | Macmillan Overview | Talk to Us